Graeme Goldsworthy

Christ-Centered Biblical Theology

HERMENEUTICAL FOUNDATIONS

AND PRINCIPLES

IVP Academic

An imprint of InterVarsity Press
Downers Grove, Illinois

InterVarsity Press
P.O. Box 1400, Downers Grove, IL 60515-1426
Internet: www.ivpress.com
E-mail: email@ivpress.com

InterVarsity Press® is the book-publishing division of InterVarsity Christian Fellowship/USA®, a movement of students and faculty active on campus at hundreds of universities, colleges and schools of nursing in the United States of America, and a member movement of the International Fellowship of Evangelical Students. For information about local and regional activities, write Public Relations Dept., InterVarsity Christian Fellowship/USA, 6400 Schroeder Rd., P.O. Box 7895, Madison, WI 53707-7895, or visit the IVCF website at <www.intervarsity.org>.

Scripture quotations, unless otherwise noted, are from The Holy Bible, English Standard Version, copyright © 2001 by Crossway Bibles, a division of Good News Publishers. Used by permission. All rights reserved.

Cover design: Cindy Kiple
Image: Alfredo Dagli Orti / The Art Archive at Art Resource, NY

ISBN 978-0-8308-3969-8

Printed in the United States of America ∞

 InterVarsity Press is committed to protecting the environment and to the responsible use of natural resources. As a member of Green Press Initiative we use recycled paper whenever possible. To learn more about the Green Press Initiative, visit <www.greenpressinitiative.org>.

Library of Congress Cataloging-in-Publication Data

Goldsworthy, Graeme.
  Christ-centered biblical theology: hermeneutical foundations and
principles / Graeme Goldsworthy.
     p. cm.
  Includes bibliographical references (p.) and indexes.
  ISBN 978-0-8308-3969-8 (pbk.: alk. paper)
  1. Bible—Theology. I. Title.
  BS543.G66 2012
  230'.041—dc23

                                                                                    2012000256

P	18	17	16	15	14	13	12	11	10	9	8	7	6	5	4	3	2	1
Y	27	26	25	24	23	22	21	20	19	18	17	16	15	14	13	12		

This book is dedicated as a tribute to Donald Robinson

I wish to acknowledge my debt of gratitude to Donald William Bradley Robinson who, though being a leading Australian New Testament scholar, lectured me in Old Testament when I was a student at Moore Theological College. This book is my attempt to spell out the rationale for the method of biblical theology that Robinson taught me, which galvanized my enthusiasm for the subject. It is my tribute to him and his tireless endeavours to make the Bible more accessible to generations of students and, through them, to ordinary Christians. It is impossible to say how my thinking and practice in biblical theology would have developed if Donald Robinson had not been my teacher. But this I do believe: a great debt is owed to him for the considerable influence on many Christians that has resulted from his teaching and writing, and from that of some of his former students. The Robinson schema has not only found much acceptance here in Australia, but also in the UK, USA, Europe and in churches in Asia and Latin America.

Donald William Bradley Robinson

Born in Sydney	1922
Graduated BA University of Sydney	1946
University of Cambridge	1947–50
Ordination by Archbishop of Sydney	1950
Lecturer, Moore College	1952–73
Vice Principal, Moore College	1959–73
Bishop of Parramatta	1973–82
Archbishop of Sydney	1982–93

CONTENTS

FIGURES AND TABLES

Figures

Tables

PREFACE

I have written this book, and write this preface, reflecting on my heritage in
evangelical Anglicanism, which began in Australia with the arrival of the first
fleet at Sydney Cove on 26 January 1788. With it came an evangelical minister
of the Church of England as Chaplain, Richard Johnson. He preached the first
Christian sermon in Australia on 3 February of the same year.[1] A monument
in the Sydney central business district marks the place and commemorates the
date of this sermon and the preacher's text: Psalm 116:12. Johnson was succeeded by another evangelical chaplain, Samuel Marsden. In 1792 a devoutly
evangelical layman, Thomas Moore, arrived on board the ship *Britannia* as its
carpenter.[2] In 1796 he became the official Boat Builder of the Colony of New
South Wales, and later went on to establish a prosperous pastoral venture

---

1. Johnson's successors were officially under the oversight of the Bishop of Calcutta
   from 1825 until 1835. In that year Australia was removed from this oversight and
   the Diocese of Australia was formed with William Grant Broughton as its first,
   and only, bishop. During Broughton's episcopate, Australia was divided into four
   dioceses in 1847 and Broughton became the first Bishop of Sydney.
2. Much of the historical detail here pertaining to Moore comes from Peter G. Bolt,
   Thomas Moore of Liverpool: One of Our Oldest Colonists, Studies in Australian Colonial
   History 1 (Camperdown, NSW: Bolt Publishing Services, 2007).

at Liverpool, 20 miles south-west of Sydney. When Moore died in 1840 his will directed that his considerable wealth should benefit the church in the colony.[3] Specifically he directed that a substantial amount should be used to establish a college 'for the education of young men of the Protestant persuasion in the principles of Christian Knowledge'. In 1856 the second bishop of Sydney, Frederic Barker, applied Moore's will to establish a theological college at the Moore property in Liverpool. Moore College, one of the oldest tertiary institutions in Australia, began with three students and, at the time of writing, had increased one hundredfold. In 1891 it moved to premises adjacent to the University of Sydney in the inner suburb of Newtown. Barker was a convinced evangelical who had been greatly influenced by Charles Simeon during his time in Cambridge. The development of evangelical Christianity in Sydney was not always smooth. But in 1934 the evangelical missionary bishop to western China, Howard Mowll, was appointed Archbishop of Sydney. He worked tirelessly to consolidate the evangelical character of Sydney Diocese. In 1935 Thomas Chatterton Hammond, director of the Irish Church Missions in Dublin, was appointed Principal of Moore College. Although Hammond was distinctive as to his emphasis and style, his determined evangelical stance has left an indelible mark on the College and the Diocese.

This heritage I have shared with generations of laity and clergy in Sydney. It is the heritage I share with Donald Robinson, to whom this volume is dedicated. I have watched its development under the leadership of the Archbishops who succeeded Mowll, and the Principals who succeeded Hammond. Archbishop Mowll ordained me to the Anglican ministry in 1958 and, in my time at Moore College as a student and junior tutor, I was privileged to sit under Hammond at the end of his ministry there. Donald Robinson and I share not only this ethos of Sydney Diocese but also that of the theology faculty at Cambridge. My debt to Robinson is the motive for this study of his approach to biblical theology as a distinct discipline. He was my teacher in theological college, became my colleague on the faculty and has remained a mentor and friend ever since.

It is fitting that I should also acknowledge my debt to other leaders and teachers who shaped my Christian thinking and living, and thus my writing. These include those who impacted me in Sydney: Marcus Loane, Broughton Knox, Alan Cole, Bruce Smith, Graham Delbridge, John Chapman and many others. In Cambridge I was privileged to be taught by Peter Ackroyd, Charlie

---

3. His wife and stepson had both predeceased him and he had no other immediate relatives.

Moule, David Winton-Thomas and Henry Hart. In later graduate studies at Union Theological Seminary in Virginia[4] I greatly benefited from the supervision of John Bright and Patrick D. Miller.

In 1973 and 1974 I was a visiting lecturer in biblical theology at Moore College. This gave me the opportunity to think through the Robinson schema and to apply it to an introductory course in the subject. The urging of the students that I should put it all in writing, a project I initially thought to be bordering on the ludicrous, finally prevailed and *Gospel and Kingdom* (1981) was the outcome. Paternoster published this and two further studies. My relationship with IVP began with the publication of *According to Plan* (1991), and I have been delighted to be able to maintain that relationship ever since. I wish to express my grateful thanks for the sensitive suggestions, comments and other help I received first from David Kingdon and, in more recent times, from Dr Philip Duce, who is Senior Commissioning Editor for theological books at IVP. My earlier Christian life was shaped by two main influences: my parish church in the Sydney Diocese, and the Sydney University Evangelical Union, an affiliate of the Australian arm of the International Fellowship of Evangelical Students. The latter had its beginnings in the Inter-Varsity Fellowship to which IVP is related. IVP, and the evangelicalism of both Sydney Diocese and Moore College, all have common roots in British evangelicalism. It is very satisfying to me to have a good working relationship with a publisher that shares my spiritual roots, my doctrinal convictions and Christian ethos. I have been encouraged to complete this present project by numbers of friends and colleagues who share my respect for Donald Robinson. To all of these I owe my gratitude, and especially to Miriam, my wife and partner in the gospel for forty-seven years, who has constantly stood by me and supported my endeavours.

Graeme Goldsworthy
Bilambil Heights, NSW

---

4. Now named Union Presbyterian Seminary.

ABBREVIATIONS

ABR	*Australian Biblical Review*
AUSS	*Andrews University Seminary Studies*
BST	The Bible Speaks Today
CTM	*Concordia Theological Monthly*
ESV	English Standard Version
Gk.	Greek
JSOTSup	Journal for the Study of the Old Testament, Supplement Series
LCC	Library of Christian Classics
LXX	Septuagint
NDBT	*New Dictionary of Biblical Theology: Exploring the Unity and Diversity of Scripture*, ed. Brian S. Rosner, T. Desmond Alexander, Graeme Goldsworthy and D. A. Carson (Downers Grove: IVP; Leicester: IVP, 2000)
NICOT	New International Commentary on the Old Testament
NIV	New International Version
NRSV	New Revised Standard Version
NSBT	New Studies in Biblical Theology
RTR	*Reformed Theological Review*
SBJT	*Southern Baptist Journal of Theology*
SBT	Studies in Biblical Theology
SHS	Scripture and Hermeneutics Series

SJT	*Scottish Journal of Theology*
TB	*Tyndale Bulletin*
tr.	translated by
WBC	Word Biblical Commentary
WTJ	*Westminster Theological Journal*

1. BIBLICAL THEOLOGY: LAME DUCK OR EAGLES' WINGS?

Confessions of a biblical theology addict

The immediate appeal of biblical theology to preachers, teachers and ordinary Christians is that it provides a 'big picture' that makes sense out of the bewildering bulk and variety of the biblical literature. It seeks to view the whole scene of God's revelation from the heights – to mount up with eagles' wings and allow God to show us his one mighty plan from creation to new creation. When the Bible ceases to be a mass of unconnected stories and other bits of writing, and begins to look like a unity that connects the narratives of Israel with those of the four Gospels, that shows up the progression from the creation to the new creation, and that highlights the life, death and resurrection of Jesus Christ as the prime focus of the whole Bible, people usually sit up and take notice. If the Bible is indeed the one word of the one God about the one way of salvation through the one saviour, Jesus Christ, it is biblical theology that will reveal this to us. Yet, for some, this exercise in biblical theology is considered to be a lame duck or, worse, a delusion.

Since the 1960s or so I have worked to refine my understanding of biblical theology that came about as a result of my experiences as a student, pastor and teacher in theological education. This approach, which is now expressed in a number of books, evokes a whole range of responses from opposition to indifference and to enthusiastic endorsement. Opposition causes me to reconsider my theory and practice and to try to understand on what grounds the rejection of my position is mounted. Indifference causes me to renew my attempts to convince people of the value of evangelical biblical theology. And endorsement encourages me to persevere without becoming self-satisfied or complacent. There are, of course, some more nuanced responses of people who do not reject the idea out of hand but may have some problems with the way I handle it. I am grateful to those who have identified aspects of my biblical theology that have caused them concern even if, in the end, I have not always felt that their criticisms warranted any radical change to my position. Nevertheless I have learned much from those who differ from me in basic approach.

I first wrote and expounded my seminal views of biblical theology in *Gospel and Kingdom*,[1] which was in essence a first-year course in biblical theology that I taught at Moore College in the early 1970s. Later, while in parish ministry, I wrote a more comprehensive outline of biblical theology for both lay people and pastors. I developed it as a course that I taught to successive groups of church members over some five years. The course was eventually published under the title *According to Plan*.[2] The schema I pursued in those two books has been the basis for my further explorations into biblical theology. Although my approach has been welcomed in some circles, it has not been without its evangelical critics.[3] Furthermore, that which has seemed to me to be a fairly obvious way of dealing with the structure of Scripture has not found much place in the literature, though, in more recent times, this situation seems to be changing.

I think that it is time to set out in more detail the rationale for this approach and thereby to seek to advance the cause of evangelical biblical theology. I hasten to add that my approach came about initially from a brief description of the structure of biblical revelation by one of my teachers when I was a theological student. Donald Robinson, a leading Australian New Testament scholar, was at that time my teacher in Old Testament.[4] He expounded his

---

1. *Gospel and Kingdom: A Christian Interpretation of the Old Testament* (Exeter: Paternoster, 1981), now published in *The Goldsworthy Trilogy* (Milton Keynes: Paternoster, 2000).

2. *According to Plan: The Unfolding Revelation of God in the Bible* (Leicester: IVP, 1991; Downers Grove: IVP, 2002).

3. The mainstream of liberal-critical scholarship has, on the whole, ignored it, which is not altogether surprising.

4. After we both had attended a meeting of the Fellowship for Biblical Studies in Sydney at which a paper on some aspect of the Old Testament was read, Robinson rather wistfully wondered if he should not have stayed with the Old Testament.

view in response to a student's question about how the whole diverse body of
Scripture fitted together. My memory of what he said in response to the question
goes something like this:

> God revealed his kingdom and the way into it in three stages: first, in the history of
> God's people particularly from Abraham to Solomon's dedication of the temple;
> second, in the eschatology of the prophets; and third, in the fulfilment of all these
> Old Testament expectations in the person and work of Christ.[5]

Donald Robinson more recently has set out something of his own odyssey
in biblical theology.[6] He expresses some indebtedness to various theologians
including three non-evangelicals: C. H. Dodd, Oscar Cullmann and Gabriel
Hebert.[7] Robinson describes how Hebert in 1957 gave lectures to the Clergy
School of the Anglican Diocese of Brisbane on the subject of 'Christ the
Fulfiller'.[8] He comments, 'In these he propounded an outline of the contents
of the Bible in three stages somewhat similar to that which I was developing in
the Moore College course.' In an earlier work Hebert attributes this schema to
Dr W. J. Phythian-Adams.[9] Robinson explains that in the development of his

---

That surely was a comment that reflected the problem of specialization in one or
other Testament for any biblical theologian who loves the whole Bible.

5. I stress that this is my memory of what was said over fifty years ago. It does,
however, agree with some more recent statements and writings of Robinson.
Though not an exact quote, I have put it as a quote to emphasize its importance
for me. Robinson's own version of this basic idea is quoted in chapter 9 and below
on pp. 22–23.

6. Donald W. B. Robinson, 'Origins and Unresolved Tensions', in R. J. Gibson (ed.),
Interpreting God's Plan: Biblical Theology and the Pastor (Carlisle: Paternoster, 1997), pp.
1–17.

7. Gabriel Hebert was an English Anglo-Catholic monk who taught for a while in
St Michael's House seminary, South Australia. During that time he developed a
friendship with Robinson and was an occasional visitor to Moore College. All of
these men, while not perhaps identifiable as evangelicals, had a high view of the
authority of Scripture.

8. A. G. Hebert, *Christ the Fulfiller: Three Studies on the Biblical Types as They Are Presented
in the Old and New Testaments* (Sydney: Anglican Truth Society, 1957).

9. Robinson, 'Origins', p. 5. Hebert's analysis in *Christ the Fulfiller* was to identify three
confessions of faith: (1) A pre-exilic confession of Israel's main story based on the
election of Abraham. This main story runs from the exodus to the sanctuary in

course, '[t]he aim was to assist [the students] in their approach to theological study in general, and to the study of the Bible in particular.'[10] He further comments that 'A distinction was drawn between the study of the Christian religion in its various aspects (including credal doctrines, church history, Prayer Book) and the study of the Bible in its own terms to discover what it is all about.'[11] This phrase 'the study of the Bible *in its own terms*' (italics mine) is, I believe, the key to Robinson's approach to biblical theology. What those terms are, to be sure, is not a matter of total agreement among biblical scholars.

Robinson developed his course into a treatment of seven main issues:[12]

1. The character of the Bible: its scope and structure.
2. The people of God; including a study of the biblical covenants.
3. The significance of Abraham and his seed. This dealt with the biblical story of the outworking of the promises to Abraham as it reached its climax with David and Solomon.
4. A treatment of the two great themes of exodus/redemption, and land/inheritance.
5. The prophetic view of promise and fulfilment.
6. The New Testament claim that all this is fulfilled in Christ.
7. Principles of biblical interpretation.

Here Robinson comments significantly:

Based on the foregoing understanding of what the Bible is 'about', we enunciated a biblical 'typology' using the three stages in the outworking of God's promise to Abraham, that is, (a) the historical experience of the fulfilment of God's promise

---

Footnote 9 (*cont.*)

Jerusalem. (2) A post-exilic confession based on the works of the writing prophets that reaffirms the first confession but adds to it the fact that God 'has a future for his chosen people' (p. 11). Hebert refers here to a second and greater exodus, and a restored temple at Jerusalem. (3) The Christian confession that reaffirms the previous two confessions and declares them fulfilled in Christ. See pp. 9–13. In his work *The Authority of the Old Testament* (London: Faber and Faber, 1947), pp. 51–52, Hebert sets out this same thesis with the footnote 'I owe the idea of this threefold scheme to Dr. Phythian-Adams, in the *Church Quarterly Review*, No. cclxix (Oct. 1942), p. 3f.'

10. Robinson, 'Origins', p. 6.
11. Ibid., p. 7.
12. Ibid., pp. 7–9.

to Abraham through the exodus to the kingdom of David's son in the land of inheritance, (b) the projection of this fulfilment into the future of the day of the Lord, by the prophets, during the period of decline, fall, exile and return, and (c) the true fulfilment in Christ and the Spirit in Jesus' incarnation, death, resurrection, exaltation and in his parousia as judge and saviour in a new heaven and new earth.[13]

It is this understanding of the 'big picture' and the role of typology that captured my imagination over fifty years ago, and that has been at the centre of my preoccupation with biblical theology ever since. It is this schema that I explore and seek to defend in this book. Any refinements I may have applied to this basic schema are, in my opinion, nothing more than fine tuning at the edges. The basic structure remains.

My purpose in writing this account is to try to establish a valid rationale for the approach to biblical theology outlined above. I am aware that some evangelical exegetes and theologians are not entirely convinced of the usefulness of such a discipline. Others are more cautious about the way to pursue and apply it. Some doubt the very basic assumptions upon which the method is based. Criticisms must be taken seriously and the doubters listened to. I am, however, far from convinced that biblical theology is a lame duck. Rather I believe that it is at the heart of evangelical hermeneutics and is absolutely indispensible in expository preaching. I also believe that it is the heartbeat of effective pastoral ministry.[14]

The big questions about the big picture

The attempt to summarize the overall message of Scripture as a 'big picture' raises certain questions we must try to answer. If we assume the unity of Scripture, on whatever basis, the obvious question is: can we represent this unity without distortion in one schematic proposal? Is an overall structure

---

13. Ibid., p. 9.
14. On this topic see Graeme Goldsworthy, 'The Pastoral Application of Biblical Theology', in David Peterson and John Pryor (eds.), *In the Fullness of Time: Biblical Studies in Honour of Archbishop Donald Robinson* (Homebush West, NSW: Lancer, 1992), pp. 301–317; 'The Pastor as Biblical Theologian', in Gibson, *Interpreting God's Plan*, pp. 110–129; 'Biblical Theology as the Heartbeat of Effective Ministry', in Scott J. Hafemann (ed.), *Biblical Theology: Retrospect and Prospect* (Downers Grove: IVP; Leicester: Apollos, 2002), pp. 280–286.

discernible in such a way that it can be represented, for example, by a diagram without being hopelessly reductionist? The schema that developed from my encounter with Donald Robinson's brief exposition appealed to me in a quite dramatic way. It radically changed my view of the Bible and how to read it. Very soon after this first encounter I was already trying to refine my ideas of it and to test its validity against Scripture.

I am a person who tends to think visually. If I can represent something or some concept with a diagram I shall do it. I am well aware that this runs the risk of avoiding details that might challenge the simplicity. Nevertheless it was not long after I was pointed in the direction of this three-stage understanding of biblical revelation that I was drawing diagrams to represent it as I came to understand it better. Once the basic shape was in place I began to use diagrams as teaching aids. It is impossible for me to estimate how many times and in what different situations I have used the basic shape of my diagrams to introduce people to the overall picture of the biblical message. To me a diagram's greatest justification lies in its explanatory power, provided it is not distorting the biblical message. To be able to feel one has got hold of some way of linking the whole diverse range of biblical documents into a coherent unity was almost overwhelming. But therein lay its danger. It would always be open to the criticism of being either simplistic or simply wrong. I found that many people responded with enthusiasm to this way of showing how the whole Bible fitted together as the one word of God. I was, of course, aware that people's enthusiasm for a schema did not necessarily mean it was accurate or defensible. But when people who had been Bible readers for years began to wonder aloud why they had not been shown years before something like this approach, it did encourage me all the more to investigate its validity. The true test of any diagrammatic, reductionist big-picture approach is whether or not it can stand up to detailed analysis derived from the close reading of the texts.

The Robinson–Hebert schema

What does this Robinson schema look like as I have understood it and developed my own version of it? It seems Robinson and Hebert initially developed their ideas independently of one another and only later compared notes. Hebert acknowledges his debt in turn to W. J. Phythian-Adams for this threefold structure.[15] Both Robinson and Hebert went on to develop

---

15. See n. 9 above.

their ideas of typology based on the threefold structure of revelation.[16] I
followed their lead and began with the basic biblical timeline from creation
to the new creation and marked it with the three main stages of revelation:
biblical history from creation, and especially from Abraham, to Solomon; the
eschatology of the writing prophets; and the fulfilment of all things in Christ.
The prophetic ministry and, in particular, the eschatological pronouncements
of the prophets, took place within the history of Israel. Specifically such prophetic ministry coincided with the post-Solomonic decline of Israel's fortunes
due to rebellion and disobedience. Whereas the history from Abraham to
Solomon's temple showed an overall advance or development in the revelation of the blessings of God's covenant made with Abraham, the history from
Solomon's apostasy (1 Kgs 11) to the exile showed an overall manifestation
of the curses of the covenant. Even the return from the Babylonian exile
did not bring the true blessings that were expected, and the nation limped
on under the judgment of God while the faithful were sustained only by his
promises.

The Old Testament, then, can be represented as a manifestation of
promise and blessing reaching a high point in David's Jerusalem as the focal
point of the land of inheritance, in Solomon as David's heir, and in the temple
representing the presence of God to dwell among and bless his people. After
Solomon's apostasy it is history primarily as a manifestation of judgment that
is overlaid with the prophetic promises that the Day of the Lord will come and
bring ultimate blessing and judgment. The story may seem to end in failure,
especially as the four hundred years between the Testaments perpetuates the
scenario of judgment with Israel's fortunes at a low ebb. It takes the person of
Jesus, his teaching and the proclamation of his apostles to restore hope in the
original promise of God.

Figure 1 below represents the most basic outline of the revelation of the
Bible. The biblical story begins with creation and ends with the new creation. Somewhere between the two is the person and work of Jesus. If it does
nothing else, this representation expresses the essential parameters of revelation within history and the unity of the story within which revelation is given.
On its own this diagram is no more than a pointer to the potential of biblical
theology. We must then move on to the structure of this revelation.

The basic structure of revelation as represented in Figure 2 has the further
advantage of representing each stage as related to the others. A summary

---

16. Hebert, *Christ the Fulfiller*, pp. 13–17, where he outlines the typology of the exodus
    as an example.

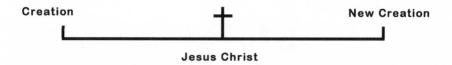

Figure 1: The basic biblical timeline (not to scale)

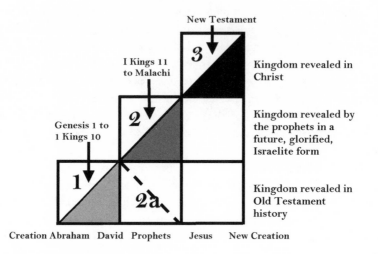

Figure 2: The structure of revelation[17]

of the major theological moments in each will show that the second stage (prophetic eschatology) recapitulates the first, and the third (fulfilment in Christ) recapitulates both the first and the second. Each successive level, however, is more than a *mere* recapitulation in that it moves the revelation to a higher level of reality. Thus the structures within the history of Israel give way to the prophetic eschatological perspective of the Day of the Lord, and this, in turn, gives way to the ultimate reality as fulfilled in Christ. The nature of the recapitulation can be seen in the juxtaposition of the key moments of redemptive revelation in each stage as shown in Table 1. Other aspects could be added, but this suffices to show the general shape of the biblical pattern.

---

17. This figure is similar to that in Goldsworthy, *Gospel and Kingdom*, in *Goldsworthy Trilogy*, p. 124.

Table 1: The content of the three-stage structure of revelation

Biblical history from creation to Solomon[18]	*Eschatology of the prophets*	*Fulfilment in Christ*
Creation	New creation	Jesus is new creation
Covenant with Abraham	New covenant	New covenant in Jesus' blood
Captivity and exodus redemption	New captivity and new exodus redemption	Jesus is the Passover lamb and new exodus
Tabernacle and temple as dwelling of God	New temple as dwelling of God	Jesus is where God and humanity dwell: the word 'tabernacles' with us
Possession of the land	Possession of the new land	Jesus fulfils the land as the dwelling place of God
Kingship of David	New Davidic king	Jesus is new David
Jerusalem (Zion)	New Jerusalem	Jesus is new temple, the new Jerusalem
Temple	New temple	

The role of Genesis 1 – 11

That the three-stage schema concentrates on events from Genesis 12 onward should not be taken to mean that Genesis 1 – 11 is neglected. This would be a serious mistake given that so much of biblical theology has its foundation in these chapters. It could even be suggested that *all* of the theology of the Bible has its foundations in these chapters. The doctrines of creation, the Fall, judgment, the progress of evil, the exhibition of God's grace, election, covenant, sovereignty and salvation history all have their beginnings here. I shall take this up in more detail when I consider the notion of salvation history. Suffice it to say at this point that Genesis 1 – 11 provides the rationale and backdrop to the calling of Abraham and the covenant of grace that God establishes with the patriarch of Israel. The terms of God's covenant with Abraham in Genesis 12:1–3 do not make a lot of sense apart from the account in the previous chapters.

There is also a deliberate and important structuring in these early chapters that clearly shows the grace of God at work in the election of a line from

---

18. Creation and Fall are the presuppositions of the history of Abraham and the covenant. See the discussion of the role of Gen. 1 – 11 below.

Adam, through Seth, Noah and Shem to Abraham.[19] This contrasts with the 'line' that exhibits the godlessness of fallen humanity: from Cain through Lamech to the humanity that is destroyed in Noah's flood. A second godless line proceeds from Noah's son Ham and comes to an important climax in the generation that builds the tower of Babel. That the people of the godly line are nevertheless fallen is always clear and provides the dynamics of typology as the shadow of salvation that cannot become the solid reality until Christ.

The question of reductionism

There are some obvious questions that will need to be addressed if this approach is to be sustained. Not least is the charge of reductionism or of being simplistic. One way to avoid facing such challenges would be to treat each section, book or corpus in isolation from the others. Such could hardly be referred to as *a* biblical theology but only a collection of fragmented studies in biblical theology. This is not without its proponents who see the diversity of Scripture and, in particular, that of its message as too strong to permit any real sense of unity. I maintain that reductionism is not inherently bad. It is merely a way of representing the under-lying structure, which is overlaid with the rich diversity of literary genres and theological themes. It should be clear from these comments that I conceive of biblical theology as the study of the Bible done in such a way as to take account of the unity of its message within its diversity. Such a study recognizes a histor-ical time line running through the Scriptures so that we can speak of its storyline as both explicit in the narrative sections, and implicit in the non-narrative ma-terial. The quest for an evangelical biblical theology begins with the presupposi-tion that the biblical literature and its historical storyline together provide the vehicle for God's revelation of himself and his purposes for creation.

If we can argue for a reductionist approach that is valid in much the same way that an X-ray image is a valid representation of the structure of the body, it will only stand if the details can be fitted in without special pleading. If the reduction is on such a grand scale that it does not even raise the question of details – such as when we schematize the entire contents of the Bible merely as promise (Old Testament) and fulfilment (New Testament) without any specifics – it has only minimal value. Our schema must be detailed enough to explain what is there, and simple enough to allow its use in teaching and in personal understanding of the Bible. If, for example, a particular salvation-

---

19. See Goldsworthy, *Gospel and Kingdom*, in *Goldsworthy Trilogy*, ch. 6, pp. 64–66.

historical schema simply cannot accommodate the wisdom literature of the Old Testament, something is lacking in the understanding of either or both.[20] Those who find wisdom problematic point to the almost complete absence of salvation history in the wisdom books.[21] They seem to have overlooked the fact that, while there is little explicit salvation history in the wisdom corpora, there is much wisdom material embedded in salvation history. Thus, for example, 1 Kings 3 – 10 is a significant wisdom pericope as it relates Solomon's getting of wisdom and its expression in his rule and the temple at a high point of salvation history.

Among evangelicals there is a certain ambivalence regarding the propriety and usefulness of biblical theology. Some seem to doubt or to deny the validity of the discipline; others give it qualified endorsement but see certain dangers. Still others, including me, regard it as simply the necessary response to the way the Bible is. Among evangelical Christians the lack of a coherent biblical theology is usually by default. Many have learned one particular way of dealing with the Bible and have not been exposed to a comprehensive biblical theology as an alternative. Some acknowledge that the Bible is a unity and that the heart of it is the gospel of Christ. But they have never been shown, or have tried to work out for themselves, the way the various parts of the Bible fit together. Reading the Bible then easily becomes the search for today's personal word from God, which is often far from what the text, within its context, is really saying.[22] The unity is then more of an existential experience that lies in the individual believer rather than an objective unity in the text.[23]

---

20. While many biblical theologians have found difficulty in incorporating the wisdom literature into the salvation-historical pattern, I believe it can be done given an adequate understanding of both salvation history and wisdom. See my *Gospel and Wisdom: Israel's Wisdom Literature in the Christian Life*, in *Goldsworthy Trilogy*, and *The Tree of Life: Reading Proverbs Today* (Sydney: Anglican Information Office, 1993; rev. ed., Sydney: Aquila, 2011).

21. So G. Ernest Wright, *God Who Acts: Biblical Theology as Recital*, SBT 8 (London: SCM, 1952), pp. 102–105.

22. George Athas has aptly described this approach as 'a narcissistic engagement with Scripture'. See his 'Reflections on Scripture Using the Distinction Between Jews and Gentiles as an Exegetical Key', in Peter G. Bolt and Mark D. Thompson (eds.), *Donald Robinson: Selected Works. Appreciation* (Camperdown, NSW: Australian Church Record; Newtown, NSW: Moore College, 2008), p. 125.

23. A reader-response hermeneutic was in vogue among pietists and other evangelicals long before it was formalized in hermeneutical theory.

Scepticism about biblical theology is not confined to liberal theologians who play down the unity of Scripture. A former student of mine, now in ministry, contacted me asking for advice and comment on a sermon he had preached on 1 Samuel 17 (David and Goliath). He had endeavoured to approach the sermon with the perspective of biblical theology by dealing with the event in question as typological of Christ. Some time later an elderly retired minister, a definite evangelical, commented to the preacher about the sermon and indicated some reserve concerning the typological approach and about biblical theology in general.[24] The issue was in essence whether or not the sermon should emphasize David's saving of the impotent and frightened Israelites as a type of Christ's saving activity, or David as an example of Christian faith trusting in the power of God. Of course, to pose the question in either–or terms is not the most helpful approach. The retired minister insisted that passages such as Hebrews 11 show that exemplary preaching is the acceptable way to go. But, it seems to me that such exemplary exposition is nevertheless a form of typology in that David is now made to be a type of every Christian believer. The problem with this approach is that it plays down the mediatorial role of Jesus.

My reply to my former student was that I did not think it was necessarily an either–or situation, but that the overwhelming evidence of the New Testament is that the testimony of the Old Testament to Christ has priority over its testimony to the authentic Christian life in today's world. Furthermore, when we use biblical characters as examples to us, there is always the problem of whether the example is good, questionable, ambiguous or bad. This is not always clear cut.[25] This approach is also problematic in that it tends to sever the text in question from the centrality of Christ and to lead to moralism, even legalism. Even if we follow the narrative of redemptive history, within the framework of which the non-narrative parts of Scripture are also to be found, it is a mistake to regard Jesus Christ as merely the foretold One who makes the fulfilment of promises and prophecies possible for us in the here and now. Rather the contention of this present study is that the pathway of the narrative

---

24. He also commented that he considered biblical theology to be the scourge of all recent Moore College graduates.
25. A classic example would be Gideon's fleece as an instrument of guidance (Judg. 6:36–40). This is often spiritualized so that a 'fleece' becomes any way of testing God for a sign. What is often ignored is that it is not at all obvious that God was pleased with Gideon's approach, or that this event can be made a pattern for Christian behaviour.

foreshadows and leads to Jesus as *the* fulfiller. There is a world of difference between Jesus making fulfilment possible and in Jesus himself *being* the fulfilment. Jesus is thus the primary goal of all the promises and prophecies of the Old Testament. It has been one of the mistakes of some Reformed theologians to emphasize the role of the church as the new Israel and the new people of God without first highlighting Jesus as the new Israel.[26] The individualistic form of this perspective is to regard ourselves as the primary subject matter of all Scripture. Yet Jesus indicated that the Old Testament was about him, and thus it is not first and foremost about us.[27] The lack of a Christocentric perspective leads to some uncertainty about eschatology and, in particular, to the eclipsing of Christ as the centre of biblical theology. It also emboldens the still considerable number of Dispensationalists who dismiss the commonly held notion that the church is the new Israel as an illegitimate 'replacement theology'. In this they do have a valid point, but the term *replacement* is somewhat pejorative and clouds the issue. I would rather see the emphasis on 'fulfilment theology', with Christ at the centre as the true Israel.[28]

The assertion of the biblical theology doubter that Hebrews 11 establishes the exemplary connection between the Testaments as primary is problematic. Hebrews 11:39–12:2a makes it clear that there is something lacking in the exemplary nature of the saints of old:

> And all these, though commended through their faith, did not receive what was promised, since God had provided something better for us, that apart from us they should not be made perfect. Therefore, since we are surrounded by so great a cloud of witnesses, let us also lay aside every weight, and sin which clings so closely, and let us run with endurance the race that is set before us, *looking to Jesus, the founder and perfecter of our faith.* (Italics mine)

By removing the intrusive chapter heading we find the wider context of the examples of faith in the Old Testament. In other words, although faith was the operative principle throughout the old dispensation, it is incomplete without the principle that operates in the New Testament, which is faith in

---

26. The question of whether or not the church can be called the new Israel will be considered later in this study; see especially chapter 10.

27. Luke 24:25–27, 44–45; John 5:39, 45–47.

28. The related issues of the relationship of Jew and Gentile and of Israel to the church are among Donald Robinson's central concerns and will be examined in greater detail in chapter 10.

Christ; looking to Jesus and his gospel. Jesus is the author and the finisher of our faith. An exemplary sermon on David's faith is incomplete and misleading if it does not bring us to great David's greater Son, who is both the subject and object of true faith. It is not legitimate for a Christian simply to imitate an Old Testament character unless this character's significance is in some way refracted through the prism of the gospel. The New Testament's primary call to Christians is that we should become more like Christ, not more like any of the Old Testament heroes. But even the imitation of Christ can be a destructive concept if it is removed from its foundation in the unique substitutionary and representative role of Christ.

Notwithstanding this emphasis, it is important not to overreact to exemplary preaching and teaching. The Bible is full of examples. Evangelical Christians may react rightly to the kind of liberal teaching that reduces Jesus' life and death to the merely exemplary. When Jesus is relegated to the role of 'good teacher' and his death is seen only as a supreme example of self-sacrificing love, we do well to object. We recognize that being imitators of Christ is a significant aspect of New Testament teaching, but Christ as the example is derivative of Christ as the unique author and finisher of our salvation. The work of Christ *for* us is the heart of the gospel and the mainspring of the Christian life. The work of Christ *in* us by his Spirit stems from that gospel and cannot operate without it.

What, then, is the alternative to an overemphasis on exemplary preaching and teaching of the Old Testament? If the characters of the Old Testament are more than examples to follow or, alternatively, to avoid, what are they and how do we penetrate to their significance? Sidney Greidanus in his treatment of the matter indicates that one alternative is the redemptive-historical approach.[29] I would stress again that the redemptive-historical does not exclude the exemplary, but rather provides the context that controls it. It is essentially canonical in the truest sense of the word in that it acknowledges quite explicitly the overall canonical context of any text of the Bible. Once that context is understood, the primacy of the Christ-centred approach is readily seen. This raises the important question of the nature of the Bible's unity within diversity, and the role of Jesus Christ as the centre to which all Scripture leads. It is my aim in this book to open out these questions.

---

29. Sidney Greidanus, *Sola Scriptura: Problems and Principles in Preaching Historical Texts* (Toronto: Wedge, 1970).

Why is biblical theology so neglected?

When I set out to write *Preaching the Whole Bible as Christian Scripture*,[30] I researched the role of biblical theology in the literature on preaching. I surveyed a considerable number of books on preaching, looking for any indication that biblical theology was regarded as significant for the sermon. Even in evangelical books emphasizing the importance of expository preaching there was little to be found that suggested that biblical theology should have a key place in the preparation of a sermon. While there has been a great revival of interest in biblical theology, especially among evangelicals of the Reformed persuasion, it seems to me that we still have a long way to go. It makes me wonder how many seminaries and Bible colleges provide basic instruction in biblical theology as a subject distinct from biblical studies in Old and New Testaments. I cannot answer this question especially with regard to the American or British theological scene. I believe that my own Alma Mater, Moore College, was for some time the only college in Australia with such a course, though this is not the case now. I suspect that the ambivalence regarding biblical theology among evangelical and Reformed preachers and teachers, and the neglect of basic introductory courses in biblical theology in seminaries is at least partly driven by several factors, including the following.

Assumptions about biblical studies curricula

First, if it is assumed that instruction in biblical theology will take place in the established courses in biblical studies, it is left to individual teachers to include it in their curricula. This assumption, in my opinion, is not always well founded. Courses in biblical studies are usually mainly concerned with questions of introduction (literary matters including dating and authorship of the documents), and with exegesis and close reading of the text. This is as it should be, but the exegesis of any text implies its canonical context and, thus, its biblical-theological function.[31] But the more division of labour there is, and the greater the concentration on individual books or corpora, the less likely it is that an overall biblical theology will be in view. The assumption needs to be replaced by the prescription. In other words, biblical studies curricula would

---

30. Graeme Goldsworthy, *Preaching the Whole Bible as Christian Scripture* (Grand Rapids: Eerdmans; Leicester: IVP, 2000).

31. See Kevin J. Vanhoozer, 'Exegesis and Hermeneutics', *NDBT*, pp. 52–64; especially p. 62, where he proposes 'a series of expanding interpretative frameworks'.

need to have issues of biblical theology made explicit. I do not think this can be done effectively without some attention to the method and application of biblical theology, preferably as a distinct subject.

Separation of Old and New Testament studies

The second reason for neglect of biblical theology is closely related to the former. The usually accepted division of labour between Old and New Testament teaching means that questions of the relationship of the Testaments are not likely to be closely considered. Theological curricula have, at least since the nineteenth century, divided the courses in a way that allows for scholarly specialization in one or other Testament. This is reflected in the fact that most of the biblical theologies written since then have been either of the Old Testament or the New Testament.[32] Theologies of the whole Bible are rare, though some useful contributions have been made in recent times.[33] The division of labour is at times ideological, especially when the principles of historical criticism are shaped by philosophical perspectives that happen to be in vogue at the time. The idea that God himself has a purpose that is accurately revealed in the redemptive-historical narrative of the Bible as a whole has been under attack since the seventeenth century. Biblical theology comes to be regarded by many as a futile exercise on the basis that there is no discernible theological unity to the canon. Evangelical seminaries tend to be either reactionary against, or carefully critical of, presuppositions in biblical studies that tend to reduce biblical theology to questions of the history of religious ideas. Yet many, perhaps most, are heirs to the conventional theological curricula that impose a hermeneutical barrier between the Testaments that is more like the Berlin Wall than a freely negotiable border crossing.

---

32. See Hans-Joachim Kraus, *Die Biblische Theologie: Ihre Geschichte und Problematik* (Neukirchen-Vluyn: Neukirchener Verlag, 1970); Wilfrid Harrington, *The Path of Biblical Theology* (Dublin: Gill & Macmillan, 1973). There are many surveys of the history of biblical theology readily available and I do not intend to deal with the matter in general.

33. Harrington, *Path*, p. 260, comments, '[T]here are practically no theologies of the whole Bible. This state of affairs is significant and is not wholly explained by the fact that scholars tend to specialise in one Testament or the other. It would seem, rather, that the complex relationship between the Testaments has not been satisfactorily worked out.'

Lack of agreement about principles and method

Thirdly, in evangelical seminaries there is the lack of consensus about the nature, the principles and the method of biblical theology. How do we design, say, a one-year introductory curriculum that will cover these matters and provide the practical guidance necessary for preachers and teachers? We shall spend some time looking at a variety of evangelical and more conservative approaches to biblical theology to try to assess their methods and the differences between them. It would be quite arrogant to suggest that there is only one valid approach to the subject or even that important insights are not also to be gained from non-evangelical biblical theologians. However, my main purpose in this investigation is to try to establish an approach that is consistent with biblical presuppositions and that is ultimately Christ-centred.

Lack of clarity about different theological disciplines

A fourth reason for the neglect of biblical theology is that in modern times it emerged on the scene as something of a novelty. The fact that Johann Philipp Gabler is usually credited with having first defined the discipline in contrast to dogmatic theology is indicative of this. His 1787 Altdorf address may have pointed up some important distinctions, but his particular brand of biblical theology was born of the Enlightenment and not really the biblical theology we are concerned with as evangelicals. Nevertheless it is true to say that the self-conscious distinctions between dogmatics and biblical theology are not so evident before Gabler. It could be argued that the distinction has not always been helpful. The early and later medieval theologians, and the reformers such as Luther and Calvin, would not have made the distinctions in the way we do today. But it is also clear that from earliest times the questions of the way the Old Testament should function for Christians as a witness to Christ were constantly raised and debated. It would seem that once Gabler's distinctions were accepted and once the philosophical presuppositions of the Enlightenment began to dominate biblical studies, the kind of biblical theology that had always been a part of biblical studies was largely eclipsed.

Failed approaches to biblical theology

A fifth reason for this neglect may well lie in the influence of neo-orthodoxy, which, in America, led to the so-called American Biblical Theology Movement. Modern evangelical biblical theology no doubt owes much to this movement. But, as Brevard Childs demonstrated, the failure of Barth and his followers really to deal with the problem of liberalism and its rejection of the Bible as the word of God was to remain a problem. Neo-orthodoxy's attempt to provide a way out of the stalemate between liberalism and evangelicalism, especially so-called fundamentalism, did not succeed. The demise of the American school was not really answered by Childs's own proposed solution in his canonical biblical theology.[34] As important as Childs's contribution is to the wider scene of biblical theology, it is nevertheless influenced by his acceptance of many of the less helpful tenets of the historical-critical method. When James Barr and others put the American school to rest it seemed to many scholars to sound the death knell for biblical theology as a whole.[35] It did seem to some that G. E. Wright and John Bright had left us with a lame duck that could have little to contribute to serious biblical studies. However, Barr does not have the last say, and the American School was certainly not devoid of merit. John Bright's extraordinary classic *The Kingdom of God* is ample proof of how much we owe to it.[36]

Obviously in the investigation of such a large and complex body of literature as the Bible there are a number of perspectives and ways of organizing the material. Some may be equally valid in being true to the Bible, but that does not make them equally useful in uncovering the inner structures of biblical revelation. There is always the danger of imposing preconceived ideas that come from our own training or our denominational subculture. It is clear that not all evangelical biblical theologies turn out the same. When we compare a Reformed covenantal biblical theology with Dispensationalism we can easily see the disparities. They are both biblical theologies, both evangelical, but poles apart in many of the conclusions reached and in the view of redemptive history constructed. This raises hermeneutical issues, particularly those of the relationship of the Old to the New Testament, and of the basic presuppositions in interpretation.

---

34. Childs's contribution is significant. I was a graduate student at Union Theological Seminary in Virginia when, in January 1972, Childs delivered the annual James Sprunt Lectures entitled 'Canon and Criticism: The Old Testament as Scripture of the Church'. In these lectures he made a preliminary statement of his Canonical Biblical Theology. Since Donald Robinson and Childs had been acquainted for some time, I sent Robinson a copy of the lectures. He had always expressed a high regard for Childs and his work. I received the following letter in reply: 'Dear Graeme, Many thanks for this. In principle, it seems to me that BSC is saying something very important. It would be good to have a staff [Moore College faculty] seminar on O.T. understanding next year. I have written to Bard Childs to express appreciation and to cheer him up. Every good wish, Don.'

35. Brevard S. Childs, *Biblical Theology in Crisis* (Philadelphia: Westminster, 1970), pp. 65–66, 71–72.

36. John Bright, *The Kingdom of God* (New York: Abingdon, 1955).

If the biblical theology Childs described as in crisis is seen by some to have bequeathed to us a lame duck, is there yet a robust and viable biblical theology? If there is, and if it is true to the very nature of God's revelation, then it has the potential to be a formidable weapon in the hands of preachers and teachers of the Bible. Furthermore, it will return the Bible as the One Word of God to ordinary Christians, many of whom seem to regard it as a very mixed collection of texts of differing value to the Christian. Too many Christians go through life with a theoretically unified canon of Scripture and a practical canon consisting of favourite and familiar snippets and extracts removed from their real canonical context.

The task, then, facing evangelical biblical theology is to endeavour to make progress in the following aspects:

- Establishing a set of acceptable working presuppositions about the nature of the Bible.
- Defining what we mean by *biblical theology*.
- Understanding what the nature of the Bible means for how we do biblical theology.
- Determining the hermeneutical procedures that stem from the supremacy of Christ and his gospel.
- Clarifying the theoretical considerations of the relationship of biblical theology to systematics and other theological disciplines.

Some of the practical issues that flow from such an endeavour would include:

- The role of biblical theology in Christian education at all levels.
- The shape of a basic academic curriculum of biblical theology.
- The pastoral applications of biblical theology in the home and local church.

I hope that the following discussions will make some small contribution to these matters. I also hope that this study will show that the Robinson–Hebert schema has great potential for the pursuit of a biblical theology that is robust in providing a firm foundation for both doctrinal formulation and practical theology of all kinds.

2. EVANGELICAL DEFINITIONS AND PRESUPPOSITIONS

Tentative steps towards a definition of biblical theology

How we refine our definition of biblical theology and develop our practice will largely depend on the doctrinal assumptions we make about the Bible. For this reason we need to be aware of our presuppositions and how we have arrived at them. We shall need to consider how this happens in more detail later in this chapter. First, let us recognize that in many cases differences of opinion and conviction come about because of differences in prior assumptions or presuppositions. In Chapter 1 I have moved towards a working definition of biblical theology. If we begin by defining it negatively, what it is not, this does not mean that we rule out connections with other disciplines. *Distinction* does not mean *separation*. Thus, the classic distinctions between biblical and systematic theology do not mean that there is no relationship between them. Indeed, some expressions of biblical theology have drawn heavily on systematic categories.[1] It could be argued that one negative result,

---

1. Some earlier biblical theologies have tended to systematize the content of either Testament under doctrinal categories. This is commonly criticized now as an unhelpful procedure. I would suggest that a positive aspect of this approach is that it suggested the importance of understanding that biblical and systematic theology

perhaps unintended, that came out of Gabler's distinction between systematic and biblical theology was the almost complete separation of the two. It is clear, however, that beyond a very broad consensus of the nature of biblical theology there are varieties of definition, approach and presuppositions that make for quite disparate and sometimes mutually exclusive outcomes. So, let us begin with a broadly consensual definition of biblical theology as the discipline that seeks to understand the theological message, or messages, communicated through the variety of literary phenomena within the various books of the Bible.

Biblical scholars have used the term *biblical theology* to apply to a range of approaches to biblical study. This fact simply makes it all the more difficult to propose a single comprehensive definition. The exegetical study of the meaning of words or word clusters within part or the whole of the canon is sometimes designated as biblical theology. The examination of the theological content of a single textual unit may be referred to as a synchronic biblical-theological study. Likewise the exegetical study of a single book also may be seen as an exercise in synchronic biblical theology. These are called synchronic because they focus on the theological message of text or texts from a particular limited time frame. But such studies will inevitably involve us in questions of the cultural, historical and theological contexts of the particular text. This will tend to drive us towards a focus on the longitudinal study in which the relationship of the text with what came before it and what comes after will be examined. Longitudinal, or diachronic, studies frequently examine the way a particular theme is evident throughout a part or the whole of the canon. The diachronic approach is more likely to be concerned with progressive use of themes or theological motifs.

There are also biblical theologies that are concerned with the whole of one or other Testament without necessarily trying to relate the two Testaments. Many Old Testament theologies are proposed on the basis of Christian presuppositions, even though these are not set out in any detail. And there are biblical theologies that seek to set out the theology of the whole Bible. Biblical theology happens when we engage part or all of the biblical text and endeavour to lay bare the theological content that is there. The immediate goal is not the formulation of Christian doctrine for today, but rather an understanding of what this biblical text reveals about God and his ways with his creation. Even if our presuppositions allow us to assume only that the text reveals what

---

should relate in a symbiotic way. How they should relate was not necessarily elucidated by this approach.

the author thought about God, it is still an exercise in biblical theology. In the wider sense biblical theology is concerned with the structures of revelation and with the ways in which the unity of the biblical canon can be described.

Because I assume an overall unity of the Scriptures as the word of God, I can define biblical theology in a way that emphasizes this unity while not overlooking the diversity. Biblical theology from this perspective is the study of how every text in the Bible relates to every other text in the Bible. It is the study of the matrix of divine revelation in the Bible as a whole. This, of course, is to make assumptions about the unity of Scripture and of its role in divine revelation, which many are unwilling to make. I make them because I believe the nature of the gospel requires me to do so. At the heart of the gospel is the person of Jesus Christ; he is the word of God come in the flesh. The nature of the gospel is such that it establishes Jesus Christ at the centre of the biblical message. Biblical theology, then, is the study of how every text in the Bible relates to Jesus and his gospel. Thus we start with Christ so that we may end with Christ; he is the Alpha and Omega (Rev. 22:13). Biblical theology is Christological, for its subject matter is the whole Bible as God's testimony to Christ. It is therefore, from start to finish, a study of Christ. But, since Christ is the mediator who makes the Father known, biblical theology is also *theological* and not solely Christological.

How biblical theology is actually done will depend a great deal on our dogmatic presuppositions about the nature of Scripture. If we do not have confidence in the Bible as the inspired word of God, we shall most likely treat it as little more that a collection of human documents. Liberalism killed biblical theology because it could not allow for the unity of Scripture as reflecting the one purpose of its one divine Author.[2] A concise definition that begins with the presupposition of revelation is given by Geerhardus Vos: 'Biblical Theology is that branch of Exegetical Theology which deals with the process of the self-revelation of God deposited in the Bible.' He goes on to explain that 'Biblical Theology deals with revelation as a divine activity, not as the finished product of that activity.'[3] He indicates significantly that revelation in the Bible is a process: it is progressive.

Evangelical presuppositions about biblical theology are of two kinds, though these are related. First, there are the theological presuppositions

---

2. See Graeme Goldsworthy, 'The Necessity and Viability of Biblical Theology', *SBJT* 12.4 (2008), pp. 7–8.

3. Geerhardus Vos, *Biblical Theology: Old and New Testaments* (Grand Rapids: Eerdmans, 1948; repr. 1963), p. 13.

concerning the nature of the Bible as the word of God. Secondly, there are hermeneutical presuppositions relating primarily to the nature and purpose of the Bible as literature, albeit inspired literature. Often evangelicals disagree about doctrine as the outcome of biblical theology because, while they agree about the theological presuppositions, their hermeneutical presuppositions and method are very different.[4] As we build a biblical theology, some of our findings will come to constitute secondary presuppositions that will lie behind the way we read and understand the Bible. It should be recognized that the hermeneutical spiral comes into play here. Thus we make certain assumptions about the nature and content of the Bible that are conditioned by our upbringing, our spiritual experiences, our Christian subculture, our unconsciously formed pre-understandings, our initial contact with specific texts, and our already formed doctrines. These then become the framework within which we proceed to read the Bible. This framework will be confirmed or challenged at various stages of our study. Ideally this requires a close reading or exegetical study involving, for best results, a good grasp of the original languages. When our framework is challenged we may seek ways to adjust our presuppositions in the light of the study of the text.

An ultimate presupposition is almost impossible to pin down because it involves us in the difficult problem of subjectivity and objectivity. As subjective, self-conscious beings, we naturally tend to start with ourselves. But is an ultimate, all-embracing presupposition one that starts with us as cognitive beings, or is it one that starts with God or some other reality external to ourselves? Can a basic presupposition be in terms of us as the knowers, or should it be in terms of the objective concern of our knowledge. Should an ultimate presupposition be about us or about God? The philosopher Descartes left us with the dilemma of total subjectivity (*cogito ergo sum*: 'I think, therefore I am'). I have suggested elsewhere that Calvin avoided such a dilemma by posing the interrelatedness of subjectivity and objectivity.[5] He did this on the basis of his Christian understanding of God and creation. We can only know the one in relation to the other or, as Calvin puts it, knowledge of God requires knowledge of self, and vice versa.[6] The evidence of Genesis 1:26–31 is that human

---

4. Differences concerning the Millennium, for example, are largely the result of different hermeneutical processes.

5. Graeme Goldsworthy, *Gospel-Centred Hermeneutics* (Nottingham: Apollos; Downers Grove: IVP, 2006), pp. 186–187.

6. John Calvin, *Institutes of the Christian Religion*, tr. Ford Lewis Battles, LCC 20–21 (Philadelphia: Westminster; London: SCM, 1960), 1.1.1.

subjectivity was to be subject to and aware of divine objectivity. Adam and Eve could know themselves truly only as beings subject to God and his word. But, however we form our presuppositions, we must be prepared to defend them in terms of their explanatory power and self-consistency. Explanatory power, in turn, must be able to deal with all truth claims and all of our notions of reality.

For a theologian to pursue a biblical theology implies some kind of already existing dogmatic framework regarding the Bible. Biblical theologians who insist that we do not need dogmatics simply have not examined their own presuppositions about the Bible. The issue is not really that of which comes first, dogmatics or biblical theology, because they are interrelated and involve the hermeneutical spiral. Because of the symbiotic relationship between them, I do not think it is possible to be competent in one without the other. A similar symbiosis exists between dogmatics and historical theology since dogmaticians cannot ignore the history of the discipline. Evangelical biblical-theological presuppositions will include some cognisance of the dogmas discussed below as the structure for progress in theologizing.

Evangelical theological presuppositions in biblical theology

The doctrine of God

We would not be interested in the theology of the Bible if we did not have some previously formed notion that the Bible can deliver a theology. It may be little more than the recognition that religious ideas about God are to be found throughout the biblical literature. But a Christian believer will find that disciplined examination of the text leads to certain conclusions. God as Creator, and humanity created in the image of God, are doctrines integral to the evangelical view of Scripture. An evangelical doctrine of God that supports both the notion of a biblical theology and the grounds for a fruitful investigation will inevitably include the dogma of the Trinity. In other words, as Christians we bring our Christian faith, including some idea of God as Trinity to the task. It also means that we go to the Old Testament with a greater or lesser formation of Christian presuppositions about it as a book that is from God and about Christ. Christians do not read the Old Testament having left all their Christian convictions behind them. We may try to suspend them for a time in order to allow the Old Testament to speak for and within itself, but its application to us requires us to recognize it as fulfilled in Christ.

The dogma of the Trinity will shape the way we understand God as the communicator of his revelation. God as a communal being is also seen to be a communicating being. A trinitarian dogmatic will inform the way we do our theology and the way we formulate principles of interpretation. The doctrine of the Trinity and its related doctrine, the incarnation of Jesus, form the basis for understanding all relationships in terms of both their unity and their distinctions. This is vital for the proper handling of a progressive dynamic in revelation and for the avoidance of a view of Scripture as a flat and static body of timeless propositions. Different parts of Scripture bear different relationships to Christ and to the Christian. From the outset we recognize that neither dogmatics nor biblical theology can be merely descriptive. That God is Trinity, with Jesus being the one mediator (1 Tim. 2:5), means that in testifying to Christ the Bible testifies to God: Father, Son and Holy Spirit.

The doctrine of the word of God

One aspect of the doctrine of the word of God begins with the creation account that asserts the creation of all things from nothing (*ex nihilo*) by the divine fiat 'Let there be . . .' That God pronounces each day's creation as good means this word achieves what he intends it to. At no point does God say, 'Oops! Scrub that one.' His word is thus a sovereign word, self-interpreting, self-authenticating, infallible and all-powerful. It is the foundation of a hermeneutic of authorial intent. It is also the foundation of our understanding of the Bible as coherent, understandable and containing the truth about the real world. The communicating God of the Bible is the God who speaks. He speaks creation into being and is said to uphold all things by his word (Pss 104:1–35; 119:89–91; John 1:3; Heb. 1:3; 2 Pet. 3:5–7). As he brings into existence the human pair as the pinnacle of his creation, God speaks to them words intended to be understood and obeyed (Gen. 1:26–30). God's relationship with people thereafter is focused on his word. The word subsequent to the creation is initially given directly to individual humans, but later, when God's people are identified as a nation, it is mainly mediated by the prophetic servants of God to all his people. It is a word that reveals, redeems and judges. The ultimate prophet, Jesus of Nazareth, is also the fullest and final word of God. He is the Word of God incarnate who is the revealer, redeemer and judge. We can either approach these data with the degree of scepticism that characterized so much historical-critical enquiry, or we can come to the biblical assertions with confidence that they are words from God. Historical criticism in its extreme form rejected the dogma that God both set in train the events of history and also acted within them. It rejected the notion of divine revelation within space and time, and thus ultimately made biblical theology impossible. In its place it put the study of the history of religious ideas.

Although the biblical account begins with God speaking in creation, it is

really no surprise to learn that God is Trinity with intra-trinitarian communication. In other words God is eternally a speaking God. God is a communal
being and the communal relationship he creates with human beings reflects
his very being. Vern Poythress has suggested that the prayer of Jesus in John
17 reflects the eternal conversation between the Father and the eternal Son.[7]
Whatever the nature of that divine conversation, it is reflected in the words
addressed by Jesus to the Father. It is reasonable to deduce, then, that the
Bible describes God's speaking the creation into being and then addressing
humans with words because that is what God is and does. In other words, we
cannot simply reduce 'And God said . . .' to a metaphor or to an anthropo-
morphism.

One area that must be considered concerns the nature of Jesus as the Word
of God incarnate and the relationship he bears to the Bible as the word of God
written. We should recognize that God does not have two conflicting words,
which would be the case if we could drive a wedge between the historical Jesus
and the biblical Jesus. This would be to separate the Bible from the real Jesus.
That the Bible is the word of God written is dependent on its relationship to
the Word of God incarnate. It is because it is the Spirit-inspired testimony to
Jesus Christ that we can know it as the word of God. Its authority is not based
only on the Spirit's role in inspiring its writing, for it is also the role of the Holy
Spirit thereby to testify to Christ, the Word (John 14:26; 15:26; 16:13–15). In
biblical theology we are constantly confronted by a humanly mediated, written
text that claims to be the word of the divine Author. Thus the relationship of
the divine to the human in this mediated revelation reflects the relationship of
the divine and human natures of Christ. The doctrine of the incarnation, and
how we understand and handle it, becomes the vital dogmatic pointer to how
we should understand certain relationships within Scripture.

It stands to reason that if the Bible is the word of God, a number of things
follow. In the Old Testament we find numerous cases where a prophet intro-
duces his words with 'Thus says Yahweh' or 'An oracle of Yahweh'. The
implication is that what the prophet says is what God says. It follows that
an inspired human mediator does not compromise the divine word simply
by being human. Nor does human language fail to communicate what God
wants to communicate, since it reflects God's speech. It further follows that
God does not contradict himself, and thus we accept the Bible as the one
word of the one God about the one way of salvation through the one medi-

---

7. Vern S. Poythress, *God-Centered Biblical Interpretation* (Phillipsburg: Presbyterian &
Reformed, 1999), pp. 16–17.

ator, Jesus Christ. The divine–human nature of the Bible reflects the divine–human nature of Jesus to whom it testifies.

The Bible as the word of God relates closely to Jesus Christ as the Word of God come in the flesh. Jesus' own conviction was that the Old Testament was a testimony to him or, to put it another way, he is the central subject matter of the Hebrew Scriptures. Although the authors did not write directly of Jesus of Nazareth, what they did write about has its final meaning determined by its relationship to Jesus. Thus Jesus can assert that Moses 'wrote of me' (John 5:46). A number of things follow from such assertions, not least that there is an essential unity to the Old Testament that carries over into the New Testament. If we allow that such Christ-centredness is indeed a key attribute of the entire biblical canon, the unity of the canon must also be asserted. That God has spoken to us, first by the prophets and then by his Son (Heb. 1:1–2), is at the centre of the quest for a biblical theology. This unity of the message of Scripture is not first and foremost arrived at empirically. When the matter is approached from the dubious presupposition that empirical evidence can be the only justification for asserting unity, the result is often scepticism. We must allow the person of Jesus to establish the basis of unity in Scripture.

The canon as the limit of inspired Scripture

This question of the actual bounds of Scripture raises several related issues. Protestant evangelical theologians have rejected the Roman Catholic claims that the church gave us the Bible and has the authority both to delineate it and to interpret it in accordance with its dogmas. The Protestant view is that God gave us his word and the church can only recognize and submit to its authority. The word created the church, not the other way round. Jesus' words in John 10:27, 'My sheep hear my voice, and I know them, and they follow me,' provide an important clue to the process. The fact that this process may have been quite drawn out until the present canon was accepted does not alter the fact that we can regard the canon as closed. The Protestant view avoids the ambiguities of the grey areas of the Roman Catholic basis of authority in canonical Scripture: deutero-canonical texts and church tradition.

Oscar Cullmann has emphasized the organic nature of the canonical message based on the coherence of its development and interpretation in the kerygma, the gospel proclamation.[8]

---

8. Oscar Cullmann, *Salvation in History* (London: SCM, 1967), pp. 122–123.

Both the limitation and the continuation of salvation history are well founded within the biblical salvation history itself. Its limitation amounts to the fixing of the canon. It seems to me impossible to justify the canon apart from salvation history and it is not by accident that its justification is inevitably questioned whenever salvation history is rejected. But the usual attempts to establish the dogmatic necessity of the canon seem insufficient to me, for they do not see how the canon is necessarily anchored in the inmost essence of the Bible itself, that is, in salvation history. It is not as though with the fixing of the canon a foreign element was imposed on the books of the Bible which was absent in its various writings. On the contrary, I would like to show here that both the idea of a canon and the manner of its realization are a crucial part of the salvation history of the Bible.[9]

Cullmann's thrust here is the important point that the storyline of the Bible is coherent and is inseparable from the kerygma in a way that makes the non-canonical conspicuous. Of course there were difficult areas that would take a while for the church finally to decide upon. Such a one is the book of Revelation. But once it was recognized that this unique piece of literature was truly consistent with the rest of the New Testament, it was accepted as canonical.

Donald Robinson's view of the canon hinges on the dual concepts of gospel and apostle. He rejects the view of his teacher C. F. D. Moule that the canon consists of those documents that provide the best evidence for Christian beginnings, a view that is very similar to John Bright's understanding of the authority of the Old Testament as resting on the best documents available.[10] Robinson's position, I believe, does not clash with Cullmann's, but it does place the emphasis elsewhere in a way that shows some differences in understanding of the authority of Scripture. In dealing with the question of canonicity he states:

The answer lies in the content of the *gospel* which the basic documents point to as their precipitating word, and in the rule of the *apostle* who was sent out to preach and teach that gospel to the world. If the rule of faith was dependent on apostolic witness, we need to identify more closely what was the essential kernel of this preached message – the gospel – and who were its prime exponents – the apostles.[11]

---

9. Ibid., p. 294.

10. John Bright, *The Authority of the Old Testament* (London: SCM, 1967), pp. 26, 28, 30.

11. Donald W. B. Robinson, *Faith's Framework: The Structure of New Testament Theology* (Exeter: Paternoster; Sutherland, NSW: Albatross, 1985), p. 39, italics his.

It is important to settle the question of the canon if we are to proceed with the search for some understanding of its structure. There is no doubt that Robinson's biblical theology depends on the acceptance of the Christian (Protestant) canon. It is also clear that his approach is centred on the gospel as witnessed to by the apostles. The canon thus defined provides the framework for our Christian faith.

The unity of the canon of Scripture

The unity of Scripture and the existence of an authoritative canon are both data of systematic theology. The biblical theologian who thinks this discipline makes systematics redundant needs to reflect on how we are able to distinguish a Bible from other literature and to privilege it with special authority. That some biblical theologians have tended to downplay the importance of systematics does not constitute an argument but rather betrays a lack of reflection on what doing biblical theology is about and how we can achieve it.

Since I have already expressed the conviction that evangelical biblical theology should proceed with the presuppositions of the unity of Scripture and the centrality of Christ, we need to examine these presuppositions further. In speaking about the unity of Scripture it is important to make clear what sort of unity is meant. The Bible, as a book, can exhibit unity in different ways. The three major dimensions of the Bible are literary, historical and theological. The literary unity cannot be usefully reduced to the fact that all sixty-six books have come to be collected under one cover. In fact there is very little by way of unity at the level of the literary genres. A collection of documents written over more than a thousand years in three different languages and containing a long list of different genres and forms does not make for much that we can call unity. There are many extra-biblical texts that closely resemble the biblical texts in terms of language and genre, and even of subject matter, but that have not been recognized as Scripture. Beyond the narrative continuity, literary unity is clearly not very meaningful. The diversity of the canon is found principally in its literary dimension. Literary diversity demands careful literary hermeneutics.

What justification, then, can we propose for the fact that these books were collected and put together as one collection? Their unity lies in both the historical and theological dimensions. The messages of the books belong together in that they concern God, his people and the historical process. When we look at the historical dimension the vexed question of salvation history arises. We must leave the discussion of what we mean by that term till later. We shall need to consider the relationship of theology and history as lying at the heart of biblical theology. At this point it suffices to say that there is a discernible timeline of the deeds of God that provides an aspect of the Bible's unity. Even those books that do not major on the narrative or story of God's workings contain links, sometimes indirect, to the overall progression of events. The Old Testament wisdom books are a case in point, as are the epistles of the New Testament.

The New Testament indicates that Jesus did not have any problems with the Scriptures (the Old Testament) but rather he asserted that they were about him, that they testified to him, that they were authoritative and that they could not be broken. It is also the clear conviction of the New Testament authors that the Scriptures find their fulfilment in Jesus. Jesus' view that 'the Scripture cannot be broken' (John 10:35) reinforces the notion that there is no problem with the authority and unity of the Scriptures. The actual nature and structure of the unity is something biblical theology addresses. With this unity as one of our basic presuppositions we proceed to examine empirically the shape and content of the canon of Scripture.

Closely relating to the historical unity of the Bible is the theological message being carried. The theology is never in the form of timeless abstraction. It is given within the historical processes of God acting within history to bring about his purposes. Broadly speaking, it is the task of biblical theology to understand the historically contextualized theology, and it is the task of dogmatics or systematic theology to understand the contemporary significance of the theology that has been thus contextualized in ancient history. I say broadly speaking because we may observe the beginning of the process of forming a systematic theology within the Scriptures themselves. Obviously doctrine is not something invented out of thin air by the sub-apostolic Christian church.

The human problem and God's response

The human problem is expressed biblically as one of rebellion against the Creator and the consequent judgment of God pronounced against this rebellion. This fact is integral to the biblical story. Our rejection of God's word has left us under the judgment of God so that we are dead in our trespasses and sins. Our receptivity to the message of the Bible is so badly damaged that none of us human beings can by nature read, understand and submit to God's word as we should. The grace of God is such that he gives his Holy Spirit in regeneration to his elect so that they repent of sin and believe the gospel. As our understanding of the gospel grows it affects our comprehension of the one message of the Bible. As Jesus opened the minds of his disciples to understand the Scriptures (Luke 24:45), so also he must open our minds to the relationships between all Scripture and his person and ministry.

The hermeneutical spiral is at work here also because understanding more of the Bible's unity will enhance one's grasp of the gospel. The gospel in turn reinforces our understanding of the unity of the biblical message. And so on.

This matter addresses the question of objectivity and empiricism. Since Bultmann and Gadamer there are few, I think, who would imagine that we can approach the study of Scripture without any prejudices and with pure objectivity. The old historical-critical catchcry of 'the assured results of biblical criticism' and the branding of those with conservative presuppositions as 'obscurantist' have become somewhat muted. The relationship of our subjectivity to the objective reality around us is the concern of both biblical theology and dogmatics. The history of modern hermeneutics shows how the focus of scholars has moved over time from objectivity to subjectivity. Those who were most convinced of an objective scientific approach leading to assured results were those that were most convinced of their own unprejudiced objectivity and presuppositional neutrality. Historical criticism claimed to get beyond even the authorial intent of the final redactor to that of the various sources that lay behind the biblical text. The subsequent move to the new literary criticism was a recognition that no such objectivity existed. Authorial intent was discarded and only the text in itself could be considered. Once this happened it was only a matter of time for the emergence of the reader-based hermeneutic that reduced understanding to subjectivity. This *either–or* approach is seen by evangelical theologians as a symptom of our estrangement from God who is Trinity and whose nature establishes a perspective of *both–and* in relationships. Claims to either complete objectivity or complete subjectivity reflect the theological hubris of humanity in rebellion against the self-revelation of God.

Evangelical hermeneutical presuppositions in biblical theology

It is not entirely accurate to say that the hermeneutical assumptions or presuppositions pick up where the theological ones leave off. Hermeneutics that focuses on the literary dimension cannot be engaged apart from the theological issues. Once again the distinctions we make between them do not mean separation and largely exist in order to clarify the issues.

The languages of the Bible
Theologically we must assess human language as a gift of the speaking God. The idea that it is inadequate to convey truth about God and his purposes

is one of the non sequiturs of both liberalism and neo-orthodoxy. While we recognize that there is mystery in God and his ways, and that the human mind and spirit cannot plum the depths of God's being, it simply does not follow that human language is not able to express such truth as God means to reveal to us. Such a negative assertion is itself a use of human language to say something that is supposed to be meaningful about God. If God chooses to reveal himself and his plan of salvation, and if he chooses to regenerate the minds of his people to receive such revelation, there is no need for us to claim exhaustive knowledge in order to understand it, for we know that the truth we have is from the one who alone has exhaustive knowledge.

Understanding the way the three biblical languages behave and were used is important for biblical interpretation. Linguistic issues of grammar and syntax are at the heart of biblical exegesis. I hasten to add that a good translation is the next best thing to recourse to the Hebrew, Aramaic and Greek texts. I have set out elsewhere my reasons for believing that the so-called formal equivalence end of the translation spectrum is more conducive to the doing of biblical theology than the so-called dynamic equivalence end.[12]

The interrelationship of hermeneutics and biblical theology can be seen when we engage in a biblical-theological study of communication and interpretation.[13] There is nothing inherently unreasonable or unbelievable about the proposition that God communicates with the authorial intent that humans who are created in his image can receive and understand his communication. Only a set of purely naturalistic presuppositions would rule this out. For the evangelical, issues of subjectivity relate to the biblical teaching about the effects of the Fall and the work of the Spirit in regeneration.

Human language, then, can be seen as reflecting the divine language of the intra-trinitarian communication. The biblical languages must therefore be looked at from both the linguistic perspectives of human languages, and also as the divinely ordained medium of divine–human communication. The rules of grammar will be seen as descriptive of linguistic usage. Such usage may or may not contain uniquely biblical manifestations in the genres of the literature. It is to be expected that there is mainly a commonality of linguistic unity shared by biblical and non-biblical texts. Such commonality does not imply that the biblical languages and their grammar and syntax are non-theological. If all human language does reflect divine discourse, and if all Scripture is inspired by the Holy Spirit, then the grammar and syntax of the

---

12. Goldsworthy, *Gospel-Centred Hermeneutics*, ch. 18.

13. This matter is considered in ibid., ch. 4.

biblical texts are not gratuitous. In the sovereign purposes of God, Hebrew, Aramaic and koine Greek are ordained by him to communicate what he wants to communicate and in the way he wants to communicate it. The serious biblical theologian will work from the original texts and, when using a translation, have recourse to one that is true to the original texts.[14]

The literary nature of the Bible

Probably the most important area of literary concern is the identification of genre differences. The issue is not that of giving a piece of text a precise name of genre identification, but rather that of understanding the variety of ways that literature can be used to communicate. Some conservative evangelicals, for example, make a basic error in assuming that the literal interpretation of all texts is both mandatory and obvious. A lot depends on what precisely is meant by *literal*.[15] Genre criticism has become an important aspect of hermeneutical investigation. This has enabled texts to be examined with greater precision than is possible without the recognition of the variety of ways human language can be used to communicate.

Genre criticism, rightly used, should avoid the kind of problem that arises when, for example, we classify Daniel and Revelation as apocalypses and assume we have thereby 'cracked the code'. Such classification is too broad to do justice to the variety of genres that may be contained in the one document. Not only do both books contain much that is not strictly apocalyptic, but it can easily be assumed that the category *apocalyptic* is a classification that follows fixed rules and conveys unambiguous meaning without complications. Some studies have drawn up lists of apocalyptic characteristics by which to test the biblical books and even to date them and to establish hermeneutical rules for them. Yet the edifice of scholarly reconstruction of apocalyptic

---

14. The spectrum of formal equivalence to dynamic (or functional) equivalence in translations from one language to another involves us in some important, if complicated, issues. I cannot go into them here but have made some comments in the work referred to in n. 5 above which indicate why I think the more 'literal' end of the spectrum is to be preferred, particularly in doing biblical theology. However, I recognize that dynamic equivalence in which ideas rather than words are in view can provide some productive leads in conceptual links between texts.

15. This is discussed by Vern S. Poythress, *Understanding Dispensationalists* (Grand Rapids: Zondervan Academie, 1987); see especially ch. 8, 'What Is Literal Interpretation?' See also Peter Cotterell and Max Turner, *Linguistics and Biblical Interpretation* (London: SPCK, 1989), ch. 9.

has in some cases resulted in something that is really not found in any of the separate texts said to be apocalyptic.

I would suggest that care is needed before drawing parallels between biblical texts and trends in secular writings that are assumed to have come from the same or a similar provenance. The important thing is not the label but the way meaning is conveyed. While background culture and history form part of the context within which we understand the meaning of the biblical texts, the overruling hermeneutical principles must come from within Scripture itself. Scripture as God's word must interpret history and culture, not the other way round.

The relationship of the two Testaments

For the biblical theologian one of the most important areas is the New Testament understanding and usage of Old Testament texts. This is only one aspect of the broader issue of the relationship of the Testaments.[16] It is a complex matter that has exercised biblical scholars since earliest times. If the New Testament authors seem to have no doubts about how this relationship works, they also present some important diversity in perspective. That in itself is not a problem. The problems for us lie in how the New Testament's uses of the Old Testament can be extended into the life and understanding of the church throughout the ages. The history of biblical interpretation shows that the matter was always problematic and still is.

The relationship of the Testaments, then, remains a key issue in the pursuit of a unified biblical theology. We must keep in mind the fact that Jesus and the apostles proclaimed from the Old Testament that Jesus was the Christ. This was apparently never seen to be some Procrustean task or, in more modern terms, a forcing of square pegs into round holes. The Scriptures testified to Jesus; their promises were fulfilled in his life, death and especially his resurrection. The biblical-theological and hermeneutical task is to try to discern how the relationship of Jesus and the gospel to the Old Testament was understood by Jesus, the apostles and the New Testament authors. The relationship of Jesus to the Scriptures was not obvious to everyone, and it was really problematic for the Jews and even for the disciples. This relationship of the texts to the person and work of Jesus is central to the unity of the Bible.

---

16. See David L. Baker, *Two Testaments, One Bible: The Theological Relationship Between the Old and New Testaments*, 3rd ed. (Nottingham: Apollos; Downers Grove: IVP, 2010).

The underlying historical framework of the Bible

The matter of history and its relationship to theology will need to be carefully examined.[17] Christianity claims to be a historic faith and thus poses the question of how God acts in history, and how we can perceive historical events as acts of God. It also raises questions about biblical historiography. It is necessary to try to understand the function and coherence of historic events as they are recorded in the biblical texts. There is little dispute that what purports to be some kind of historic timeline can be discerned within the canon of Scripture. There is a storyline that functions as a framework for what is perceived to be the works of God in space and time.

An evangelical hermeneutic differs from a rationalist-empiricist one. While the two will overlap, they differ in that the rules for judging historical truth claims are based on essentially different grounds. When we talk of the historical framework of the Bible we begin by taking seriously the word of the Lord of history as he pronounces on all history from eternity to eternity. We accept that God can tell us, and indeed does tell us about history that is beyond the scope of modern secular research and historiography. This includes the history of creation and the early history of the world and humanity, and also the history that has not yet occurred but is certain because God is also the Lord of future history.

It should be noted that, although the biblical history focuses on one nation and on the people of God in the early church, its scope is universal. The history of Genesis 1 – 11 is a history of all the nations of the world either explicitly or implicitly. That it is a schematized history that does not follow the lines of modern historiography does not alter the fact that it is set forth as historical.[18] The promises to Abraham that follow are universal in scope in that they are directed not only to Abraham's actual descendants, but also to all the nations of the world. The story in the Acts of the Apostles is of the universalizing of the gospel throughout the whole world. And the final salvation and judgment that figure so prominently in the book of Revelation bring all world history to an end.

---

17. See chapter 3.

18. Questions of biblical historiography are discussed by a number of evangelical authors including V. Philips Long, *The Art of Biblical History*, Foundations of Contemporary Interpretation 5 (Grand Rapids: Zondervan, 1994), and Iain Provan, V. Philips Long and Tremper Longman III, *A Biblical History of Israel* (Louisville: Westminster, 2003). See also Craig G. Bartholomew, C. Stephen Evans, Mary Healy and Murray Rae (eds.), *'Behind' the Text: History and Biblical Interpretation*, SHS 4 (Carlisle: Paternoster; Grand Rapids: Zondervan, 2003).

The theological content of the Bible

By 'theology' we mean that which is revealed of God and his ways. Some
may write this off as nothing more significant than what people have thought
about God or gods. The extreme form of this perspective is that there is no
theology in the Bible but only the records of religious ideas. We also need
to recognize that the history of Israel's religious ideas does not necessarily
coincide with the theology of the Old Testament. In fact, there is frequently
tension between what is set out prophetically as normative revealed truth and
the actual beliefs and behaviour of the professing recipients of the revelation
in both Old and New Testaments. This becomes increasingly obvious in the
tension between Jesus' interpretation of the Old Testament and that of his
Jewish contemporaries. The reality that made it a gross inaccuracy to assess
the early church as merely an insignificant sect within Judaism is the radical
hermeneutical divide between the emerging Rabbinic Judaism and the gospel
proclamation of Jesus as the Christ, the Messiah of Israel.

Evangelical biblical theology works on the presupposition that the Bible
is revelatory. There is some dispute as to how the revelation of theological
content occurs. The idea that it is propositional has come under scrutiny
especially since there is a lot of non-propositional language in the Bible. Some
argue that non-propositional forms of language, such as metaphors, poetic
imagery, commands and suppositions mean that we cannot characterize the
Bible as propositional revelation. However, there are also grounds for asserting that such modes of speech that are not in the indicative can be understood
for their propositional force in the context in which they occur. The development of the speech-act theory has been taken up by a number of theologians,
including some evangelicals, as a useful analysis of the way language works. Its
limitations have also been expressed.[19] Speech-act theory has the potential of
working against the broader scene within which 'speech-acts' occur. But this
broader view, the big picture, is the very thing biblical theology seeks to deal
with. I think it is true to say that generations of Bible-believing Christians have
instinctively asked questions about the way the biblical texts convey revelation
and applicable truth. That many mistakes have been made does not alter the
fact that the written word of God has not been discarded as indecipherable.

Having acknowledged the non-indicative modes, we can nevertheless

---

19. There are those who provide important caveats to the application of speech-act
    theory to the Bible. See, for example, Vern Poythress, 'Canon and Speech Act:
    Limitations in Speech-Act Theory, with Implications for a Putative Theory of
    Canonical Speech Acts', *WTJ* 70 (2008), pp. 337–354.

assert that the indicative framework of salvation history is so pervasive as to provide the safe context from within which to deal with all the metaphors, poetic images, analogies, symbolic expressions, imperatives, subjunctives, optatives, and the like. This is even more pronounced when we recognize the normative nature of the indicatives regarding the life, death and resurrection of Jesus of Nazareth. In other words, salvation history is, in the final analysis, the history of Jesus the Christ.

* * *

There are no doubt other presuppositions to evangelical biblical theology that we might consider. I think those dealt with above provide a framework for both the theory and practice of sound biblical theology. It is time now to turn to some of the specifics that make for a legitimate approach to the whole subject, and that may be said to justify a particular method. I must stress that the Robinson–Hebert schema on which I have modelled my own approach is not put forward with any sense that it is the only possible way to proceed. But it has commended itself to me as probably one of the best ways of arriving at a credible evangelical modus operandi with enormous practical implications.

3. SALVATION AND HISTORY

The idea of salvation history

There has always been a tension between the idea that God acts within time and space and those views that attempt to circumvent or supersede history. This tension goes back to early biblical times in which the historical view of Israel that God has acted in a linear progression of events in the real world was at variance with the Canaanite mentality that tied history into mythic cycles.[1] It is seen in the Christology of the New Testament that is founded on the reality of the incarnation of God in Christ. Even in the primitive church the tension existed between this historical understanding of Christ and the

---

1. G. Ernest Wright championed this contrast between Hebrew and Canaanite views of history in his monographs *The Old Testament Against its Environment*, SBT 2 (London: SCM, 1950), and *God Who Acts: Biblical Theology as Recital*, SBT 8 (London: SCM, 1952). Wright, a leader of the so-called American School of Biblical Theology, followed a view of 'history as revelation', which weakened the notion of revelation by word that interprets history. This idea that the biblical witness consists of inferences and deductions made by people reflecting on their own historical situations is also stated in Wright's book *The Old Testament and Theology* (New York: Harper & Row, 1969), ch. 2.

Hellenistic Docetism that John combats in his first epistle (1 John 4:1–6). Irenaeus (second century) refutes the Gnostics by appealing to the apostolic tradition and to their use of the Old Testament. The Antiocene hermeneutic that engaged a history-based typology rejected the ahistorical allegorizing that prevailed right up to the Reformation. Arlis John Ehlen in his survey of *Heilsgeschichte* in Old Testament theology draws a line of progression in the idea of salvation history from the Bible to the apostles, and then to Irenaeus. He refers to Irenaeus' view of historical 'recapitulation' as his argument against Gnosticism.[2] Like the Hebrews the Greeks were also interested in history but, as Ehlen points out, it was humanistic, glorifying the Greeks, never 'holy history'.[3] The Reformation restored a biblical view of history only to have it squandered in post-Reformation orthodoxy's 'resurgence of an almost purely systematic, doctrinal approach'.[4] It was the emergence of covenant theology with the federal theology of men like Cocceius in the seventeenth century that really established salvation history in Protestant theology. The modern use of the term *Heilsgeschichte* is usually attributed to the Lutheran J. C. K. von Hofmann in the nineteenth century.

That biblical history is salvation history is a commonly held evangelical position. A key dimension of the Bible is its historical narrative that is viewed theologically. The Bible is concerned with a specific history of God's actions in the world. It is history under the sovereign control of God. Thus evangelical biblical theology is frequently associated with the notion of redemptive history or salvation history. In broadest terms this conveys some concept of God's actions to save or redeem that take place within human history. It also implies that God's revelation of his redemptive plan involves a discernible historical framework. This raises the question of the status of the Bible's historical truth claims and theology. But even the idea of an overarching salvation history in the Bible has not always been well received.

Much of the problem involves the relationship of biblical history to, for want of a better term, *secular history*. The historical-critical method of investigation led to varying degrees of scepticism about the reliability of the biblical account of history. As a result, some solutions posed a salvation history that was on a completely different plane from real history. The history of faith was seen to be something that bore the weight of theological interpretation

---

2. Arlis John Ehlen, 'Old Testament Theology as *Heilsgeschichte*', *CTM* 35.9 (October 1964), p. 520.

3. Ibid.

4. Ibid., p. 522.

but not necessarily the weight of historical investigation and fact. Taken this way, salvation history simply means that people wrote an account of God's redemptive work as a story, a story that may have little to do with real human history. Some have reduced it to the level of etiological myth used as a means of explaining in theistic terms the situation contemporary to the writers.[5]

An evangelical concept of salvation history is that the Bible contains a perceptible historical timeline that reaches from creation to the new creation. This is not to suggest that this timeline has no gaps or no mystery. And, strictly speaking, *salvation history* would not include the events before the fall into sin. Nevertheless the term is useful to express the entire biblical timeline because the story of creation and Eden constitute the necessary background for God's redemptive work. We can assert its comprehensive range simply because the Bible does. Some may question the joining of the words *salvation* (used adjectivally) or *redemptive* to history because of the problem of the relationship of theology to history. I can see no real difficulty in doing so. I understand these terms to mean that God's work of salvation or redemption is done within human history, and that the biblical account of salvation is given within the framework of historical narrative. The incarnation of God the Son is the ultimate declaration that God works among us in space and time. Jesus of Nazareth as a historical figure establishes the validity of the story that leads to him and that flows from him. Not only does salvation take place within our history, but the purposes of God are what constitute human history in the first place. I take a Reformed position here in that I do not contemplate God as the helpless observer of human affairs, including folly and evil, but as totally sovereign in all things. Thus we are not conceiving of human history as having an existence in itself within which God decides to interfere and to inject the story of sin and redemption. If the biblical account is correct, all history is involved in salvation history. The biblical story focuses on a particular part of world history, but it states explicitly, and also implies, the relationship of all human history to the work of God in salvation. In systematic theology we would be concerned here with what is referred to as common grace: God's plan and purpose being active for the preservation of the whole of human-

---

5. Alan R. Millard rightly challenges James Barr's assertion that etiological narratives have no place in history writing: 'On a larger scale, it may be noted, all history writing is a specie of etiology, and analogy is basic to the work of modern historians' (Alan R. Millard, James K. Hoffmeier and David W. Baker [eds.], *Faith, Tradition, and History: Old Testament Historiography in its Near Eastern Context* [Winona Lake, Ind.: Eisenbrauns, 1994], p. 40).

ity. The important thing is that the story begins, continues and ends with the universal scope of God's work. The specifics show the process by which the history of the cosmos goes from creation to new creation.

To qualify history with the terms *salvation* or *redemptive* implies that the history includes, or at least presupposes, a situation from which people need to be saved or redeemed. The biblical story includes much that is negative and could therefore just as easily be dubbed judgment history.[6] It is one of the marvels of God's grace that it continues unabated within the life of a people that is full of ambivalence, rebellion and evil. But then, of course, the thing that makes grace gracious is that it is undeserved mercy to those who deserve only the judgment of condemnation. That redemption is the other side of condemnation is the consistent picture throughout Scripture. Salvation, it emerges, is effected only when it is accompanied by acts of judgment. In fact salvation itself is also an act of God's judgment in which those saved are declared to be just and guiltless. The supreme example of negative judgment is the cross of Christ, which demonstrates the full weight of God's wrath against sinful rebellion. Given that human sin or covenant-breaking is a constant part of biblical history, there is no reason why it should not be included in the general concept of salvation history.

When I say that all history is salvation history I am, of course, introducing the theological interpretation I believe the Bible intends. It is important to see that all human history from creation to new creation belongs to God's sovereign work and purpose.[7] While the biblical focus is on the history of a

6. Elmer Martens notes the problem Claus Westermann had with salvation history because history in the Old Testament is also a history of judging: 'The Oscillating Fortunes of "History" Within Old Testament Theology', in Millard, Hoffmeier and Baker, *Faith, Tradition, and History*, p. 321. I believe the problem is purely one of semantics and does not alter the view that the Old Testament contains a historical structure. Martens also looks at some of the problems the idea of salvation history poses. Martens concludes, 'In short, my appeal is for the kind of balance exhibited in Westermann's approach. In his approach history is neither dismissed nor over-played' (ibid., p. 340). Cullmann is fully aware that his term *salvation history* must also embrace disaster and judgment (*Salvation in History* [London: SCM], p. 123).
7. Gerald O'Collins, S. J., *Foundations of Theology* (Chicago: Loyola University Press, 1971), ch. 5, 'Salvation History', p. 87, refers to the distinction between general (or universal) salvation history and special (or official) salvation history: 'No one asserts that the events of Israel and the New Testament "explain" in any proper sense of the word the whole of human history. At best they provide the warrant for

specifically chosen people of God, the whole of human history is indirectly
included. This is seen in the first eleven chapters of Genesis, which concern
the whole world and its people. The election and calling of Abraham does not
alter this reality in that the one man is chosen ultimately to bring blessing to all
the nations of the world. The inclusiveness of the plan is seen in the Adam–
Christ typology in the New Testament (Rom. 5:12–21; 1 Cor. 15:42–49), and
in the goal of the gospel to create one new man in Christ uniting both Jew and
Gentile (Eph. 2:14–16; Col. 3:10–11). It is also seen in the grand vision of the
book of Revelation of a new humanity and the return to Edenic bliss in the
new Jerusalem at the centre of the new creation.

The focus on Israel in the Old Testament, and on Jesus and those who
believe in him in the New, does not alter the fact that what God did in Israel
had ramifications for the church of Jesus Christ and, through it, for the
whole world. If we are correct in maintaining that the New Testament sees
the death and resurrection of Jesus as the *telos*, the intended goal of history,
then we have to conclude that the meaning of history is to be found in Christ.
Historical critics often reverse this perspective to make the significance of
Jesus dependent upon secularist historians' interpretations of the Gospels
and the early church within their cultural milieu. Given that the biblical focus
outside Genesis 1 – 11, including the perspective of the New Testament narratives, is upon one small nation of the ancient Near East, Israel, we can easily
come to think of salvation history as completely separate from all other world
history. This is a mistake, for, even if Israel had a very limited perception of
the nations among whom Yahweh would act, all the nations of the world are
implied. The biblical view is comprehensive: all nations belong to the one
world history that finds its meaning in Jesus Christ.

Gerald O'Collins helpfully summarizes six major constitutive elements in
Heilsgeschichte theology, which I believe are in full agreement with an evangelical view.[8] These are:

1. [A *Heilsgeschichte* theology] commits us to the view that God acts and
   reveals himself in history.[9]

Footnote 7 (*cont.*)

    such very general assertions as that Jesus is (and will be seen to be) the meaning
    of all history.'

8. Ibid., pp. 93–94.
9. O'Collins has already asserted the role of the revealing word in salvation history
    (ibid., p. 89).

2. A theology of salvation history makes a positive assessment of the Old Testament's function for Christian faith.

3. The life, death and resurrection of Jesus form the heart of salvation history. A theology of *Heilsgeschichte* necessarily excludes any 'liberal' appraisal of Jesus' role as the initiator and model of human faith.

4. A salvation-historical view stands committed to a genuinely futurist eschatology that involves both man and his world. In other words, a *Heilsgeschichte* theology implies an *Endgeschichte* (a final history) still to come.

5. Salvation history is opposed to an individualizing of the gospel.

6. A *Heilsgeschichte* approach clearly safeguards the fact that the saving events are independent of our faith.

The biblical history as salvation history

Salvation history can be summarized simply by following the biblical story. The non-narrative parts of the Bible, such as the wisdom literature and many psalms, belong to the life of the nation of Israel and thus are part of its salvation history.[10] Since biblical theology is concerned with both the 'big picture' and the details, we might start by proposing the broad scenario within the Old Testament, as in Table 2 overleaf.

The period between the Testaments is important for biblical studies for a number of reasons. The apocryphal books and other 'second temple' literature enable us to fill in much of the gap of some four hundred years in history between the Testaments. They show the struggles of the Jews against the encroachments of Hellenism after the conquests of Alexander the Great. They provide the cultural framework against which we understand the scenario in Roman-occupied Judea as portrayed by the four canonical Gospels and Acts. They show the growing gap between the developing hermeneutics of Rabbinic Judaism and what would emerge as the Christological hermeneutics of Jesus and the apostles.

From the data available in the books of the Old Testament it is possible to

---

10. Some psalms include narrative or narrative references that show the wider salvation-historical context to which they belong. Many psalms are put into their historical context by titles that may include the author or some event that evoked the psalm. Unlike our English versions, the Hebrew and lxx both include the titles as part of the psalm and thus indicate them as part of holy Scripture.

Table 2: The biblical narrative

Biblical books or corpora	The biblical story
Genesis	Creation and human fellowship with God in Eden Rebellion and judgment: humanity ejected from Eden Increase in human wickedness: • The flood and Noah's salvation • The table of nations • Babel and the confusion of languages The call of Abraham and covenant promises: • A great nation, blessed by God • The possession of the land • Blessing to the nations of the world Abraham's descendants and frustration of the promises Joseph's and the patriarchs' migration to Egypt
Exodus	Abraham's descendants in captivity and slavery in Egypt The call of Moses: his ministry to lead Israel out of Egypt The exodus and sojourn at Sinai The covenant of Sinai: instruction for redeemed Israel
Leviticus	More of the Sinai instruction
Numbers	Israel refuses to enter the Promised Land The nation condemned to forty years of wandering in the wilderness
Deuteronomy	Moses gives new instruction as preparation for the next generation's entry into the Promised Land
Joshua	The conquest of Canaan and division of land for the tribes
Judges	Disobedience, judgment and the grace of God shown in deliverance The Judges function as mini-saviours sent by God
Ruth	The account of a faithful Moabite ancestress of David
1 and 2 Samuel	First moves towards a monarchy for national stability Saul's failure as king of Israel David chosen by God to be king; his initial rejection and eventual ascent to the throne Jerusalem established as the focus of the Promised Land God's covenant with David
1 and 2 Kings	Solomon succeeds David

Biblical books or corpora	The biblical story
	Solomon's wisdom displayed in his kingdom and the temple
	Solomon's apostasy and the decline of the kingdom
	Schism: separation of Israel and Judah
	Prophetic ministries of Elijah and Elisha
	Destruction of northern kingdom, exile to Assyria
	Destruction of southern kingdom, exile to Babylon
1 and 2 Chronicles	The history of David's line up to the return from exile
Ezra and Nehemiah	The story of the return and re-establishment of Judah; Jerusalem and the temple reconstructed
Daniel	Accounts of life in exile under Babylon and Persia Visions of the future
Esther	An account of the Jews in exile under the Persian king

Latter Prophets	Pre-exilic:
	  • Indictment and judgment for covenant-breaking
	  • Future hope of salvation
	Exilic:
	  • Reason for exile into Babylon
	  • Future hope of salvation
	Post-exilic:
	  • Reason for disappointment in the return from exile
	  • Future hope of salvation

represent the timeline of biblical history diagrammatically broadly as in Figure 3 overleaf.

This representation shows the content of the biblical story. It is not significant that there are gaps in the details in biblical narrative since the continuity of the story is clearly to be seen. The fact that the narrative is full of rebellion and judgment does not detract from the account of God's triumphant grace and his lordship over history. The period of some four hundred years between the end of the Old Testament story and the New Testament must be understood for what it is. The canonical texts do not deal with it in its details. The book of Daniel in one of its apocalyptic and futuristic visions stretches the

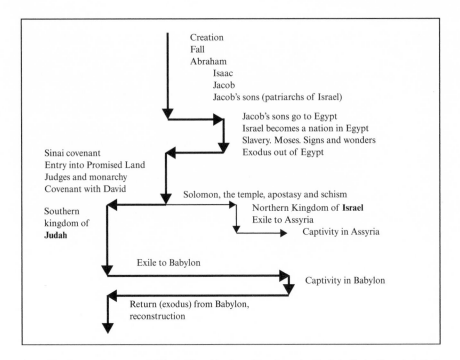

Note: Timeline not drawn to scale. The northern kingdom of Israel remains theologically significant in both the narrative and in prophecy. However, the ultimate saving purposes of God would be worked out in connection with the southern kingdom and, specifically, the tribe of Judah.

Figure 3: Outline of Old Testament history

range to take in the future kingdoms of the world.[11] The prophetic eschatology presents a multifaceted view of the future of God's people when God will finally act to bring in the fullness of salvation. It would remain for the New Testament to inform us of the time and place of the ultimate fulfilment of the prophetic promises.

The tension that exists between the prophetic expectations and the reality of Israel's life has existed all through biblical history. God is acting in time and space to deal with the descendants of rebellious Adam. While being recipients of God's gracious covenant love, Israel continues to display its sinfulness.

---

11. This is one reason for the critical assessment of many that Daniel is not a book from the sixth century BC, as it purports to be, but rather post-dates the future prophecies and comes from the second century.

Biblical history is a 'warts and all' portrayal of a continuous line of people from Adam, through Abraham and his descendants until we come to the Saviour, Jesus Christ. We need to examine the New Testament for the way it treats the historical timeline we have observed in the Old Testament.

We have recognized the value of intertestamental texts for understanding the history and culture of the Jews and thus as a background to the New Testament. However in the canonical perspective, irrespective of the value of the various literary works of that period, the prophetic value of these texts is nil. Protestant churches have always resisted the notion that the collection of Jewish works, known as the Apocrypha, belongs in the canon of Scripture. Thus, as Article 6 of the Anglican Thirty-Nine Articles states concerning these books: 'the church doth read [them] for example of life and instruction of manners; but yet doth it not apply them to establish any doctrine'. Chapter 1 of the Westminster Confession states the matter more bluntly: 'The books commonly called Apocrypha, not being of divine inspiration, are no part of the canon of Scripture, and therefore are of no authority in the Church of God, nor to be any otherwise approved or made use of than other human writings.'

The New Testament timeline proceeds from the narratives of the life, death and resurrection of Jesus, to the founding and spread of the early church of the apostles. Beyond that the timeline is a projection to an eschatological event of the return of Jesus and the consequent consummation of all the promises and expectations relating to the salvation purposes of God. Similar to the future projections of the book of Daniel in the Old Testament are those of the book of Revelation in the New. The New Testament, despite confident assertions sometimes made to the contrary, gives us no indication how long a period of the history of the church there will be before the return of Christ and the revealing of his kingdom. But given that God is Lord of history and that all history serves his purpose, we are justified in allowing biblically portrayed future history to be part of the overall picture of salvation history.

It will, I hope, be clear from the foregoing discussion, that what I understand by the terms 'salvation history' and 'redemptive history' is very different from the use of the terms by some biblical theologians. Nevertheless I think there is a degree of commonality in the recognition of a narrative structure that provides an underlying framework for the theological ideas of the Bible. The precise relationship of that discernible framework to what modern historians would accept as historical is an area of dispute. An evangelical understanding of Scripture and its inspiration by the Holy Spirit means that we are not sceptical about the historical claims of the Bible.

Salvation history within Scripture: Old Testament

It has long been recognized that not only does the Old Testament provide us with a discernible historical structure in its narratives but also that the history of salvation became a part of Israel's confession of faith. Gerhard von Rad drew attention to this in his landmark *Old Testament Theology*.[12] He begins with the salvation history recorded in Deuteronomy 26:5–10:

> And you shall make response before the LORD your God, 'A wandering Aramean was
> my father. And he went down into Egypt and sojourned there, few in number, and
> there he became a nation, great, mighty, and populous. And the Egyptians treated us
> harshly and humiliated us and laid on us hard labor. Then we cried to the LORD, the
> God of our fathers, and the LORD heard our voice and saw our affliction, our toil, and
> our oppression. And the LORD brought us out of Egypt with a mighty hand and an
> outstretched arm, with great deeds of terror, with signs and wonders. And he brought
> us into this place and gave us this land, a land flowing with milk and honey. And behold,
> now I bring the first of the fruit of the ground, which you, O LORD, have given me.'

We have here a recital that is integral to an act of worship, in this case the bringing of the offering of first-fruits. It is evident that the history of salvation was understood to provide the identity of the worshipper and the reason for worship. Having been brought to the land of milk and honey, they now present the first-fruits in thanksgiving to God.

The covenant was always understood as identifiable by its historical circumstance. The studies since the 1950s of covenant formulas of the ancient Near East, and the light they have thrown on biblical covenants, have shown the historical prologue as a conventional part of the formulation of covenant. This is reflected in the preamble to the Sinai law in Exodus 20:2, 'I am the LORD your God, who brought you out of the land of Egypt, out of the house of slavery.' Some scholars suggest that the whole book of Deuteronomy is cast in covenant form, and the first four chapters provide the same kind of historical prologue as the preamble to the Ten Commandments in Deuteronomy 5.[13] This I believe is a sustainable view. It is born out by the use of a salvation-

---

12. G. von Rad, *Old Testament Theology*, vol. 1, tr. D. M. G. Stalker (Edinburgh: Oliver & Boyd, 1962), pt. 2, 'The Theology of Israel's Historical Traditions', pp. 121–128.

13. See, for example, Meredith G. Kline, *Treaty of the Great King: The Covenant Structure of Deuteronomy* (Grand Rapids: Eerdmans, 1963), and P. C. Craigie, *The Book of Deuteronomy*, NICOT (Grand Rapids: Eerdmans, 1976).

historical recital by Joshua in the covenant-renewal ceremony at Shechem (Josh. 24:1–13). This can be seen as an expanded version of Deuteronomy 26:5–9. It is significant in that covenant renewals were part of the tradition as one leader departed and another was poised to bring in the new regime. Deuteronomy 1 – 31 contains the covenant statement before Moses dies. After Joshua leads the people into Canaan, various covenant-linked ceremonies are performed including the circumcision of the new generation who will possess the land of promise (Josh. 5). Then, as Joshua is about to leave, the covenant renewal takes the form of a salvation history summary followed by a challenge to serve the Lord (Josh. 24:1–28). The main points of the history of salvation as Joshua relates it are as follows:

- The call of Abraham to Canaan (vv. 2–3).
- The offspring of Abraham in Egypt (vv. 3–5).
- The exodus from Egypt (vv. 5–7).
- The wilderness experience (vv. 8–10).
- The entry into Canaan and its conquest (vv. 11–13).

Because this is all the gracious doing of Yahweh, the only reasonable response is to eschew idolatry and serve the Lord (vv. 14–28).

The recital of God's victory and gracious covenant with a wayward people continues to be a feature of Israel's worship. We see it in certain psalms. For example, Psalm 78:2–4 expresses its aim thus:

> I will open my mouth in a parable;
> I will utter dark sayings from of old,
> things that we have heard and known,
> that our fathers have told us.
> We will not hide them from their children,
> but tell to the coming generation
> the glorious deeds of the LORD, and his might,
> and the wonders that he has done.

The recital of the 'glorious deeds of the LORD' is integral to Israel's understanding of itself as defined by the history of God's saving deeds. Such recital is also integral to the way Israel worshipped God. The actual recital in Psalm 78 is interesting in that the lesson for the children of the coming generation is first expressed in retelling the sordid history of Israel's sin in the face of God's mercy and saving works. It emphasizes the judgment of God on his people for their forgetting of the miracles in Egypt and beyond. They had sinned even though God preserved them in the wilderness. Eventually judgment had some effect and the people repented. But even in the act of repentance they are lying and turning away (Ps. 78:5–39). Again the recital is made going back to the events in Egypt, the exodus and the entry to Canaan. Nevertheless the whole sorry tale is leading to its solution: God chose Judah, Zion, his sanctuary and David (Ps. 78:40–72). There is a tenderness that almost seems to idealize the coming of David. Yet its theology is clear whatever the ongoing experience of Israel will be.

> He chose David his servant
>   and took him from the sheepfolds;
> from following the nursing ewes he brought him
>   to shepherd Jacob his people,
>   Israel his inheritance.
> With upright heart he shepherded them
>   and guided them with his skilful hand.[14]

David is seen as the solution to all the problems of Israel's rebellious ways. This can only express an eschatological hope, so far is it from the actual experience of Israel even during the heyday of the reigns of David and Solomon. Of course this raises the interesting question of the way history and theology are brought together in the thinking of the psalmist.

Other psalms that have a salvation-historical perspective are Psalms 104, 105, 106, 111, 114 and 136. Further allusions and references in Psalms to the acts of God in Israel's history are too numerous to list here. It is clear that the worship of God was never an abstract reference to 'God', but was solidly grounded in the conviction that Yahweh, the God of Israel, was the Lord of history and had revealed his ways within the events of relatable history. Feasts such as Passover (Exod. 12:3–20; Lev. 23:6; Deut. 16:1–8) and Tabernacles (Lev. 23:34; Deut. 16:13) related worship to great saving events of the past. It is also clear that Israel had a sense of continuity in its history, which, in its written and oral traditions, it traced all the way back to the creation.

Another significant salvation-historical recital took place on the occasion

---

14. This psalm expresses the folly of Israel's rebellion, which is met by David's shepherd role. In v. 72b *skilful* (*tĕbûnôt*) is a wisdom term; *hand* (*kap*) can express the power of rule, especially in this context where David is the *shepherd*: another term for the ruler of Israel. Thus the answer to Israel's folly is the wisdom of David's kingship.

of a great public and corporate confession of sin by the exiles who returned from Babylon. Ezra reads the Book of the Law to the people with the result that the Feast of Booths is re-established (Neh. 8). This is followed by a great fast and confession of sins (Neh. 9). This confession, led by the Levites, involves a lengthy retelling of the past deeds of the Lord in bringing them to the present situation. Beginning with the creation, it follows the now familiar series of events: the call of Abraham, the affliction in Egypt and the exodus, the Sinai lawgiving and the conquest of the land. This recital is filled with qualifications as the past sins and rebellions of Israel are recounted. At the same time they marvel at God's covenant mercies:

> But you are a God ready to forgive, gracious and merciful, slow to anger and abounding in steadfast love, and did not forsake them. (Neh. 9:17)

> Nevertheless, in your great mercies you did not make an end of them or forsake them, for you are a gracious and merciful God. (Neh. 9:31)

They are forced to acknowledge that, even in their new-found freedom from captivity, they are still subject to a foreign power.

> Behold, we are slaves this day; in the land that you gave to our fathers to enjoy its fruit and its good gifts, behold, we are slaves. (Neh. 9:36)

This highlights the tension between prophetically driven expectations that the return from Babylon would herald the fullness of God's salvation and his kingdom, and the reality of their present situation. The tension between promises and their non-fulfilment remains throughout the Old Testament, but it in no wise compromises the notion of salvation history.

Another aspect of the sense of salvation history is related to the use of genealogies. In the Old Testament they serve a variety of purposes. They generally set out to establish some kind of continuity between persons of the past and those contemporary with the writer. The best example of this is 1 Chronicles 1 – 9, which is far more significant than it may appear to the ordinary Bible reader. The first name is Adam (1 Chr. 1:1), from whom the genealogical link is made to Abraham (1 Chr. 1:27). The sons of Abraham lead us to the various kings and nations that impacted on Israel's history (1 Chr. 1:28–54). Chapter 2 takes up with the sons of Israel through to David (v. 15). Chapter 3 provides a list of the descendants of David. Further genealogies trace the lineage of the various tribes from their progenitors, the sons of Israel. Given the tone of Chronicles it is clear that these genealogies serve to link the contemporaries of the Chronicler, through the line of David, with the covenant history of Israel and right back to the primeval origins of humanity.

The genealogies of Genesis may serve as one source for the chronicler. The early ones are clearly schematized and show the development of two lines of humanity, one godless and the other the recipient of grace.[15] The latter includes Seth, Noah, Shem and then Abraham. It shows that the increase in human evil does not prevent God from following his purposes of salvation that will be formally expressed as a covenant beginning with Abraham.

As to the non-narrative parts of the Old Testament, I do not believe they present insurmountable difficulties as is sometimes suggested. Many biblical theologians have expressed the difficulty of positioning the wisdom literature into a biblical-theological account, especially one that centres on a concept of salvation history. But even if the wisdom books contain little that is overtly covenantal or salvation historical, they are linked in other ways to the theology of the Old Testament. We need mention only the following. First, the narratives relating to David and Solomon contain links to the wisdom traditions of Israel. Secondly, there are covenantal links such as 'The fear of Yahweh' (e.g. Prov. 1:7; 9:10; 15:33; Ps. 111:10; Job 28:28). The idea that the wise men of Israel had no understanding of the covenant simply does not stack up with the evidence. Thirdly, many biblical scholars have suggested that the focus of wisdom is on the creation rather than salvation. But creation is the start of the narrative history and to focus on the world, as it was and as it is, does not constitute a departure from covenant faith. Fourthly, over the last seventy to eighty years there has been much scholarly activity in trying to understand what makes wisdom distinct both as a genre and as a way of thinking. Numerous suggestions have been made of wisdom influences in just about every other part of the Old Testament including narratives and prophetic oracles. Wisdom and the hymns of Israel in the Psalms express in various ways the authentic everyday life of faith within the covenant and salvation history.

Salvation history within Scripture: New Testament

Each Gospel writer has a distinct way of linking the narratives of Jesus to the past deeds of God in Old Testament salvation history. As Brian Rosner states

---

15. See Graeme Goldsworthy, *Gospel and Kingdom: A Christian Interpretation of the Old Testament* (Exeter: Paternoster, 1981), in Graeme Goldsworthy, *The Goldsworthy Trilogy* (Milton Keynes: Paternoster, 2000), pp. 64–65.

it, 'Even a cursory survey indicates that each of the Gospels is firmly yet distinctively embedded in Israel's story through its respective selection and use of OT texts.'[16] Matthew does it with a genealogy linking Jesus, through David, to Abraham. We must return to consider the actual form of this genealogy later. Mark's link is through Old Testament prophecy. For him the gospel of Jesus Christ begins with the promises of the prophets, especially Isaiah and the prophecy of a new exodus. The process of fulfilment begins with John the Baptist. Luke's introductory narratives deal with the temple theology of the Old Testament and how Jesus fulfils its purpose. Luke also employs a genealogy to show what is meant by Jesus being called God's Son (Luke 3:21–38). It clearly indicates that this title means that Jesus is the true Adam and the true Israel. John takes us back to creation, which was effected by the Word who becomes flesh to dwell among us. This dwelling, the locus of God's glory, links theologically to the dwelling of God among his people Israel in the tabernacle and temple. That is why Jesus can cleanse the temple of Herod and indicate that he is the true temple that will be raised up on the third day (John 2:19–22).

The many references to Jesus being the fulfilment of Old Testament promises and prophecies make a theological link between the person of Christ and the salvation history of Israel. The prophecies and promises are never made in a vacuum but consistently refer to the ongoing historical experience of Israel as God's elect. Such promises, despite the disastrous rebellion of the people, inevitably will be brought to pass by the grace of God through a faithful remnant. These isolated backward references have a cumulative effect. But they indicate that the evangelists are always aware that Jesus belongs in a long series of historical events in which God has acted. He is, furthermore, the goal to which these events were intended to lead, and the ultimate act of God.

The clearest examples of the gospel events as the goal of the history of salvation occur in Acts. First, Peter's sermon on the day of Pentecost (Acts 2:14–36) begins by anchoring the curious phenomena accompanying the outpouring of the Spirit of God to the fulfilment of an Old Testament prophecy. The history of Jesus, including his deeds, death and resurrection, brings Peter to focus on the exaltation of the crucified Jesus. Ultimately he asserts that the resurrection is the fulfilment of God's covenant with David (2 Sam. 7:14; Acts 2:30–31).

Stephen's speech in Acts 7 is given in his defence when he is arraigned

---

16. Brian Rosner, 'Salvation, History of', in Kevin J. Vanhoozer (ed.), *Dictionary for Theological Interpretation of the Bible* (Grand Rapids: Baker; London: SPCK, 2005), pp. 714–717.

before the Jewish council accused of speaking against the temple and the law. He begins with a reference to the summons to Abraham to leave Mesopotamia. Then he rehearses the history of the patriarchs, the sons of Jacob. He relates in some detail the story of the sojourn and captivity in Egypt, and the ministry of Moses. Again there is a movement out, this time from Egypt. But the people rebelled and lusted to go back to Egypt. Nevertheless the purposes of God are fulfilled in the possession of the Promised Land, the rule of David and Solomon's building of the temple. The temple, the focus of the Jews' accusation against Stephen, becomes Stephen's focus of defence. The clear implication of his counter-accusation that the Jews are resisting the Holy Spirit is that it is now time for them to move on again, this time to the temple not made with hands, but one built 'by my Spirit, says the LORD of hosts' (Zech. 4:6). The prophecy of Isaiah 66:1, that Stephen quotes (Acts 7:49–50), indicates that a temple made with human hands is never the true temple:

> Thus says the LORD:
> 'Heaven is my throne,
>   and the earth is my footstool;
> what is the house that you would build for me,
>   and what is the place of my rest?'

It is important to note that Stephen's recourse to salvation history is necessary in order to enable the theological integrity of the apostolic gospel to be maintained. Israel's failure has been one of resisting the call to move on to God's goal for them. The new has arrived in Jesus Christ and they refuse to let go of the shadows of the reality that he has brought. As William Manson put it:

> It is plain that Stephen's passionate outburst at this point is not against Solomon's act in itself, for he quotes Solomon's words in defence of his own thesis. His indignation is rather at the blindness of the Jewish people at this time of crisis, at the failure of his opponents to see that with the coming of the Messiah the hour had struck for the moving on from the temple and the Jewish institutions . . .

> [T]he central theme of Stephen's retrospect of history is that Israel has consistently and in every age opposed the saviours sent to it from God, and this opposition has culminated in the crucifixion of Jesus.[17]

---

17. William Manson, *The Epistle to the Hebrews: An Historical and Theological Reconsideration* (London: Hodder & Stoughton, 1951), pp. 34–45. Manson sees this emphasis

Paul's account of salvation history in Acts 13:16–41 is equally significant. While Paul and Barnabas are attending a synagogue in Antioch of Pisidia, Paul is invited to speak. He grasps the opportunity to preach Jesus and does so by linking Jesus to all the hopes of Israel. The outline is familiar: God chose the fathers, made them great in Egypt, led them out and into the Promised Land. He sent them judges, Samuel the prophet and Saul as king. The historical climax is David who is the direct link to Jesus:

> [H]e raised up David to be their king, of whom he testified and said, 'I have found in David the son of Jesse a man after my heart, who will do all my will.' Of this man's offspring God has brought to Israel a Saviour, Jesus, as he promised. (Acts 13:22–23)

He then tells of John the Baptist's preparation for Jesus' ministry, and the Jewish leaders' unbelief and inability to understand their prophetic Scriptures. Their condemnation and crucifixion of Jesus were actually the fulfilment of prophecy. The climax of Paul's presentation is the resurrection and the significant claim of its central importance:

> And we bring you the good news that what God promised to the fathers, this he has fulfilled to us their children by raising Jesus, as also it is written in the second Psalm,
>> 'You are my Son,
>> today I have begotten you.' (Acts 13:32–33)

On this premise Paul goes on to preach the forgiveness of sins to all who believe. It was a watershed proclamation in that the Jews reviled Paul (Acts 13:45) and as a result Paul declared that he would henceforth turn to the Gentiles (Acts 13:46–47). He cites Isaiah 49:6:

> I have made you a light for the Gentiles,
> that you may bring salvation to the ends of the earth.

It is surely significant that Paul sees the ministry of Israel, the Servant of the Lord, as fulfilled in his own gospel proclamation. But the overall significance of Paul's use of salvation history is the way in which the history of the people of Israel is interpreted theologically. Its goal is Christ. The theme of the *hope*

---

of Stephen repeated in the epistle to the Hebrews, which is addressed to Jewish Christians in danger of staying with the 'earthly securities and fixtures'.

of Israel occurs again in Paul's defence, first before Agrippa (Acts 26:6–8), and then before the Jewish leaders in Rome (Acts 28:20). The hope of Israel, as set out in the promises and prophecies of the Old Testament, is integral to the history of redemption. For Paul its focus now is the resurrection of Jesus. Thus, in Paul's view, the hope of Israel is nothing other than the gospel of Jesus Christ that he preached. This, of course, is of great significance for how we understand Old Testament promises to be fulfilled, for everything that Israel hoped for is declared to be fulfilled in Christ.

Paul's epistles reflect this anchoring of the message in the history of redemption. This connection is more explicit in some places but always implied. Perhaps the most obvious examples are in the epistles to the Galatians and to the Romans. I think the point has been made that the New Testament consists of documents that belong overall to a movement that saw itself as fulfilling the hope of Israel and, thus, as bringing the salvation history of the Old Testament to a climax. There is no sense of a new religion being created, only that of the faith of Israel finding its completion in the person of Jesus of Nazareth. We cannot divorce the theological ideas of either Old or New Testament from salvation history without reducing them to abstractions and timeless concepts. Redemptive history, far from being an alien framework, is the very warp and woof of biblical revelation.

Conclusions

Biblical revelation without some framework of salvation history would, I believe, be reduced to timeless religious ideals. The fact of the incarnation that speaks of God being with us points us in the direction of such a framework. Of itself the incarnation might be conceived of as a momentary intrusion with timeless implications. Such would be a mistake. The nature of the incarnation in bringing us the God-Man, Jesus of Nazareth, is no mere idealism. He is clearly identified as the link between all that has been recorded in the Scriptures and the final purpose of God to bring in his kingdom. The incarnation brought to its climax the reality that God has always been with his people, starting with Adam in the garden. Its consummation is the grand vision of Revelation 21:3: 'Behold, the dwelling place of God is with man. He will dwell with them, and they will be with his people, and God himself will be with them as their God.' Some have proposed the doctrine of God or the concept of the sovereignty of God as the real centre of Scripture. But these are abstractions and belong in the realm of dogmatics. To explain what they mean we need to allow Scripture to clothe the abstractions in the garments of salvation history and the related theology of all the biblical texts. Thus I stand by my initial suggestion that the central theme of Scripture is the kingdom of God defined simply as God's people in God's place under God's rule.

4. EVANGELICAL PRACTICE

The lack of consensus among evangelicals

In this chapter we shall examine the method of some evangelical biblical theologians. One of the problems we face is the lack of consensus about some major issues in the discipline. I have proposed that one of the reasons why biblical theology as a subject has not always been prominent in evangelical Bible colleges and seminaries is this inability to pin down exactly what the method should entail and what a curriculum for biblical theology should contain. This is not to suggest that there is only one right way of doing biblical theology, but the choices and relative advantages of each need to be reviewed.

The term *evangelical* itself is open to different meanings. However it usually indicates a position that regards the Bible as the reliable and authoritative source of our knowledge of God and of his will for us. For the purposes of this study I shall use a fairly broad definition of *evangelical* to include those who raise questions of literary genre in relation to the type of historical truth claims being made. Thus, for example, there are many who own the label 'evangelical' but who regard the creation account not as a literal account, but as a unique and stylized representation with a clear theological import. Some may regard the unity of the authorship of Isaiah as not seminal for its theological interpretation. Others may assess the narratives of the book of Daniel as of a different order from the historical narratives of the Former Prophets. The historicity of Job is another area where evangelical views may differ. In most such cases it is not only historicity that is the issue, but also that of genre identification. What we understand by the literal meaning of the text is another area of contention.

The name 'evangelical' properly belongs to those who see the *evangel*, the gospel of Jesus Christ, as the governing principle for the understanding and interpretation of all Scripture. This usually extends to include the acceptance of the uniquely authoritative role of the Bible. This implies that there is an essential unity that centres on Jesus Christ within the diversity of the range of biblical texts. It means that the whole Bible is accepted as God's word to humanity revealing God's plan and purpose for the salvation of his people and the establishment of his kingdom.

Because biblical theology does involve us in descriptive analysis, there are many biblical theologians who would not be thought of as in any sense of the word evangelical. Their presuppositions concerning the Bible may be very different from those of an evangelical, and yet they undertake the descriptive task with great dedication. We cannot simply ignore their often considerable contribution to our study.

I have been writing about biblical theology for some years now, and have devised curricula that I have taught to theological students and local church members in various places. I think it right, therefore, that I should first briefly outline something of my own position and how I came to it. This will, I trust, assist the reader in understanding where I am coming from and why I propose the approach that I do. To do this I need to enlarge a little on my introductory comments in chapter 1.

The shaping of a biblical theologian: my debt to Donald Robinson

When I entered theological college in 1956 I had never heard of biblical theology as a distinct discipline. I had been nurtured in an evangelical church since my conversion at the age of 16. The curriculum at Moore College contained the usual compulsory subjects as preparation for ordination to the Anglican ministry. The biblical studies were divided between Old and New Testaments, and the respective curricula did not really provide for the relationship between the two to be explored in any detail. It was thus up to the individual lecturers to deal with the matter as they saw fit. We were, however, urged by one lecturer to read John Bright's *The Kingdom of*

God.[1] This, as my first taste of a brief but comprehensive biblical theology, was for me an enthralling experience in that Bright gave to me a sense of the unity of the Bible and of the fulfilment of the Old Testament in the person and work of Jesus Christ. The approach made sense even though it still did not have for me the label of 'biblical theology'. I was also made familiar with G. Ernest Wright's *God Who Acts*,[2] which had been published in 1952 as an early volume of the SCM Studies in Biblical Theology, and gradually the terminology of biblical theology began to take hold. After some overseas study I returned to Moore College as a lecturer in 1963, the year in which Geerhardus Vos's *Biblical Theology* was reprinted.[3] The idea of biblical theology as a distinct discipline was now becoming firmly established in the circles in which I moved.

As I have previously indicated, my own engagement with biblical theology actually began a few years earlier. In my final year as a student at Moore College our Old Testament lecturer, Donald Robinson, responded to a student's question about the unity of the Bible in a way that captured my imagination and started me on the quest for my own better understanding of the unified message of the Bible. I have outlined Robinson's explanation in chapter 1 and need not repeat it here. Why this analysis came to mean more to me than other evangelical and reformed assessments will become clearer with the progress of this study.

One interesting thing about Donald Robinson's position is that he has indicated that there were some considerable influences on his thinking from outside the evangelical camp.[4] He mentions in particular Oscar Cullmann, C. H. Dodd and Gabriel Hebert. Robinson had attended Dodd's New Testament seminars in Cambridge. We students felt the influence of Dodd when urged

---

1. John Bright, *The Kingdom of God* (New York: Abingdon, 1955). It should be recognized that Bright, though conservative, accepts many of the tenets of historical criticism. I would agree with those who regard his *History of Israel* as a classic. Yet, as a historian he is rather non-committal about the early chapters of Genesis and thus begins his treatment with Israel entering the Promised Land. Nevertheless I was greatly privileged to have John Bright supervise my doctoral studies at Union Theological Seminary in Virginia (1970–72).

2. G. Ernest Wright, *God Who Acts: Biblical Theology as Recital*, SBT 1 (London: SCM, 1952).

3. Geerhardus Vos, *Biblical Theology: Old and New Testaments* (Grand Rapids: Eerdmans, 1948; repr. 1963).

4. See above chapter 1.

to read his masterful study in biblical theology, *The Apostolic Preaching and its Developments*.[5] Cullmann's work *Christ and Time*[6] engaged biblical theology thematically and with the perspective of salvation history. Gabriel Hebert lectured in a seminary in South Australia and made a number of visits to Moore College. His studies on *Christ the Fulfiller* and his *The Throne of David* give us an insight into his understanding of salvation history.[7] Robinson describes his own journey in biblical theology and the establishment of it as part of the curriculum at Moore College in a lecture he gave in 1996 at an Annual School of Theology at Moore devoted in that year to the topic of biblical theology.[8]

Let me remind you that Robinson's key statement about his formation of biblical theology involved a division of the biblical material into three stages of revelation. I began to compare this understanding with others and, over a period of time, concluded that this had more to commend it than some other approaches I was aware of. It is this approach that I have subsequently employed in my own works.[9] It was on this basis that I proposed one way

---

5. C. H. Dodd, *The Apostolic Preaching and its Developments* (London: Hodder & Stoughton, 1936).

6. Oscar Cullmann, *Christ and Time: The Primitive Christian Conception of Time and History* (London: SCM, 1951).

7. A. G. Hebert, *Christ the Fulfiller: Three Studies on the Biblical Types as They Are Presented in the Old and New Testaments* (Sydney: Anglican Truth Society, 1957); *The Throne of David: A Study of the Fulfilment of the Old Testament in Jesus Christ and His Church* (London: Faber and Faber, 1941).

8. This lecture along with the others given at this School of Theology by various faculty members of Moore College are reprinted in Richard J. Gibson (ed.), *Interpreting God's Plan: Biblical Theology and the Pastor*, Explorations 11 (Adelaide: Open Book; Carlisle: Paternoster, 1997). Other sources of information concerning Robinson's development of biblical theology at Moore are *Faith's Framework: The Structure of New Testament Theology* (Exeter: Paternoster; Sutherland, NSW: Albatross, 1985), and '"The Church" Revisited: An Autobiographical Fragment', in Peter G. Bolt and Mark D. Thompson (eds.), *Donald Robinson Selected Works* (Camperdown, NSW: Australian Church Record; Newtown, NSW: Moore College, 2008), vol. 1, pp. 259–271.

9. This analysis shapes my books *Gospel and Kingdom: A Christian Interpretation of the Old Testament* (Exeter: Paternoster, 1981), now published in Graeme Goldsworthy, *The Goldsworthy Trilogy*, Milton Keynes: Paternoster, 2000; *According to Plan: The Unfolding Revelation of God in the Bible* (Leicester: IVP, 1991); *Preaching the Whole Bible as Christian Scripture: The Application of Biblical Theology to Expository Preaching* (Grand

of defining biblical theology. In response to an enquiry from a pastor in California I gave the following descriptive definition of biblical theology as I understand it:[10]

> Biblical theology is the study of how every text in the Bible relates to every other text in the Bible. It is the study of the matrix of divine revelation. At the heart of the gospel is the person of Jesus Christ; he is the word of God come in the flesh. The nature of the gospel is such that it demands that it be at the centre of the biblical message. Biblical theology is, then, the study of how every text in the Bible relates to Jesus and his gospel. Thus we start with Christ so that we may end with Christ. Biblical theology is Christological, for its subject matter is the Scriptures as God's testimony to Christ. It is therefore, from start to finish, a study of Christ.[11]
>
> How biblical theology is actually done will depend a great deal on our dogmatic presuppositions about the nature of Scripture. If we do not have confidence in the Bible as the inspired word of God, we will treat it as a collection of human documents. Liberalism killed biblical theology because it could not allow for the unity of Scripture as reflecting the one purpose of its one Author.

The threefold structure proposed by Robinson and Hebert clearly differs in some respects from the epochal structure espoused by Geerhardus Vos and taken up by Edmund Clowney and others. If this is a valid observation the question then arises as to the relative advantages or disadvantages of the different perspectives. It will, I think, be useful to outline and compare the procedures of some of the leading evangelical biblical theologians.

Some leading evangelical biblical theologians

Geerhardus Vos

A great debt is owed to this defender of the evangelical Reformed faith. Geerhardus Vos was installed as professor of Biblical Theology at Princeton

---

Footnote 9 (cont.)

Rapids: Eerdmans; Leicester: IVP, 2000); and *Prayer and the Knowledge of God: What the Whole Bible Teaches* (Leicester: IVP, 2003).

10. Justin Buzzard blog <http://buzzardblog.typepad.com>, accessed 26 Feb. 2007.

11. This statement could lay me open to a charge of Christomonism, a position that I emphatically reject. Biblical theology *is* a study of Christ, but not that alone. Jesus is the mediator of our knowledge of God and therefore of theology.

Seminary in 1894. In his inaugural lecture he propounded his view of the nature of biblical theology. He then went on to say, 'I have not forgotten, however, that you have called me to teach this science for the eminently practical purpose of training young men for the ministry of the Gospel.'[12] I shall only comment here on the best known of his works, his *Biblical Theology*. It was a formative book for many of us in the 1960s as it provided us with one of our early introductions to evangelical biblical theology as a distinct discipline. Vos's definition stems from his prior delineation of exegetical theology. This involves the study of the content of the Bible, the origins of the various texts, the unity of the canon of Scripture, and

> the study of the actual self-disclosures of God in time and space which lie back of even the first committal to writing of any Biblical document, and which for a long time continued to run alongside of the inscripturation of revealed material; this last-named procedure is called the study of Biblical Theology.[13]

From the foregoing Vos concludes that biblical theology 'is that branch of exegetical theology which deals with the process of the self-revelation of God deposited in the Bible'.[14] This emphasis on the *process* of self-revelation is, in my view, one of his more important contributions to the study of biblical theology. Vos wrote other things that no doubt give a fuller understanding of his views on biblical theology. Nevertheless I believe it is fair to examine the book that made Vos a byword for many students in the second half of the twentieth century. In what sense is his *Biblical Theology* to be regarded as a satisfactory text on the subject, and what kind of biblical theology does it set out?

From the perspective of a biblical theologian writing in the early stages of the twenty-first century, Vos's work is in some respects quite dated. As professor of biblical theology at Princeton he taught some of those who would go on to establish Westminster Theological Seminary. This occurred in a decisive period of the challenge of historical-critical theory to traditional views of the Bible. Vos was a leading opponent of the encroaching liberalism at Princeton in the early twentieth century. His *Biblical Theology* will remain a classic in the

---

12. Geerhardus Vos, 'The Idea of Biblical Theology as a Science and as a Theological Discipline', in Richard B. Gaffin (ed.), *Redemptive History and Biblical Interpretation: The Shorter Writings of Geerhardus Vos* (Phillipsburg: Presbyterian & Reformed, 1980), p. 21.

13. Vos, *Biblical Theology*, p. 13.

14. Ibid.

literature, yet it is curiously incomplete as an example of a biblical theology of
the Old and New Testaments. The opening chapters contain important discussions of the principles and presuppositions of a Reformed theologian, and
there is a fair amount of interaction with Vos's dogmatics here. His account
of the biblical story really begins with the principle of probation in the Garden
of Eden. Curiously the theology of creation in Genesis 1 is not his starting
point, and nor is the gospel explicitly nominated as his pre-understanding,
though it becomes clear that this is implicitly the case. Vos's covenantal
theology informs the method of approach to what he calls pre-redemptive
special revelation and redemptive special revelation. These are nominated as
the covenant of works and the covenant of grace respectively. Subsequent
chapters deal with the Noachian revelation, the period between Noah and
the patriarchs, and the patriarchal period. The final chapter in the first section
of the book is a lengthy treatment of revelation in the period of Moses. This
latter chapter rightly expounds the Mosaic period, and the ministry of Moses,
as foundational for understanding the relationship of God to Israel and the
purposes of God for his people.

It is when we come to Vos's second section that I have some serious
questions. He calls it 'The Prophetic Epoch of Revelation'. There is first a
discussion of the theological nature of the prophetic office, including the
early prophets such as Samuel. But the events leading to this development
of prophetism, including the whole history of Israel recorded in Joshua and
Judges, are omitted. A chapter is spent on etymological considerations of the
prophetic role, and another chapter on the critical theories extant in Vos's day.
Then there is a discussion of various theories about the mode of reception of
the prophetic revelation. When we come to the one chapter devoted to the
content of prophetic revelation Vos organizes it systematically rather than in
terms of redemptive history. The theology of the historical narratives of the
former prophets does not come into his discussion. Nothing is really said
about David or Solomon, or about the building of the temple.[15]

Perhaps the strangest feature to the thinking of a modern biblical theologian is Vos's treatment of the New Testament. It raises questions of what a
biblical theology may fairly be expected to investigate. It seems strange that
Vos decided to treat only the incarnation and public ministry of Jesus. The
passion, death, resurrection, ascension and Christ's expected return are not
specifically dealt with and do not even occur in the index of subjects. The
period of the Acts and the apostolic ministry is excluded as are questions relat-

---

15. The index has no entry for David, Solomon or the temple.

ing to the parousia. The reader should not take these comments as a criticism of the material that *is* in Vos's book. Nevertheless the absence of the theology of the former prophets, the Psalms and the wisdom literature, and the exclusion of the entire New Testament except the life and teachings of Jesus, seems to me to disqualify this otherwise classic volume from being regarded as a comprehensive biblical theology. It is a biblical-theological study of some parts of the Bible and contains some useful discussions of the principles of the discipline. But it is not, as such, a biblical theology of the Old and New Testaments.

Having said all that, I shall summarize what Vos says about the structure of revelation. He begins with four assertions about biblical revelation.[16] First, it is progressive. He rightly points out that revelation is not to be understood apart from God's redemptive acts. Because redemption takes place in history, revelation will follow the stages by which redemption occurs. The two are not coterminous or co-extensive, because redemption continues after revelation ceases. Vos does refer to the objective, central acts of redemption, including the incarnation, atonement and resurrection of Christ. Yet he curiously omits these from his treatment of New Testament biblical theology.

Secondly, revelation is 'incarnate' in history. He correctly asserts that for the events of history to have a revealing significance they require the word-revelation to indicate that significance. Strangely this redemptive-historical framework does not really inform his actual execution of the task of biblical theology. As already indicated, large parts of theologically oriented biblical history are not represented in his *Biblical Theology*.

Thirdly, the revelation process in history is organic so that the progression is 'from seed-form to the attainment of full growth'. The progression is 'epochal' not a gradual dawning of revelation. The organic nature is seen in that 'in the seed form the minimum of indispensable knowledge was already present'.

Fourthly, revelation has 'practical adaptability'. Vos explains this by contrasting the intellectual concept of knowledge with that of the covenant relationship. Biblical revelation is not intellectual attainment but knowing God and being known by him. To properly engage in biblical theology is to engage with God.

When it comes to the actual method of doing biblical theology, Vos again refers to the principle of historic progression.[17] He asserts that the periods

---

16. Vos, *Biblical Theology*, pp. 14–17.

17. Ibid., pp. 25–26.

of the historic progression should not be determined at random but 'in strict agreement with the lines of cleavage drawn by revelation itself'. The actual lines of cleavage remain to be seen from his way of delineating the periods. They turn out to be those noted above. His own stated criterion for his divisions is, 'The principle of successive Berith-makings [covenant-makings], as marking the introduction of new periods . . .'[18] Questions remain about the actual shape of Vos's biblical theology and the reasons for his significant omissions. His other major works indicate that he understood full well the significance of the New Testament teaching on such matters as eschatology and the people of God.[19] My criticism is directed only at his volume designated as a biblical theology of the Old and New Testaments, which, in my opinion, does not provide us with a satisfactory example of a comprehensive biblical theology.

Edmund P. Clowney

Clowney's ministry at Westminster Seminary in Pennsylvania has obviously been a fruitful one in which his concern for biblical theology has been decisive. He held the professorship of Practical Theology of which discipline preaching was a prime concern. Two of his books in particular provide us with his understanding of the structure of revelation that is uncovered by biblical theology. These are his *Preaching and Biblical Theology* and *The Unfolding Mystery*.[20] The former volume contains a greater degree of the discussion of the principles of biblical theology.[21] Clowney follows Vos's lead with reference to the progressive nature of revelation that results in its having 'an epochal structure'.[22]

Regarding epochs Clowney states:

---

18. Ibid., p. 25.

19. See, for example, Geerhardus Vos, *The Pauline Eschatology* (Grand Rapids: Eerdmans, 1972), a reprint of the original 1930 publication; *The Kingdom of God and the Church* (Nutley, N.J.: Presbyterian & Reformed, 1972), a reprint with additions and corrections.

20. Edmund P. Clowney, *Preaching and Biblical Theology* (Grand Rapids: Eerdmans, 1961; London: Tyndale, 1962); *The Unfolding Mystery: Discovering Christ in the Old Testament* (Leicester: IVP, 1988).

21. These principles are largely repeated in Clowney's more recent volume *Preaching Christ in All of Scripture* (Wheaton: Crossway, 2003).

22. Edmund P. Clowney, *Preaching and Biblical Theology* (Grand Rapids: Eerdmans, 1961; London: Tyndale, 1962), p. 15.

The development of biblical theology is redemptive-historical. The divisions of biblical theology are the historical periods of redemption, marked by creation, the fall, the flood, the call of Abraham, the exodus, and the coming of Christ.[23]

He rightly asserts that biblical theology must understand each of the epochs in its own terms, but seems to regard the epochs he has listed as self-evident. Of course in one sense they are, for none can deny the importance of these events in the overall biblical history of salvation. The criteria for delineating the epochs need to be examined as to whether they are essentially theological or more historical, and to what extent they expose the overall structure of revelation. Clowney does not really develop his biblical theology in this earlier volume. The bulk of the book concerns preaching, and the application of the basics of the discerned epochal structure. This structure is his way of understanding the real unity of the Bible, which finds its centre in Christ. It also determines his use of typology.

Clowney is correct in saying that 'we discover that each epoch has a coherent and organic structure and also that there is organic progression from period to period as the plan of God is revealed'.[24] His concern is that preaching should be 'genuinely theological and christocentric'. For this we need to understand the theological horizon of the particular epoch in view. Otherwise 'we will fall into thin moralizing which misses the progress of redemptive history and fails to see Christ in the midst'.[25] It is clear Clowney sees that the valid link between the various parts of revelation and the contemporary Christian is to be found in this progressive series of epochs. It is this that enables him to make the connection between the two Testaments and to find Christ in the Old Testament. Biblical theology 'serves to unlock the objective significance of the history of salvation. It focuses on the core of redemptive history in Christ.'[26]

The significance of the epochal structure is underlined in this important statement of Clowney's:

Our hermeneutical method, therefore, must always begin by finding the immediate theological horizon and then relating that to the broader biblical-theological perspectives. When this is done, the specific force of the text in its horizon will

---

23. Ibid., p. 16.
24. Ibid., p. 75.
25. Ibid.
26. Ibid., p. 78.

become evident. Each event of redemption, each portion of God's revelation, makes its distinctive contribution to the whole. When we choose a text from Scripture, we do not arbitrarily impose a unity upon the Word of God. We discover the unity that is already present. That unity is already articulated into larger and larger unities in the organic interrelationships of Scripture.[27]

I concur with this assessment, but questions still remain. How do we determine the immediate theological horizon? As with earth's horizon, we take one step up and it recedes. What epochal structural analysis will best serve the purpose of providing the hermeneutical framework for dealing with Scripture? Are there grounds for preferring one structural picture over another? If this epochal structural analysis is to have optimum applicability the immediate theological horizons Clowney emphasizes will need to have real unity. But if there are important distinctions to be drawn we may not allow unity to override them. It is here that I think Clowney's analysis, following Vos's, does not serve us as well as Robinson's does. The theological horizon of the Latter Prophets differs significantly from the horizons of the period of Moses and of the Former Prophets. In other words, we operate not only on the presupposition of the unity of Scripture, but also by trying to understand the most useful distinctions within that unity.

Clowney's later book *The Unfolding Mystery*[28] does not purport to be a full biblical theology. It is more of a devotional study based on a biblical-theological structure. Clowney's method is to trace the main points of the Old Testament story and to make frequent links to the New Testament that indicate his understanding of the way the Old Testament points us to Christ and his gospel. Unlike Vos, he takes us into the realms of the creation narratives, and also into the history of the former prophets. He treats both David and Solomon with some care and, as he goes, he picks up the psalms and wisdom literature as they are linked to these two kings. The final chapter of this book outlines the decline in Israel after Solomon, and touches briefly on prophetic eschatology.

It would be unfair to criticize this book for not being what it was not intended to be. However, I think it fair to point out that one does not find the structural analysis in this book unambiguously set out, nor find the basis for the links with the New Testament other than the ones that the New Testament itself explicitly makes. The same can be said of Clowney's *Preaching*

---

27. Ibid., p. 92.
28. *The Unfolding Mystery: Discovering Christ in the Old Testament* (Leicester: IVP, 1988).

Christ in All of Scripture. In an introductory chapter he reiterates the principles he set out in his earlier works, especially in *Preaching and Biblical Theology*. In both cases he expresses the need to understand the epochs of God's action and revelation in history but gives little justification for his choice of epochs. His choice is possibly explicable in terms of the Reformed understanding of the unity of the covenants within salvation history. The dispensationalist, by contrast, so separates the epochs (dispensations) that their delineation is both exact and necessary.

When we turn to Clowney's theory in practice we have a better idea of the way his understanding of the relationship of the Old Testament to Christ materializes. Thus his sermons, which form the bulk of *Preaching Christ in All of Scripture*, show us his theory in practice. In those chapters given over to expositions from the Old Testament certain features emerge. First of all Clowney emphasizes the presence of Christ in the Old Testament. This is sometimes seen in actual theophanies or, more accurately, Christophanies. Encounters with the Angel of the Lord are interpreted as Christophanies. In terms of trinitarian theology it is hard to avoid some such recognition of the presence of the second person of the Trinity provided it does not pre-empt the incarnation of Jesus *as* incarnation. Nor does this detract from the typological value of these events. There is nothing inherently objectionable to the notion that God the Son is present in a way that is typological of a clearer revelation or epiphany in the fullness of time. Clowney asserts that we find longitudinal themes in the context of epochs.[29] But it is just this development of longitudinal themes that indicates the need for a refinement in the designation of the period from Moses to Christ as one epoch. This perspective does not really allow for the change from the salvation-historical perspective of Torah and the Former Prophets to the eschatological perspective of the Latter Prophets.

Secondly, when we turn to the examples of sermons in *Preaching Christ in All of Scripture*, there is a clear preference for one kind of link between the Old Testament and Christ. The predominant link is through explicit biblical typology. Thus the sermon on Genesis 22:1–19 focuses on the overt links between Abraham and Christ that we find in the New Testament. Clowney's sermon on Joshua 5:13–15 focuses narrowly on the Christophany of the Angel of the Lord. This provides the direct link with the New Testament. While he states that Joshua begins a new epoch it seems that this is not understood in the more structural way in which the epoch of Moses to Christ is proposed. It is not clear what advantage there is in preaching about the Joshua episode, as it

---

29. *Preaching Christ*, pp. 32, 35.

seems to be little more than a point of entry to New Testament teaching. My overall impression is that Clowney is careful to avoid overstepping the mark in identifying the Christian significance of Old Testament people and events. It also seems to me that he does not really use his epochal structure as a way to understand the full typological potentials of his chosen Old Testament texts.

The designation of epochs in the works of Vos and Clowney is based on two undeniable factors. The one is the progressive nature of revelation, and the other is the existence of discernible stages in this progressiveness. This is an important aspect of the theology of the Old Testament as it affects our understanding of the way the message leads to the New Testament's assertions of being the fulfilment of the Old Testament. Without some sense of the structure of the revelation in the Old Testament it would be very difficult to arrive at a workable hermeneutic for understanding the Christian significance of the Hebrew Scriptures. The questions remaining concern the best way to a valid analysis of this structure, the relationship of each epoch to the others, and whether or not *epoch*, implying a period of time, is the best way to describe the structuring. It is questions such as these that I want to address in this study.

Dennis E. Johnson

Dennis Johnson was taught by Clowney at Westminster Seminary in Pennsylvania and is himself now a professor at the California campus of Westminster. He has written a significant work, *Him We Proclaim*, which in many ways develops the insights and method of Clowney.[30] Johnson's work sets out in greater detail the theoretical implications of the kind of Christocentric preaching that Clowney so faithfully promoted. I think it is true to say that Johnson has filled in some of the gaps by working out and stating explicitly much of the theory implicit in Clowney's biblical-theological approach to preaching. Whereas Clowney provides a theoretical assessment of symbolism and typology (including a useful diagram),[31] Johnson has provided a more detailed treatment of the basis of typology in the way the

---

30. Dennis E. Johnson, *Him We Proclaim: Preaching Christ from All the Scriptures* (Phillipsburg: Presbyterian & Reformed, 2007). Johnson has also edited a volume of sermons by former students of Clowney that serve to illustrate the impact of Clowney's teaching on a number of pastors now proclaiming the gospel: Dennis E. Johnson (ed.), *Heralds of the King: Christ-Centered Sermons in the Tradition of Edmund P. Clowney* (Wheaton: Crossway, 2009).

31. *Preaching Christ*, p. 32.

prophets recapitulate the major moments of the earlier covenant history.[32] Whether he learned this directly from Clowney, or whether he followed up on Clowney's principles to develop these perspectives himself, I do not know. Whichever it is, Johnson's book demonstrates the importance of Clowney's contribution and develops a comprehensive theoretical structure for Christocentric preaching. It provides some more detailed analysis of the redemptive-historical matrix of revelation and of the rationale of typology in a way that I do not think is so obvious in Clowney's writings.

Willem VanGemeren

VanGemeren's biblical theology *The Progress of Redemption* was published in 1988.[33] This is a more detailed and comprehensive biblical theology than Clowney's or Vos's. In his preface he quotes the words with which G. E. Ladd concludes his book *The Pattern of New Testament Truth*.[34] Ladd asserts that *Heilsgeschichte*, or holy history, is what gives the Bible its unity. 'It is a record and interpretation of the events in which God visits men in history to redeem them as persons and also to redeem them in society – in history.' He also concludes that diversity in Scripture is a function of the 'different stages along the redemption line'.

VanGemeren expresses appreciation of Vos, Clowney and Richard Gaffin for introducing him to the redemptive-historical approach at Westminster Theological Seminary. So it is no surprise that his approach is similar to that of both Vos and Clowney. His concern is likewise Christological: 'Christian students of the Old Testament *must pass by the cross of Jesus Christ on their return to the Old Testament*, and as such they can never lose their identity as a Christian.'[35]

VanGemeren's analysis involves the delineation of twelve periods of redemptive history. Each, he asserts, is distinct but relates organically to the previous and succeeding epochs.[36] The logic is based more on the events in biblical history, a fact that indicates a possible alternative approach to Clowney's, which seeks to understand the epochs of revelatory activity in

---

32. *Him We Proclaim*, ch. 7, and particularly pp. 217–238. Johnson's use of Clowney's diagram indicates his indebtedness to his teacher.

33. Willem VanGemeren, *The Progress of Redemption: The Story of Salvation from Creation to the New Jerusalem* (Grand Rapids: Zondervan Acadamie, 1988).

34. Ibid., p. 15. The quote comes from Ladd's *The Pattern of New Testament Truth* (Grand Rapids: Eerdmans, 1968), p. 110.

35. VanGemeren, *Progress of Redemption*, p. 21 (italics his).

36. Ibid., p. 32.

terms of the prophetic word. It is also hard to argue with VanGemeren's twelve epochs. They fit his criteria of distinctiveness and connectedness. But the epochs are not so much illustrative of the matrix of revelation as of a succession of important stages in the history of God's people. They serve to focus on the major books of the Bible and to divide the big picture into manageable portions that follow, on the whole, the narrative order of the books of the canon.

VanGemeren is a careful expositor of the literary structures and theology of the biblical books, and is understandably drawn to the covenant as a central guiding theme. He relates the parts of the story and their theological significance as a continuous development of the purposes of God. In dealing with the Old Testament he allows the various texts and corpora to tell their own story without making constant connections with the New Testament. He leaves that aspect to the New Testament authors themselves. In every sense of the term, then, this is a *biblical theology*. It seeks to uncover the whole story of the Bible from creation to new creation. Its method is clearly grounded in the notion of salvation history. His reflections and conclusions on the hermeneutical issues, particularly with regard to the relationship of the two Testaments, are confined to a few pages in the introduction. This is not a criticism; VanGemeren succeeds admirably in what he sets out to do. He has given us a concise and exegetically sound analysis of most of the canon of Scripture within a salvation-historical framework. It is noteworthy, however, that in adopting this approach he has left us without biblical theological assessments of the wisdom books and the Psalms.

William J. Dumbrell

Dumbrell is a thorough evangelical exegete who has examined a number of topics from a biblical-theological perspective. He is an important Australian contributor to modern biblical theology. His first major work of this kind is his study of the covenant.[37] In this he examines the Old Testament covenants following a fairly traditional and biblically based structure: the covenants with Noah, and Abraham; the covenant at Sinai; the covenant with David; and the new covenant of prophetic eschatology. He does not set out to follow through into the role of Jesus as fulfiller of these Old Testament expressions of covenant. This work is thus a thematically focused theology of the Old Testament. In a similar way *The Faith of Israel* sets out the teaching of the indi-

---

37. William J. Dumbrell, *Covenant and Creation: An Old Testament Covenantal Theology* (Exeter: Paternoster, 1984).

vidual books of the Old Testament in turn, following the order of the Hebrew canon.[38] This extremely readable and useful book does not seek to answer the question of the relationship of the two Testaments.

Dumbrell's Moore College Lectures of 1983 focused on Revelation 21 – 22 and were published in 1985.[39] Of all his major works, this one probably gives the best indication of his biblical-theological method as shown in his understanding of the Old Testament background to an important part of the New Testament. In these studies Dumbrell explores the Old Testament allusions in Revelation 21 – 22 in order to answer the question 'How did the seer of Revelation arrive at the content of his panoramic final vision?'[40] He indicates that his biblical-theological method is based on the presupposition of diversity within unity, which 'is most clearly seen through a consideration of the historical development of theological themes'.[41] Importantly it is the consideration of the origins and development of themes that is the issue. In the first four verses of Revelation 21 he identifies five major themes: the new Jerusalem, the new temple, the new covenant, the new Israel and the new creation. Each of these is followed up in turn by examining its Old Testament antecedents. While the aim is to elucidate the form and content of Revelation 21 – 22, these studies stand as classic thematically organized biblical theologies in themselves. It just so happens that each of the themes reaches its consummation in the climax to the biblical story.

Dumbrell's study of biblical eschatology, *The Search for Order*, follows his assertion that 'In very broad terms, the biblical sweep is from creation to the new creation by way of redemption.'[42] He accepts a broad definition of eschatology to involve 'the goal of history toward which the Bible moves and biblical factors and events bearing on that goal'.[43] The study involves

---

38. William J. Dumbrell, *The Faith of Israel: Its Expression in the Books of the Old Testament*, 2nd ed. (Grand Rapids: Baker; Leicester: Apollos, 2002).

39. The Moore College Lectures are given as an annual series of public lectures by some renowned or well-known theologian and by members of the College faculty. The 1983 lectures are published as William J. Dumbrell, *The End of the Beginning: Revelation 21–22 and the Old Testament* (Homebush West, NSW: Lancer; Grand Rapids: Baker, 1985).

40. Ibid., introduction, n.p.

41. Ibid.

42. William J. Dumbrell, *The Search for Order: Biblical Eschatology in Focus* (Grand Rapids: Baker, 1994), p. 9.

43. Ibid.

the investigation of some major eschatological themes in the Old Testament (creation, Fall, covenant, kingship, Zion) and the eschatology of the various New Testament authors. The eschatological teaching of Jesus thus comes under the treatment of each of the four Gospels. Once again Dumbrell's chosen method is simply to work through the biblical canon as we have it, highlighting the eschatological teaching as he goes. He waits until he focuses on the New Testament corpora before tackling any of the issues of the relationship of the two Testaments. His chosen theme of *order* is based on the creation of order and loss of it in the Fall, and the fact that 'God patiently bore with sinful humankind until finally imposing order at the end of the canon.'[44] Eschatology, then, is the progressive revelation of the order that will one day be fully restored.

> The movement of the Bible from creation to the new creation was made possible only by the fact that God was in Christ, in the historical factor of the cross outside the city of Jerusalem in the midpoint of salvation history, reconciling the world unto himself.[45]

Sidney Greidanus

Sidney Greidanus has been an important contributor to the understanding of biblical theology. His first major work *Sola Scriptura*, based on his doctoral thesis, examined an earlier debate in the Reformed Churches of the Netherlands over the relative value of exemplary and redemptive-historical preaching.[46] His concern was the preaching of narrative portions of the Old Testament and the application these have to the contemporary Christian. This concern is also found in the later work *The Modern Preacher and the Ancient Text*.[47] He explains that 'In fusing hermeneutics and homiletics, I am building on my doctoral dissertation of 1970.'[48] This work is a practical guide to preachers for the handling of the various dimensions of the biblical text in preaching. He shows the close connection between preaching and hermeneutics and thus includes much that relates to biblical theology. Significantly

---

44. Ibid., p. 346.
45. Ibid.
46. Sidney Greidanus, *Sola Scriptura: Problems and Principles in Preaching Historical Texts* (Toronto: Wedge, 1970).
47. Sidney Greidanus, *The Modern Preacher and the Ancient Text* (Grand Rapids: Eerdmans; Leicester: IVP, 1988).
48. Ibid., p. xi.

Greidanus refers to an important feature of the Old Testament prophetic proclamation: the continuity of past and future. The prophets project the future acts of God in terms of the past events of Israel's history.[49]

However, it is not until his book *Preaching Christ from the Old Testament* that he really lays out in detail his understanding of the relationship of the two Testaments.[50] Greidanus here explains his understanding of how the preacher gets from an Old Testament text to Christ. The heart of this is his designation of a number of different 'roads' from the Old Testament through to the New Testament and Christ. As I deal with so-called multiplex approaches in chapter 5 I shall leave further comment on Greidanus's approach until then.

Charles H. H. Scobie[51]

Scobie's biblical theology *The Ways of Our God*[52] is a monumental achievement of a comprehensive biblical theology of the whole Bible. This massive undertaking must surely rank as one of most significant evangelical works of this kind ever produced. The first section sets out the author's understanding of his work within the context of the history of biblical theology, and gives a detailed outline of the principles behind his method. In discussing the structure of biblical theology he indicates three different approaches: systematic, historical and thematic. That Scobie worked out his own approach some time ago is clearly seen from his essay of 1991.[53] Here he assesses each of the three approaches referred to. In the systematic approach, '[t]he standard practice was to arrange the texts under the principal topics or subjects (*loci communes*) dealt with in Protestant dogmatic theology.'[54] The historic approach was affected by the prevailing critical mood that began to question

---

49. Ibid., p. 236.

50. Sidney Greidanus, *Preaching Christ from the Old Testament: A Contemporary Hermeneutical Method* (Grand Rapids: Eerdmans, 1999).

51. Scobie proposes a multi-thematic approach that could well be treated in chapter 5 but I shall consider him here as a major exponent of evangelical biblical theology.

52. Charles H. H. Scobie, *The Ways of Our God: An Approach to Biblical Theology* (Grand Rapids: Eerdmans, 2003). Much of what follows is an edited version of a book review I wrote in the book reviews section of *RTR* 63.1 (April 2004), pp. 50–52, used here with permission.

53. Charles H. H. Scobie, 'The Structure of Biblical Theology', *TB* 42.1 (1991), pp. 163–194.

54. Ibid., p. 167. Here Scobie cites a number of biblical theologies from the nineteenth and twentieth centuries that are clearly organized on the basis of doctrinal topics.

the historiography of the biblical writers. Consequently the historical-critical method had a radical effect on the writing of biblical theologies. Scobie notes:

> The Bible began to look less and less like a textbook of systematic theology and more and more like a history book. The only order it contains, it was argued, is the historical and chronological order on which God's people (Israel and the Early Church) received the divine revelation and committed it to writing in the various books.[55]

The reassessments of the history of the Bible by the historical-critical school led to a variety of rewritings of the order of events, which radically affected the structure of biblical theology.

Of the third approach Scobie remarks:

> A thematic approach to Biblical Theology seeks to structure its treatment around themes or topics which arise from the biblical material itself rather than being imposed upon it on the basis of a predetermined dogmatic system.[56]

The matter of dispute here is whether there is a single theme that can function as an organizing principle that does justice to both the unity and the great diversity in Scripture.

> If finding one central theme for the Old Testament and for the New Testament poses difficulties, this is even more the case in relation to one theme which could serve as an organizing principle for a Biblical Theology.[57]

Scobie cites here my own early attempt at using the kingdom of God as a central controlling theme.[58] He has reservations about this use of the *kingdom of God* theme because the term is not found in the Old Testament and in the New Testament is mainly used in the Synoptic Gospels.[59] He does not seem to appreciate that I was not concerned with the actual words but with the

---

55. Ibid., p. 169.
56. Ibid., p. 173.
57. Ibid., p. 176.
58. Goldsworthy, *Gospel and Kingdom.*
59. Charles H. H. Scobie, *The Ways of Our God: An Approach to Biblical Theology* (Grand Rapids: Eerdmans, 2003), pp. 86, 94.

concept to which they apply.[60] Scobie mentions also the themes of 'covenant' and 'salvation history'. The latter he dismisses because it is not found in the wisdom literature. The obvious rejoinder to that is that the wisdom literature may not use the history of Israel as a central theme, but it emerges within the history of Israel and cannot be divorced from the redemptive history that surrounds it. The 'fear of Yahweh' as the beginning of wisdom and knowledge means little if it is removed from its salvation-historical context.[61] Furthermore, as I have indicated in the previous chapter, the wisdom tradition is firmly anchored in Solomon, whose function in salvation history is extremely important.

Having assessed the systematic, historical and thematic approaches as inadequate, Scobie proposes a multi-thematic approach. Here he is in agreement with writers such as Elmer A. Martens, Sidney Greidanus and Gerhard F. Hasel. He also refers to Dumbrell's *The End of the Beginning* as such an approach. While he recognizes that Dumbrell is not setting out to write a full biblical theology, he seems to overlook Dumbrell's stated intention to trace the five themes he identifies in Revelation 21 – 22. In the end Scobie proposes four major themes around which a full biblical theology may be based, and it is these themes that he uses in his own monumental Biblical Theology.[62] These are God's order, God's servant, God's people and God's way. Each chapter is organized under four headings: Old Testament proclamation, Old Testament promise, New Testament fulfilment, New Testament consummation. He thus deals with his chosen themes within their Old Testament contemporary context, secondly in terms of eschatology and promise, thirdly in contemporary New Testament context, and finally in New Testament eschatological context. This arrangement has the advantage of highlighting the broad dynamic progression of revelation. This bears some slight resemblance to the Robinson–Hebert schema. But this treatment of numerous strands, while uncovering insightful links between the Old and New Testaments, I believe tends to mute the lateral relationships between the themes.

---

60. My suggestion was that 'God's people in God's place under God's rule', though somewhat reductionist, adequately expresses the essence of the various and progressively revealed biblical expressions of God's kingdom.

61. See Joachim Becker, *Gottesfurcht im Alten Testament* (Rome: Päpstliches Bibelinstitut, 1965); Stanley E. Porter, 'Fear', *NDBT*, p. 497; John Goldingay, *Old Testament Theology*, vol. 3: *Israel's Life* (Downers Grove, IVP, 2009), pp. 75–79.

62. 'Structure', pp. 187–194.

There is an overall 'now – not yet' structure which in my opinion is too broad. The treatment of the various themes is conducted within the four categories mentioned above. The result is that any development in themes and, thus, in the whole progress of revelation, tends to be somewhat obscured. It is as if no real difference exists between, say, the Pentateuch and the Former Prophets in the development of any given theme. This, it seems to me, tends to obscure the overall matrix of revelation. It is certainly at variance with the epochal approach of Vos, Clowney and Johnson. For example, in the first chapter of part 2 Scobie deals with the sub-theme 'The Lord is King'. The Scripture passages cited in these two pages go from 1 Chronicles to Numbers, then to a whole range of latter prophets, then to Daniel and back to 1 Kings, and so on. This tends to abstract the theme from its developing historical contexts and remove the sense of any epochal structure beyond the chosen one involving proclamation or promise – fulfilment or consummation.

I return to Scobie's apparent nervousness on the matter of a discernible centre to biblical theology. At times this is more of an outright rejection: 'It is difficult to understand the obsession with finding one single theme or "center" for OT or NT theology, and more so for an entire BT.'[63] And yet, his stated presuppositions and the method he follows seem to me to admit of such an entity. If the Bible is a unity the obvious question concerns what gives it this unity.

> The presuppositions of this study include belief that the Bible conveys a divine revelation, that the word of God in Scripture constitutes the norm of Christian faith and life, and that all the varied material of the OT and NT can in some way be related to the plan and purpose of the one God of the whole Bible.[64]

Surely it follows from such presuppositions that the plan and purpose of the one God of the whole Bible would constitute a centre that one can determine. Otherwise, how can we possibly know that 'all the varied material of the OT and NT' relates to it? Scobie's chosen categories – God's Order, God's Servant, God's People and God's Way – seem to me to be very close to my own schematizing of the kingdom of God as a central theme using 'God's people in God's place under God's rule'. Notwithstanding these criticisms I believe Scobie's monumental work will be a long-term classic.

---

63. Scobie, *Ways of Our God*, p. 87.

64. Ibid., p. 47.

Craig G. Bartholomew and Michael W. Goheen[65]

I include Bartholomew and Goheen as providing us with an example of another approach to biblical theology. Adapting an idea borrowed from N. T. Wright, they conceive of the unity of Scripture as a drama, a story in six acts from creation to new creation. By adopting the drama model the authors tie the book into the narrative structure of the Bible, which is of course their aim. The story is told with a focus on the key theme of the kingdom of God with the covenant as a subsidiary theme. They clearly do not share Scobie's problem with the kingdom of God as a central theme.

The narrative focus of the book is at the one time both its strength and a weakness. Its strength lies in the way it gives the broad sweep of events and key people that figure in the metanarrative of the Bible. It makes clear that we have to do, not with mere ideas, but with events in time and space that form the grand drama of God acting in Christ for our redemption. It is true that moving to a diachronic synthesis should not displace an analysis of the details of the story. But it is also true that the narrative shape must be integrated into such a synthesis.

To me, one weakness of the approach in this book is that it has allowed those parts of the Old Testament that sit within the broader or implied narrative context, but which themselves contain either minimal or no explicit narrative pointers, to fade somewhat into the background. Thus the wisdom literature and, surprisingly, the Latter Prophets become almost part of the passing scenery. A glance at the index of references will show what I mean. Wisdom is briefly mentioned in connection with Solomon. The Latter Prophets, about one third of the bulk of the Old Testament, are dealt with in eight pages, half the space taken to give an outline of the intertestamental period, which is assumed by the overall biblical narrative but not actually part of it. To be fair, much greater attention is paid to the New Testament claims to the fulfilment of the prophets' message in Christ. But this tends to give the impression that the prophets had little theological relevance for their own times.

The story of Jesus and the apostles, in the fourth and fifth acts of the conceived Drama, is told in some detail and with attention to the key elements of the gospel message in the life, death and resurrection of Jesus. This leads to

---

65. Craig G. Bartholomew and Michael W. Goheen, *The Drama of Scripture: Finding Our Place in the Biblical Story* (Grand Rapids: Baker, 2004). This section is an edited version of a book review I wrote for the website Biblical Theology Briefings <http://beginningwithmoses.org>, used with permission.

the mission of the church and to the crucial question about where we today
fit into the story. The hermeneutic value of this is rather understated. Where
we find our place in the biblical story affects not only all the questions of faith
and Christian living in the modern (or postmodern) world, but also the whole
approach that biblical theology demands of us towards those texts that belong
to the times previous to our joining the narrative.

What I think is missing in this book, as an intended introduction to biblical theology, is any reflection on the theological structures of the message
that lie behind and drive the narrative structures. The perfunctory treatment
of the message of the prophets at the time of the kingdom's decline is a
case in point. It is here that I think the drama scheme fails. Biblical theology
consists in more than simply relating the events of the story in order, even if
accompanied in the process by theological comment of the kind the authors
provide. It needs to be analytical of the theological dynamics within the story.
Theological analysis and synthesis are not the sole property of dogmatics.
I also miss some theological reflection that would help us to see the great
recurring themes, both in their unity and diversity. I miss the sense that the
prophets deliberately recapitulate the earlier history of redemption in their
eschatological projections. I miss the analysis of the nature of the theological
transition between the several Acts of the Drama. Act 3, which covers the
whole redemptive story of the Old Testament, needs some fine-tuning to
point up these structures. How do the several expressions of covenant relate
to a unifying covenant theme? How are the writing prophets related to the
failure under Solomon? Are there significant differences between the messages and function of the pre-exilic, exilic and post-exilic prophets? I also miss
any analysis of the dynamics of prophetic fulfilment and typology. However,
this work is to be commended for its clarity, for its uncomplicated acceptance of the integrity of the scriptural account, for its important sense of the
universal significance of the biblical story and the way it should shape our
self-understanding and world view.

Conclusions

One conclusion I draw from this brief encounter with a number of modern
evangelical biblical theologians is that none of us can claim to have the final
word on the matter. There is much work to be done in clarifying the important issues of aims and method. Most evangelicals would agree that the task
should never be undertaken for its own sake but for the better equipping of
the people of God in the truths of the Scriptures for the life and ministry of

Christ's church. This assessment may possibly be seen as an endorsement of multifaceted approaches, such as those I consider in the next chapter. It will become clear, I hope, that I am not really saying that. Rather I consider the multifaceted approaches to constitute one among a number of different viable ways of looking at biblical theology. Advocates of different approaches, and here I include myself as an advocate of the basic Robinson–Hebert schema, need to continue to talk to each other and to seek to learn from the different perspectives involved in evangelical biblical theology.

A biblical theological method that cannot deal with all the texts of the Bible is to some extent defective. It should be clear by now that I mean by that more than doing sound exegesis. The interconnectedness of all texts and, above all, their relatedness to Christ and his people must be served by whatever method we adopt and with whatever schema we represent the totality of revelation in the Bible.

5. MULTIPLEX BIBLICAL THEOLOGY

The problem of unity and diversity in method

In this chapter we shall consider the positions of some leading evangelical biblical theologians who maintain that a multiplex, or multifaceted, approach is demanded by the material of the biblical texts. Key exponents of this position include Gerhard Hasel, Charles Scobie and Sidney Greidanus. Among biblical theologians we find that there is some criticism of the attempt to designate any kind of unitary understanding of the structure of biblical theology. I think it should be clear that in most things it is never a case of unity *or* distinction, but rather of unity *and* distinction. In considering the relationship of the Old Testament to the New Testament, or of any biblical book to the whole canon, we need to understand the nature of both the unity and the distinction involved. The Bible is very diverse in all its dimensions, yet we base so much on a perceived unity in these things. The question we must address here is whether or not the overall unity of the Bible can be understood in terms of some central theological principle or theme. Is it possible to take the variety of approaches to the relationship of the two Testaments as complementary within that unity? Or does the diversity mean there is no real discernible unity?

Another related matter is whether or not some kind of multifaceted approach is incompatible with the idea of a centre or controlling theme of biblical theology. I am not persuaded that it is. If we believe in the unity of Scripture the obvious question is, what gives it its unity? It is not good enough in my opinion to leave it at the level of the accepted canon, for that still leaves open the question of why the canon came to be recognized in the form it did. Few, if any, would deny that there is great diversity in Scripture. But many have denied Scripture's unity, implying that the church's acceptance of our canon of the Old and New Testaments is based on a superficial unity that modern critical study refuses to be bound by. There are two distinct matters here that may easily be confused. One is the variety of ways that the links between the Old and New Testaments may be discerned. The other is how a biblical theology can be structured to exploit these links and provide a comprehensive and unified 'big picture' of the theology of the Bible. The two are not the same.

Proponents of the multiplex approach

Gerhard F. Hasel

The Seventh-Day Adventist theologian Gerhard Hasel (1935–94) has been a major exponent of what he called a multiplex approach and, with it, a truly canonical biblical theology. He has defined canonical biblical theology in negative terms by contrasting it with the older 'concepts of doctrine' and the 'dogmatic-didactic' approaches.[1] He also finds the notion of a centre inadequate for the structuring of a biblical theology.

> [The multiplex approach] avoids the pitfalls of structuring a theology of the Old Testament by means of a center, theme, key concept, or focal point but allows the various motifs, themes, and concepts to emerge in all their variety and richness without elevating any of these longitudinal perspectives into a single structuring concept, whether it be communion, covenant, promise, kingdom of God, or something else. The multiplex approach allows aside from this and in the first instance that the theologies of the various OT books and blocks of writings emerge and stand next to each other in all their variety and richness.[2]

It is not clear what Hasel considers are the pitfalls of structuring according to a centre except that of the risk of failing to allow the individual corpora to

---

1. Gerhard F. Hasel, *Old Testament Theology: Basic Issues in the Current Debate*, rev. 4th ed. (Grand Rapids: Eerdmans, 1991), p. 113.
2. Ibid.

yield their own theological perspectives. In this case the 'centre' would thus
be a presupposition imported from outside a particular document and would
adversely control the exegesis of it. It is difficult to see why this has to be.
Furthermore, it seems that Hasel does favour a 'both/and' approach:

> The final aim of the canonical approach to Old Testament theology is to penetrate
> through the various theologies of the individual books and groups of writings and the
> various longitudinal themes to the dynamic unity that binds all theologies and themes
> together.[3]

But how do the theologies of the various books or corpora stand next to each
other in all their variety and richness? What is their relationship to each other
beyond 'standing next to each other'? What gives them the 'dynamic unity' he
speaks of? Hasel leaves no doubt that dealing with individual books or themes
of the Old Testament is not the whole task since the Christian theologian has
the task of relating the Old Testament to the New Testament. While Hasel
outlines his canonical approach, it is regrettable that he never produced his
own Biblical Theology, as this would have clarified, and shown in practice,
the principles he laid down. He set out his proposals for a canonical biblical
theology (as distinct from an Old Testament theology) in a posthumously
published article.[4] Here he states seven theses concerning such a theology.
These include delimiting the task by confining it to the Protestant canon
of sixty-six books; understanding the task as theological-historical and not
merely historical; an acceptance of God's self-revelation in Scripture; a focus
on the biblical faith revealed in Scripture; the dual task of dealing with the final
form of the individual corpora, and presenting longitudinal themes and motifs
that emerge from the Bible; and providing a structure that can encompass the
multiform materials of the Bible.[5]

In dealing with the multiform materials of the Bible, Hasel surveys a range
of suggestions from various biblical scholars regarding a centre: 'This sam-
pling of suggestions indicates that there is no consensus on what is the alleged
"center" of the Bible.'[6] The reason, he says, rests in the variety of biblical

---

3. Ibid., p. 114. The two quotations above appear to me to involve something of a
   conflict of ideas.
4. Gerhard F. Hasel, 'Proposals for a Canonical Biblical Theology', *AUSS* 34.1 (1996),
   pp. 23–33.
5. Ibid.
6. Ibid., p. 32.

revelation. But might not lack of consensus be due to the variety of possible perspectives on a centre? Hasel makes an important point that is needed to clarify this issue, since terms like 'center' require careful definition:

> On the positive side, the OT indeed betrays an all-pervading center. God is the beginning, center, and future of the OT. The NT likewise betrays an all-pervading center in Jesus Christ, in whom God has revealed Himself. But we must make a significant distinction with regard to the matter of the center. The fact of the center and unity of biblical thought, i.e., the issue of whether there is something that appears as providing an overriding unity in spite of all variety, must be clearly separated from the question of a center, theme, concept, or the like, on the basis of which one engages in 'content criticism,' distils an 'authoritative core,' or finds a 'canon with the canon.'[7]

It seems his concern here is that identifying a centre may have the effect of excluding some texts that cannot easily be included in it.[8] His concern that a centre could lead to a canon within the canon may be well founded, but there is no reason why it should have this outcome. Hasel goes on to define the centre of both Testaments as 'the triune God who revealed Himself in the OT in multiple ways and who has manifested Himself in the NT in the incarnation of Jesus Christ as the God-man'. On the basis of this understanding Hasel proposes two steps regarding the structure of biblical theology: first, the presentation of the theologies of the various corpora in both Testaments 'so that each witness stands next to the others in all its richness and variety'. Secondly, there is 'a multitrack treatment of the longitudinal themes, motifs, and concepts that have emerged from the book-by-book and group-by-group presentation'.[9] The question of how the underlying unity can be discerned and expressed still remains.

It is clear that Hasel has a great concern that the integrity of each individual witness be preserved. We can only applaud this concern as it is all too easy for the Christian interpreter, particularly in dealing with the Old Testament, to rush to a Christological interpretation or a personal Christian application before doing a careful and close exegesis of the text itself. The distinction

---

7. Ibid.

8. A case in point may well be the difficulty, mentioned above, that biblical theologians have expressed in accommodating the OT wisdom literature into a schema that centres in the idea of salvation history.

9. Hasel, 'Proposals', p. 33.

between a theological centre and the overall basis for structuring biblical theology is an important one. From the evidence we have in his writings, it seems Hasel's main approach to linking the Testaments and finding their unity lies in his multifaceted (or multitrack) examination of longitudinal themes. It is not clear to me how that works out. He does not seem concerned with the epochal and broadly synchronic structures within which the longitudinal themes have a certain progressive dynamic. Charles Scobie, in proposing a similar approach, notes:

> This [multi-thematic approach] is in line with the 'multitrack treatment of the longitudinal themes, motifs, and concepts' frequently advocated by G. F. Hasel.[10] Hasel, however gives little or no indication of how the themes should be co-ordinated in any overall structure of a Biblical Theology.[11]

We shall need to revisit this matter when we examine the role of typology in biblical theology. Reformed biblical scholars, such as Vos or Clowney, who propose dynamic epochal structures do not really feature in Hasel's assessment of the legitimate way to proceed.[12] He does not discuss the key to the structuring of biblical theology in terms of such epochs after the manner of these two influential scholars in modern evangelical biblical theology. Thus his synchronic examinations would appear to be at the level of individual books and corpora. An epochal approach would require a diachronic integration of corpora in a way that uncovers significant stages in progressive revelation.

Sidney Greidanus

Sidney Geidanus has contributed a great deal to the subject of preaching and how biblical theology functions in relation to Christian proclamation. His first major publication (his doctoral thesis) was a consideration of how the historical narratives of the Bible, particularly in the Old Testament, should be handled in preaching.[13] His second offering builds on his doctoral disserta-

---

10. Here he refers to Hasel's article 'Biblical Theology: Then, Now and Tomorrow', *HBT* 4.1 (1982), p. 80.

11. Charles H. H. Scobie, 'The Structure of Biblical Theology', *TB* 42.1 (1991), p. 179, n. 50.

12. In *Old Testament Theology* Hasel refers to Vos three times but only to note in passing that he is a biblical theologian.

13. Sidney Greidanus, *Sola Scriptura: Problems and Principles in Preaching Historical Texts* (Toronto: Wedge, 1970).

tion but presents his approach as it is applied more widely to biblical genres.[14] His further works may be seen as a refining of his essential approach to the Christian preaching of the Old Testament.[15] It appears to me that the later works of Greidanus indicate that his essential position on the relationship between the Testaments and consequent approach to biblical theology was established quite early in his career. His later books represent a honing of this and an application of his method to the practical issues of preaching.

An interview with Greidanus by *Preaching* magazine in 2010 indicates that his position has remained essentially unchanged.[16] His biblical theology is most clearly set out in *Preaching Christ from the Old Testament*. Once again, we need to distinguish between a biblical-theological approach to texts for the purpose of preaching, and the task of structuring a biblical theology written to give a comprehensive perspective of the unity of the whole Bible. Unlike Scobie, Greidanus has not apparently attempted the latter. His focus has been consistently on the matter of preaching and application of texts in a Christian manner. If he were to write a Biblical Theology I can only conjecture that he would probably concentrate on the major longitudinal approaches he nominates.

One of Greidanus's strengths is his determination to establish a thoroughly Christocentric approach to preaching. He is a strong advocate of a redemptive-historical approach to the texts, yet he does not seem to exploit the full potential of this perspective. He wants, as he says,

> to do justice to the fact that God's story of bringing his kingdom on earth is centered in Christ: Christ the center of redemptive history, Christ the center of the Scriptures. In preaching any part of Scripture, one must understand its message in the light of that center, Jesus Christ.[17]

The nominated roads that lead from the Old Testament to Christ are as follows:

---

14. *The Modern Preacher and the Ancient Text* (Grand Rapids: Eerdmans; Leicester: IVP, 1988).

15. *Preaching Christ from the Old Testament: A Contemporary Hermeneutical Method* (Grand Rapids: Eerdmans, 1999); *Preaching Christ from Genesis: Foundations for Expository Sermons* (Grand Rapids: Eerdmans, 2007); *Preaching Christ from Ecclesiastes: Foundations for Expository Sermons* (Grand Rapids: Eerdmans, 2010).

16. Online <http://www.preaching.com/resources/articles/11584086>, accessed 7 July 2011.

17. *Preaching Christ from the Old Testament*, p. 227.

1. The way of redemptive-historical progression.
2. The way of promise-fulfilment.
3. The way of typology.
4. The way of analogy.
5. The way of longitudinal themes.
6. The way of New Testament references.
7. The way of contrast.

Although he finds these approaches in the New Testament, Greidanus seems somewhat ambivalent about it all when he warns us that the New Testament is not a textbook of hermeneutics.[18] That is true enough, for, strictly speaking, it is not a textbook on anything. But if we cannot determine our hermeneutics of the Old Testament from the way Jesus, the apostles and the inspired authors of the New Testament interpreted it, have we any firm basis at all on which to proceed?

While Greidanus has a keen sense of redemptive history, he does not follow the lead of Vos, Clowney and others in determining epochs that differentiate the stages in progressive revelation within redemptive history. He states that 'A major New Testament presupposition for interpreting the Old Testament is that God acts uniformly but progressively in redemptive history.'[19] But when it comes to the nature of this progression he seems not to be in favour of any kind of epochal structure as a guide. This New Testament presupposition of redemptive history links with a second presupposition, namely, the conviction that Jesus came to bring in the new messianic age.[20] So what kind of progression does Greidanus recognize in this redemptive history?

'The Way of Redemptive-Historical Progression' is Greidanus's first road that leads from Old to New Testament.[21] This is essentially the matrix that allows us to 'link Christ to Old Testament redemptive events which find their climax in him'.[22] Specific examples given include Matthew's use of his genealogy to link Jesus back through history to David and Abraham. In referring to Luke, Greidanus notes the two broad aeons of the time of Israel and the time of fulfilment. Acts contains a number of records of apostolic preaching that link Jesus to the great redemptive events of the past.[23]

---

18. Ibid., pp. 189–191.
19. Ibid., p. 191.
20. Ibid., p. 195.
21. Ibid., p. 203.
22. Ibid., p. 204.
23. Ibid.

'The Way of Promise-Fulfillment' is the second road Greidanus proposes. He rightly points out that fulfilment in the New Testament documents is a broad concept. Some New Testament authors use the idea of fulfilment in a way that at first seems to go beyond what is reasonable in that a number of Old Testament statements that are not typological or promissory are said to be fulfilled by what Jesus says or does. Concerning Matthew, Greidanus quotes from Christopher Wright thus: 'Matthew sees the whole Old Testament as the embodiment of promise – in the sense of presenting to us a God of gracious and saving purpose, liberating action, and covenant faithfulness to his people.'[24] Again drawing on Wright he gives us the example of progressive fulfilment of the promise to Abraham's descendants of becoming a great nation. In this there is an indisputable straight line of development. Thus he diagrammatically shows this progression from Abraham to Isaac, then to Jacob, Egypt, Canaan, David, Exile, Remnant, and into the future.[25] But there is no differentiation between the significance of each of these events beyond being part of a progression towards fulfilment. I would contend that to understand promise-fulfilment more fully we need to differentiate between the epochs of historical events and prophetic eschatology.

I do not propose to go through all of the roads between the two Testaments that Greidanus nominates. His analysis is incontrovertible, as each proposal can easily be demonstrated from Scripture. What I do propose, however, is that we can go further to identify a structural unity into which all these different aspects fit. I am well aware that there are those who think that this is to be in danger of imposing an alien grid or a simplistic structure onto the Bible. But let us, for example, take the above-quoted passage from Christopher Wright in which he proposes that Matthew sees the whole Old Testament 'as the embodiment of promise'. If we take a broad view of what promise is, it seems to me that we can see a sense in which all of Greidanus's proposed roads are subsumed under it.

To be more specific, I would propose that promise is implicit in many ways as well as being explicit in the obvious places. I think this is what Wright is referring to in Matthew. Thus promise is implicit in creation, a fact that is confirmed by the gracious act of God to allow the human race and the created order to survive the fall into sin. The indicative of Genesis 3:15 that

---

24. *Preaching Christ from the Old Testament*, p. 207, quoting from Christopher J. H. Wright, *Knowing Jesus Through the Old Testament: Rediscovering the Roots of Our Faith* (Downers Grove: IVP, 1992), pp. 63–64.

25. *Preaching Christ from the Old Testament*, p. 208.

the seed of the woman would bruise the head of the serpent is full of promise. Every indication of the plan and purposes of God, even when not given as verbal promise, is promissory. We could without violence subsume all of Greidanus's roads from Old to New Testament under the notion of explicit or implicit promise. Notwithstanding these criticisms, we are indebted to Greidanus for the skill and clarity with which he pursues the task of showing what it means for us as Christians to appropriate the Old Testament as part of our canon of Scripture.

Elmer A. Martens

Charles Scobie names Elmer A. Martens's book *Plot and Purpose in the Old Testament* as an example of a multifaceted approach to biblical theology.[26] Martens proposes Exodus 5:22 – 6:8 as a passage that outlines and 'clarifies the central message of the Old Testament'.[27] What this passage does is really to reiterate the covenant promises to Abraham with the added dimension of deliverance from the Egyptian captivity. This only underlines the fact that there is a unity to the themes before we start. Martens structures his book on four themes drawn from this passage: salvation or deliverance, the covenant community, the experience and knowledge of God, and the land. Scobie finds Martens's use of the theme of 'the land' rather forced since it does not feature much in the New Testament. He similarly doubted my wisdom in nominating the *kingdom of God* as the centre because the term is not mentioned as such in the Old Testament. I think Scobie misses the point here. The centre of biblical theology does not have to be a theme defined by a single specific term. We are not concerned with word studies here. Rather we can look for the binding concept that may be expressed by a variety of terms. Thus the land is the place of God's dwelling with his people. The significance of the Promised Land can be alternatively expressed as God's dwelling with his people in Eden, the tabernacle (focal point of the Promised Land), the temple, the new temple which is Christ, and the consummation in the new Eden (the new creation). As the 'Immanuel' the dwelling place of God with his people, Jesus fulfils all the significance of Eden and the Promised Land.

Martens, then, structures his analysis in four parts: God's design *articulated*,

---

26. 'Structure', pp. 179–180. Since Scobie wrote this article a later edition of Martens's work has appeared; see n. 27 below.

27. Elmer A. Martens, *Plot and Purpose in the Old Testament* (Leicester: IVP, 1981), ch. 1; 2nd ed., *God's Design: A Focus on Old Testament Theology* (Grand Rapids: Baker; Leicester: Apollos, 1994).

God's design *implemented* in the pre-monarchy period, God's design *tested* in the monarchy period, and God's design *reaffirmed* in the post-monarchy period. Scobie has remarked on the multifaceted approach at the synchronic levels indicated, but does not seem to notice that Martens has also given these an epochal structure. Without saying as much, Martens has shown that the testing time of the monarchy and the judgment that falls on it requires the reaffirmation that follows. Thus particularly in his fourth section Martens in effect highlights the recapitulation by the prophets of the promises that go right back to Abraham and that were developed in Israel's historical experience up to the zenith preceding the decline and exile in Babylon. Martens, it seems, is not far from the epochal approach or Donald Robinson's threefold schema.

Conclusions

The following conclusions can be drawn from this survey:

1. Our examination of these representatives of the multiplex approach suggests that such a method is not inherently incompatible with the recognition of important epochs or stages in biblical revelation that enable us to structure an overview of the theology of the Bible.
2. There is a distinction to be drawn between the discernment of different nuances in the ways the Old Testament texts relate to the New Testament, and the delineation of the centre of biblical theology that gives Scripture its unity.
3. A further important distinction needs to be drawn between the question of such links between the Testaments and the structure one might choose to employ in the writing of a Biblical Theology.
4. The different *roads*, to use Greidanus's term, are essentially based on the literary examination of what is there in the written text. The question remains with regard to each as to what principle is being applied by the New Testament writers that enables them to make particular links between the Old Testament and Christ.
5. The question to be put to those evangelicals who reject a 'centre' in favour of a multiplex approach is, what gives the Bible its unity? Once we undertake to describe 'A Biblical Theology', as opposed to 'Biblical Theologies', we are bound to attempt to organize our material on the basis of some central principle, theme or person. We cannot assert the unity of the word of God and at the same time relegate its description to the too-hard basket.

I am concerned now to go on to examine the possibility of some kind of overarching unifying structure that accommodates the proposed variety of links between the two Testaments. I would not want to suggest, for example, that Greidanus's different roads and Hasel's multiplex approach are merely exercises in semantics. These multiplex methods do make real and important distinctions. My primary concern is whether or not there is some basic structure that allows us to find the Christ-centred significance of any text from any part of the Bible. As Hebrews 1:1–2 reminds us:

> Long ago, at many times and in many ways, God spoke to our fathers by the
> prophets, but in these last days he has spoken to us by his Son, whom he appointed
> the heir of all things, through whom also he created the world.

This text indicates the diversity – 'in many ways' – in the prophetic speech of God in the Old Testament that is given unity in Christ. The question raised here, and presumably answered in the rest of Hebrews, is that of the relationship between the two ways God has spoken. I suspect, also, that for Jesus to be 'heir of all things' implies that all things are defined by their relationship to him. 'All things' is a phrase that includes all that the Bible contains. The nature of those relationships is what we wish to uncover.

6. LETTING THE OLD TESTAMENT SPEAK I: BIBLICAL HISTORY

What kind of epoch?

Does the Old Testament provide any evidence of some kind of internal structuring of the revealed message? Does it, from its internal evidence, support one biblical-theological schema over another? My aim in this chapter is to try to answer this question by enquiring into the manner of reflection within the Old Testament texts on what has happened in the process of salvation history. The notion of epochs in biblical revelation stems from observing the parameters of significant periods in salvation history. These parameters are established by key persons or events in the narrative. For Vos it was 'Berith-makings' (covenants).[1] The usefulness of such a schema lies not only in highlighting the distinctive theology of the epochs but also in showing the overall structure of revelation. We want to know not only what makes one epoch distinct from the others, but also how they relate. The term *epoch* has reference primarily to time and to notable sequences of events that distinguish a particular period of time from others.

The historical dimensions of the Bible provide the greatest opportunity

---

1. Geerhardus Vos, *Biblical Theology: Old and New Testaments* (Grand Rapids: Eerdmans, 1948; repr. 1963), p. 25.

for the useful delineation of epochs simply because *epoch* is about time and significant periods in history. Furthermore it becomes fairly obvious that the historical narratives of the Old Testament are written from the point of view that God is behind history and, in a real sense, in front of it as well. That is, biblical history purports to be the history of God's doings. God can be regarded as the principal character in the biblical narratives. History is what it is because of God's plan and purpose for his creation. For this reason alone we cannot really separate issues of history from issues of theology in the Old Testament. The non-narrative texts have enough pointers to their broad relationship to the historical process to enable us to include them in the consideration of epochs. What, then, can be said to constitute the significant events that characterize epochs or stages of revelation, and what criteria are applicable to discern them? The object of our enquiry is to discover what, if any, matrix of revelation exists in the Old Testament. Are there inherent structures or epochs that can be discerned from some overarching emphasis in the various texts?

Since we are dealing with the history of the acts of God, the epochs will be characterized by theological history. We have seen that Clowney's approach to epochs is similar to Vos's:

> The development of biblical theology is redemptive-historical. The divisions of biblical theology are the historical periods of redemption, marked by creation, the fall, the flood, the call of Abraham, Moses and the exodus, and the coming of Christ.[2]

But while Clowney follows Vos he is more comprehensive in beginning with creation. The Fall is clearly a significant event that reveals the need for redemption. The immediate post-Fall history climaxes in the judgment of the flood and the salvation of God's elect, Noah and his family. There can be no argument about this. The pre-patriarchal period follows on with the table of nations and the confusion of languages at Babel. Then the patriarchal period stretches from Abraham to the enslavement of the patriarch's descendants in Egypt. Finally both Vos and Clowney nominate the period from Moses to the coming of Christ as the last great epoch of the Old Testament.

---

2. Edmund P. Clowney, *Preaching and Biblical Theology* (Grand Rapids: Eerdmans, 1961; London: Tyndale, 1962), p. 16. In *Preaching Christ in All of Scripture* (Wheaton: Crossway, 2003), p. 17, Clowney refers to the same schema as taught by John Murray at Westminster Seminary.

There is no doubt that the promises to Abraham and the setting up of the covenant relationship between his people and his God constitute a significant event. What is more, the storyline from Abraham to the end of the Old Testament is, on the whole, detailed and continuous in a way that the story from the Fall to Babel is not. I want to propose that the way to allow the Old Testament to speak for itself is to follow its lead as to whether or not it exhibits such an epochal structure. The sense of continuity in the biblical dynamic is such that it becomes obvious whenever this continuity brings us to significant or critical events in the flow of things. But do such watershed events mark periods that warrant the status of epoch? There is little doubt that creation and Eden have a continuity broken by the Fall. The flood could be said to break the continuity of the post-Fall age. Abraham is a new beginning in a way Moses is not. And yet the outstanding nature of Moses' ministry suggests we at least consider how the period before Moses differs from the Mosaic age. We should be wary of making too keen a distinction between the Mosaic and pre-Mosaic epochs. Scott Hafemann aptly remarks:

> The historical development within the Bible does not proceed from a creation order with humanity based on obedience to a qualitatively different order with Abraham based on faith, only to return to an obedience-based relationship with Israel. Rather, God's original covenant relationship with humanity before the fall based on creation is re-established with both Abraham and Israel as an act of redemption.[3]

Distinctions between epochs can easily lead to separations and consequent distortions in theology. This, of course, is what covenant theologians believe happened in the rigid separation of dispensations in Dispensationalism. Let us then, try to follow the way the Old Testament itself understands epochs. How significant does each of the nominated possible epochal markers or foci turn out to be in the later reflections of Israel?

---

3. 'The Covenant Relationship', in Scott J. Hafemann and Paul R. House (eds.), *Central Themes in Biblical Theology: Mapping Unity in Diversity* (Nottingham: Apollos, 2007), p. 47. Hafemann's comment would seem to be in broad agreement with the controversial thesis of Holmes Rolston III, *John Calvin Versus the Westminster Confession* (Richmond, Va.: John Knox, 1972). Rolston asserts that this kind of separation has led to a legalistic tendency in the Westminster Confession that is opposed to Calvin's understanding of the faith principle in the OT.

The main foci in Old Testament history

Since Vos and Clowney seem to regard their delineation of epochs as self-evident I propose in this and the next chapter to follow a very simple procedure to see if their nominated epochs are as obvious as they suggest. I shall look at the main biblical foci in historical order, including those used in Clowney's scheme as marking the parameters of the epochs of revelation. I shall then examine the way these events are handled subsequently in the Old Testament texts. My aim is to uncover something of the way the Old Testament writers themselves saw the structure of revelation unfolding.

Creation

Creation and Fall are everywhere presupposed in subsequent texts. After Genesis 1 – 2 there are a number of significant references I shall note without trying to comment on them all. It is not my concern to analyse the topics in any detail, but only to point up the apparent significance they came to have for Israel and, particularly, for those agents of God's Spirit who wrote the biblical texts.[4]

After the Genesis accounts of creation, there is not much specific reflection on the event until the Psalms and the Latter Prophets. It is clearly an important doctrine in the later stages of Israel's theological reflection. Psalms 8, 89, 100, 136, 144 and Job 38 – 39 all make reference to God's majesty and sovereignty as creator. Psalm 8 expresses wonder at the dignity of human beings as the pinnacle of God's creation. Psalms 89 and 144 both link the sovereignty of God in creation with his covenant relationship with Israel and, specifically, to the covenant with David. Psalm 100 makes a similar link between creation and covenant. The first part of Psalm 136 establishes the link between creation and the covenant faithfulness of God to Israel. The second part links the redemptive event of the exodus from Egypt to God's steadfast love or covenant faithfulness (ḥesed). Creation, then, is mainly reflected on in relationship to the redemptive work of God.

---

4. A useful survey of the creation theme is Brevard S. Childs's 'Creation Tradition Within the Rest of the Old Testament', in *Biblical Theology of the Old and New Testaments* (London: SCM, 1992), pp. 113–122. This contrasts with Vos's omission of creation from his biblical theology.

Fall

We might be surprised by the dearth of direct references to Adam and the Fall. Nevertheless creation and rebellion against God are part of Israel's reflection on her past. Adam receives little attention after the accounts of his descendants in Genesis 4 and 5. In Deuteronomy 32:8 a reference to the sons of Adam simply means the human race. Adam's is the first name in the genealogy of 1 Chronicles 1:1, a reference that has no direct reflection on Adam in the Fall. The reference to Adam (*kĕ'ādām*: 'as Adam') in Hosea 6:7 is treated as a place name in the NRSV. The NIV and ESV both translate it as the personal name: 'Like Adam they transgressed (NIV: have broken) the covenant.'[5] The exact translation of the Hebrew is disputed. The specific events of the Fall as recorded in Genesis 3, then, are not very prominent in other parts of the Old Testament. Israel's reflection on the Fall comes to be enlarged by the idea of exile. Outside Eden there is an important sense that God's people are always in exile. The dimensions of this exile are clarified by the promise of a land that reflects the reality of Eden. The Egyptian bondage further demonstrates what exile is and how it is met by redemptive grace. Deuteronomy's covenant curses are always present as the threat of a new exile.

Nevertheless we need only to reflect on the prominence of the theme of Israel's rebellion against God, the many words for sin and transgression in the Hebrew text, the role of the Law and the curses of the covenant, to recognize that the Fall is one of the main presuppositions of the whole economy of salvation in the Old Testament. Covenant and redemption have in mind the Promised Land and a return to Eden. This return presupposes the ejection from Eden and that the disaster is to be redressed. What we as Christians might discuss under the doctrinal heading of Original Sin is not much of a concern, still less the more philosophical mystery of the origins of evil. The presuppositions that underpin the demands for obedience and faithfulness are most frequently stated in terms of election, covenant and redemption. The doctrine of creation is also used as a powerful reminder of God's sovereign rights and of human responsibility before him.

With the Fall come both the judgment and the word of grace in Genesis 3:15. The conflict between the seed of the serpent and the seed of the woman is clearly promissory of a redress of the disaster of the Fall. The great conflict

---

5. Douglas Stuart, *Hosea–Jonah*, WBC 31 (Waco: Word, 1987), pp. 98–99, takes *'ādām* as a reference to 'dirt': 'they have walked on my covenant like dirt'. There is, of course, the linguistic link between the name Adam and the words for 'red' and 'earth'.

becomes a central theme with varying expressions throughout the Old
Testament. The suffering Servant of the Lord is one among many.

The flood

There is very little reflection on Noah and the deluge in the Old Testament.
The post-flood accounts in Genesis 9 – 11 demonstrate that the flood did
not rectify the problem of human rebellion against God. This rather stylized
narrative shows that, though the godless line of Cain is annihilated in the
flood, the line of Ham takes over as representing the godless mass of humanity. After the Genesis occurrences the name of Noah appears early in the 1
Chronicles genealogy and four times in the Latter Prophets. In Isaiah 54:9
God's faithfulness to his covenant with Israel is compared with the covenant
with Noah. In Ezekiel the terrible judgment to come cannot be averted even
by the existence of some righteous men. Thus if Noah, Daniel and Job were
there, their righteousness would save only themselves.

The account of Noah and the flood makes abundantly clear the displeas-
ure of God at the rebellion of humanity, and the inevitability of judgment.
Also highlighted in these narratives is the operation of grace among the few
I have already referred to as constituting a 'godly' line of people. This 'godli-
ness' is not their own virtue but the choice of God. That Noah 'finds grace'
in the eyes of the Lord requires us to begin to search out the meaning and
significance of grace.[6] Thus while grace sometimes is given to those whose
demeanour is described positively (Noah, Abraham), they are nevertheless
flawed human beings. That Noah is a righteous man who walks with God is
not given as the cause of God's favour towards him. Others, such as Jacob
and Samson, do not commend themselves, certainly not to begin with. Still
others, Saul, David and Solomon, are chosen by God, are the objects of his
grace, and yet show enormous defects of character. Grace is clearly a gift of
God. We note also that the Old Testament does not reflect on the covenant
with Noah as a new beginning.

Abraham and the patriarchs

Abraham, by becoming the father of the race chosen by God for his purposes, stands above all others as a towering figure. The subsequent narratives
and reflections on God's choice of Israel frequently refer to the patriarchs,
if not to Abraham alone, then to Abraham, Isaac and Jacob. If we can speak

---

6. The first occurrence of ḥēn (grace, favour) is in Gen. 6:8: 'But Noah found favour
   in the eyes of the LORD.'

of a covenant with creation or with Adam, this is mainly by inference. The covenant with Noah is couched in positive terms before the flood when God announces his intention to save Noah and his family. It is then given in negative terms; that is, God promises never again to destroy the earth by flood.[7]

The covenant to Abraham is remarkable for its specificity. A direct genealogical line is drawn between Noah and his son Shem, and Terah the father of Abraham. Thus there is direct line of continuity from the theology of the covenant with Noah and the patriarchal covenant. But it is with the latter that the larger story of salvation history begins. It is reasonable to suggest that Genesis 3 – 11 demonstrates the necessity for the kind of saving activity that is given its initial expression with God's covenant with Abraham. The salvation experience of Noah appears to provide a fresh beginning, and it is an important foretaste of what is to come. But apart from its direct line to Abraham it peters out since things are really no better after the flood than before it and there is no revealed programme for further redemption until Abraham. The fact of salvation is illustrated with Noah but not its pattern. It is surely with Abraham that the new beginning is presented. Later it came to be seen thus in the credo in Deuteronomy 26:5–9:

> A wandering Aramean was my father. And he went down into Egypt and sojourned there, few in number, and there he became a nation, great, mighty, and populous. And the Egyptians treated us harshly and humiliated us and laid on us hard labour. Then we cried to the LORD, the God of our fathers, and the LORD heard our voice and saw our affliction, our toil, and our oppression. And the LORD brought us out of Egypt with a mighty hand and an outstretched arm, with great deeds of terror, with signs and wonders. And he brought us into this place and gave us this land, a land flowing with milk and honey.

The Abrahamic covenant is given its main expressions in Genesis 12:1–3; 15:1–6, 17–21; and 17:1–8. While it is not referred to as a covenant in the first passage these promises come to be recognized as explicitly covenantal. The gist of these statements is that God assures Abraham, when he and his wife are old and childless, that they will be progenitors of a great nation that will possess the Promised Land and know the blessing of God. Through these descendants of Abraham blessing will come to all the nations of the world. The patriarchal narratives (Gen. 12 – 50) take us through the events that rather frustrate the

---

7. The first reference to *běrît* (covenant) is in Gen. 6:17–18. The sign of the rainbow and the promise not to destroy again by flood are in Gen. 9:8–17.

outworking of these promises in the lives of Isaac and Jacob (Israel), and the eventual migration of the sons of Jacob to Egypt where their descendants become slaves. Thus the marvellous promises of God to the patriarchs appear to have come to nothing with the captivity in Egypt. Yet, as Elmer Martens points out, the rationale for the exodus redemption is given in Exodus 5:22 – 6:8 as the covenant promises to Abraham, Isaac and Jacob.[8] He goes further to nominate this passage as a grid for the whole message of the Old Testament. The promise to Abraham is recalled at certain significant points in Israel's history. Thus Moses' intercession for the people after the golden calf incident pleads not only the exodus from Egypt but the promises to Abraham (Exod. 32:11–14). Then the command to leave Sinai is given so that the people might possess the land as promised to Abraham (Exod. 33:1). In Numbers 32:11–12 God indicates that only Caleb and Joshua of the adults of the present rebellious generation will see the land he swore to give to Abraham, Isaac and Jacob.

A significant salvation-historical recital occurs in Joshua 24:1–13. The occasion is a covenant-renewal ceremony at Shechem after the settlement of the tribes in the newly possessed land of Canaan. The ceremony is predicated on the dealings of Israel's God with Abraham, which, as in the Deuteronomy 26 credo, is presented as the new beginning:

> Thus says the LORD, the God of Israel, 'Long ago, your fathers lived beyond the Euphrates, Terah, the father of Abraham and of Nahor; and they served other gods. Then I took your father Abraham from beyond the River and led him through all the land of Canaan, and made his offspring many.' (Josh. 24:2–3)

The account continues with a summary of the stay in Egypt, the plagues and the release from Egypt, the wilderness sojourn and, finally, the entry and possession of the land. Joshua then calls on the people to choose whom they will serve; either the gods their fathers served beyond the River (Euphrates) or Yahweh. It is interesting that Moses is mentioned only as the one sent as the agent of the plagues in Egypt (Josh. 24:5), and there is no reference to Sinai or the Law of Moses. The Book of the Law of God is referred to as that which Joshua wrote after making a covenant with the people and putting in place statutes and rules (Josh. 24:25–26). For Joshua, God relates a salvation history that begins with the call of Abraham out of paganism and ends with his current situation in the land.

---

8. See chapter 5 above and Elmer A. Martens, *God's Design: A Focus on Old Testament Theology* (Grand Rapids: Baker; Leicester: Apollos, 1994), ch. 1.

When Elijah meets the priests of Baal on Mount Carmel (1 Kgs 18) his response to the frantic ravings of the pagans is to repair the altar of the Lord and to re-establish the Sinai requirements for the burnt offering for sin. In that sense he is calling the Israelites back to obedience to the Law as revealed to Moses. His prayer, however, that evokes the response of God's fire from heaven to consume the offering, is a prayer to the God of Abraham. This, I believe, is significant in that it shows that the Mosaic instruction (*tôrâ*) is subsumed under the call of Abraham. Later, during the reign of Jehoahaz and after the death of Elisha, the king of Syria oppresses the people of Israel. The basis of God's gracious action is his promise to Abraham:

> But the LORD was gracious to them and had compassion on them, and he turned toward them, because of his covenant with Abraham, Isaac, and Jacob, and would not destroy them, nor has he cast them from his presence until now. (2 Kgs 13:23)

When David finally achieved his kingship he brought the Ark of the Covenant to Jerusalem. 1 Chronicles 16 contains the song David directed should be sung as a thanksgiving by Asaph and his brothers. The words of this song are also found in Psalms 105:1–15; 96:1–13. It calls on the people to give thanks to God for his deeds, to remember his works, miracles and judgments, and then:

> Remember his covenant forever,
>   the word that he commanded, for a thousand generations,
> the covenant that he made with Abraham,
>   his sworn promise to Isaac,
> which he confirmed as a statute to Jacob,
>   as an everlasting covenant to Israel,
> saying, 'To you I will give the land of Canaan,
>   as your portion for an inheritance.'
> (1 Chr. 16:15–18; see also Ps. 105:8–11)

The part also found in Psalm 96 focuses a good deal on the Lord as Creator. This is to remind the people of the futility of idolatry (Ps. 96:2–6) and to assure them of their security as the people of Yahweh. There is little doubt, then, that Abraham is *the* figure in salvation history's new beginning for the people of God.[9]

---

9. There are too many references to God's covenant with Abraham to deal with here. I think it is significant that in the narratives that deal with the period after

Ronald Clements's study using the method of tradition history concludes that David was understood in close relationship with the traditions
of Abraham. This included not only the geographical association of both
Abraham and David with Mamre-Hebron, but the portrayal of David as the
one who, more than any before him, took control of the land of promise.[10]

Moses and the exodus

A new king arose over Egypt, who did not know Joseph (Exod. 1:8). The
constant string of frustrations of the covenant promises to Abraham that so
characterize the lives of the patriarchs now reaches a climax. Being captives
of a heathen king in a strange land seems a long way from possessing the land
of promise and being a great nation that experiences God's blessing. The
account of Moses, his birth, preparation and commissioning to lead God's
people out of captivity, signals the promise of a new start. The plagues, the
Passover sacrifice and the flight from Egypt across the Red Sea will come
to provide the paradigm of redemption that will last into the message of the
New Testament. Moses is not only the one whom God uses to precipitate
the exodus; he is above all the definitive prophet of God. His role as lawgiver
shows him to be God's mouthpiece for the purpose of instructing Israel as to
its status before God. It is easy to see why Vos and Clowney regard Moses as
beginning a new epoch in redemptive history.

The law given at Sinai, then, does stand as a critical event in the salvation history of the Old Testament. The points of distinction between the
patriarchal period and that of Israel under the instruction of Moses must be
acknowledged. For our purposes we must also enquire about the continuity
between these two epochs. Do the Old Testament texts that reflect on these

---

Footnote 9 (*cont.*)

the patriarchal history in Genesis there is frequent reference to the Abrahamic
covenant as the basis for God's activity in Israel. For example, Exod. 2:24; 3:6,
15–16; 4:5; 6:3, 8; 33:1; Lev. 26:42; Num. 32:11; Deut. 1:8; 6:10; 9:5, 27; 29:13;
30:20; 34:4; Josh. 24:2–3; Neh. 9:7. There are also references in Psalms, Isaiah and
Jeremiah.

10. Ronald Clements, *Abraham and David: Genesis 15 and its Meaning for Israelite Tradition*,
SBT, Second Series 5 (London: SCM, 1967), p. 51. Clements's tradition-historical
approach leads him to conclude that Gen. 15 is a Yahwistic post-David tradition
and is partly shaped by the conviction that the Abrahamic covenant foretold the
rise of the kingdom over which David ruled (p. 80). While not agreeing with this
latter assessment I agree with his showing of the link between David and Abraham.

periods and their significance emphasize one over the other? Vos, Murray and Clowney would all seem to favour the distinctions in their designation of Moses to Christ as a distinct epoch. If we run with this as a useful line of approach for the purposes of understanding the structure or template of revelation, there is still the question of the possible need to make other distinctions *within* this epoch.

This point need not be laboured, but it certainly demands recognition. The promises to Abraham are constantly stated as the explicit basis for all that happens in the exodus and the giving of the Law at Sinai. The narrative in the book of Exodus indicates that all the events surrounding the liberation of the Israelites from Egypt and what follows happen because 'God remembered his covenant with Abraham, with Isaac, and with Jacob' (Exod. 2:24). In the events that follow, the link with Abraham is specifically stated a number of times (e.g. Exod. 3:6, 15–16; 4:5; 6:3–8). Moses' intercession after the golden calf incident is an opportunity for him to plead with God to remember the covenant with Abraham (Exod. 32:13–14). The command to leave Sinai is based on God's willingness to fulfil the promises to Abraham (Exod. 33:1–3). It should also be remembered that the preamble to the Decalogue states the basis for this instruction is the redemption from Egypt, which, as we have already noted, was based on the Abrahamic promises (Exod. 2:24; 20:1–2).

Leviticus is likewise clearly linked with the Abrahamic covenant. This is explicitly stated towards the end of the book. Obedience will bring the blessings of the covenant (Lev. 26:3–13).

> And I will walk among you and will be your God, and you shall be my people. I am the LORD your God, who brought you out of the land of Egypt, that you should not be their slaves. (Lev. 26:12–13)

The covenant, as stated in Genesis 17:7, is that God should be 'God to you'. The covenant summary, as given in Exodus 6:7–8 and Leviticus 26:12, links the promises to Abraham with the exodus and everything that follows in the epoch of Israel under the law. Leviticus 26:1–13 not only has overtones of the promise to Abraham but also emphasizes fruitfulness of the Promised Land. This oft-repeated theme of the Promised Land, the land flowing with milk and honey, implies a return to the fruitfulness of Eden. The two are more explicitly linked in the prophets (e.g. Isa. 51:3; Ezek. 36:35; 47:1–12).

The historical prologue to the book of Deuteronomy (Deut. 1 – 3), which claims to be the words of Moses, deals only with the events after the exodus and the Sinai experience. The reiteration of the law, the 'second instruction (*tôrâ*)' would indicate that Moses' prophetic ministry that came to the fore at

Sinai does indeed begin an epoch. Nevertheless the continuity with God's covenant promises to Abraham is constantly being referred to. The idea that the theology of Deuteronomy stresses the Mosaic period as the start of an epoch certainly reinforces the theory of the Deuteronomic History as a theological interpretation of events from Moses to the monarchy. The idea of a Deuteronomic History presupposes that the traditional notion of a Pentateuch is inaccurate. Accordingly we should rather conceive of a Tetrateuch followed by the Deuteronomic History. This is not universally accepted; von Rad, for example, prefers to speak of a Hexateuch to include Joshua with the five books of Moses. These disagreements serve only to show that establishing epochs, whether theological or narrative-historical, is difficult. This difficulty surely arises, at least in part, because there are clear points of continuity as well as of discontinuity in the narrative texts.

We cannot consider the exodus in isolation. The redemption from captivity is not simply a 'get out of jail free' move. The Israelites are freed so that they can take possession of the Promised Land and become the people to whom the promises to Abraham become a reality. Thus the apparent hiatus of the forty years in the wilderness is not the final word. Deuteronomy anticipates the new beginning in the Promised Land. The crossing of the Jordan is achieved through a miracle similar to that of the Red Sea even if it is less spectacular. This crossing under the leadership of Joshua marks a new beginning that leads to conquest, occupation and possession of the land.[11] No matter how much the events that follow are confused and bedevilled by Israel's rebellion and lack of faith, the movement is towards the ultimate glories of the kingdom of David and Solomon as the fulfilment of the promises to Abraham.

These considerations suggest that, as important as the events surrounding the leadership of Moses are, these are all recognized as stemming from the faithfulness of God to the covenant with Abraham. None of the events from the death of Abraham onwards, and especially those that involve Moses, make any sense without the promises to Abraham. However much the Israelites in Canaan reflect on Moses and the Law, they can never see that event as the beginning of their experience of God or of themselves as the people of God. The Abrahamic covenant of grace is the necessary basis for Sinai if it is not to be corrupted by legalism. The emergence of a great nation during the captivity does not take away from the initial significance of its progenitors, the patriarchs.

---

11. This new beginning is possibly behind John the Baptist's choice of the Jordan as the place where Israel needs another new beginning, marked by the baptism of repentance, before they can enter into possession of the promises.

David

The so-called Deuteronomic History and the books of Chronicles place great emphasis on the person and achievements of David. In the former, the account of events following the death of Moses includes the entry into Canaan, the conquest of the inhabitants and the settling of the people in allocated tribal areas. There are many setbacks in the fortunes of the nation, and many blemishes on the character of its heroes. But, nevertheless, the progress towards the greatness of the kingdoms of David and Solomon is inexorable. There is a direct theological link from Abraham to David and Solomon. The narratives of the exodus, entry and possession of the land ride on the back of the covenant with Abraham through to the climax in the Davidic dynasty of rule.

The corpus we refer to, following the Hebrew canon, as the Former Prophets provides a coherent account of Israel's move from a desert nomadic existence to a highly developed and relatively stable monarchy with a complex national infrastructure. One of the features of the biblical narrative is its brutal realism. The great heroes of faith are consistently portrayed with warts-and-all detail. A characteristic of the salvation-historical narrative is that the human involvement in the outworking of God's plans is never without blemishes. This serves only to emphasize the reality of God's grace as he continues to achieve his purposes. Also the progress of salvation history is not without the occasional serious interruption due to the waywardness and rebelliousness of the people of God. These setbacks serve only to demonstrate why history needs to be salvation history. There are other challenges to the fulfilment of promises that are more a part of God's sovereign working. Thus the narrative of Genesis 12 – 50 presents a series of apparent frustrations to fulfilment, not all of which are due to human intervention. In retrospect we see at least two things implicit in this situation. First the patriarchs have to learn to live by faith in the promises of God even when old age and failure to possess the Promised Land challenge the integrity of the promises (so Gen. 15:1–6). Secondly, the captivity provides the stage for the great drama and paradigm of redemption in the exodus.

The ambiguity in the processes of fulfilment, so clear in the rebellion in the wilderness, continues into the period of the Former Prophets. The book of Joshua is fairly positive about the events it records. Yet it must also relate the rebellion that leads to the defeat at Ai. At the end of the book we find Joshua having to challenge the Israelites to choose Yahweh and serve him only. The book of Judges makes it clear that the conquest has not been completed and that the result is a continual cycle of rebellious idolatry, judgment and deliverance (Judg. 2:10–23). The judges God uses to deliver his people from the

various oppressing enemies are themselves often badly flawed in their character. In the end, the lack of leadership has serious consequences: 'In those
days there was no king in Israel. Everyone did what was right in his own eyes'
(Judg. 21:25).

The books of Samuel provide some of the most detailed and skilfully crafted
narrative in the Bible. But the picture drawn is not all rosy. Thus there is no clear
prophecy in the land until Samuel. The priesthood is corrupt. The Israelites, by
a gross act of superstitious folly, lose the Ark of the Covenant to the Philistines.
The request for a king is motivated by a desire to be 'like the nations'. The first
king, Saul, is a failure even though he starts well. The narrative takes a turn
when it reaches a denouement in the anointing of David. Yet even then the
tension rises between him and Saul and is not resolved until Saul's death. Only
when David is anointed as king over all Israel do we arrive at some sense that
this is what it has all been leading to since the calling of Abraham.

Yet David also is a flawed character. It is difficult to see why Saul comes in for
such opprobrium and is removed from his kingship while David, an adulterer
and murderer, remains the favoured king 'after God's own heart'. Some readers
may not be satisfied with my judgment that the sovereign purpose of God for
the messianic pattern of kingship rests with David despite his shortcomings.
His flaws only highlight the fact that his position is all of grace and that he certainly does not bring in the final glory of God's kingdom. Yet we may not lightly
dismiss David's achievements: a capital city strategically placed on the borders
between north and south; secure borders of the largest extent of territory ever
achieved by Israel; a permanent standing army; a permanent public administra-
tion and advisory council; the sanctification of the city as the city of God with
the Ark of the Covenant present. An impressive record indeed!

Central to the theology of the books of Samuel is the covenant made
with David (2 Sam. 7:4–16). David expresses the desire to finish the glory of
the city of God by building a permanent sanctuary for Yahweh. Nathan the
prophet is instructed to tell David that, far from his building God a house,
God will build him a house; that is, a dynasty.[12] David's son will build the
sanctuary, and the throne of his kingdom will be established for ever. God
declares of this son of David, 'I will be to him a father, and he shall be to me
a son' (v. 14). There is a clear reference here to the covenant with Abraham
and God's intention 'To be God to you' (Gen. 17:7). The covenant summary,

---

12. This famous play on the meaning of the word *bayît* (house) also applies to the
    English usage for the word 'house'. In both Hebrew and English the reference
    can be to a domicile or a dynasty.

as it was first expressed in Leviticus 26:12, 'I will walk among you and will be your God, and you shall be my people,' is now personalized in reference to the royal offspring. David's son is to be the son of God. This sonship is not here a reference to deity. Israel is God's son (Exod. 4:22; Hos. 11:1), and the son of David is the representative Israelite upon whom the favour of God rests.

The tragic irony of the narrative is that the moral fall of David and the challenges to his power take place soon after the pronouncement of the covenant promises. The narrative moves from David's adultery with Bathsheba to the revolt of Absalom and his death. The rebellion of Sheba also indicates that David's kingdom is not as stable as it first appeared. Nevertheless he manages to pass on a thriving kingdom to his successor. Notwithstanding all these blemishes, the covenant with David is remembered as a key feature of the gracious way God deals with Israel in years that follow. David does not build the temple, for that is left for his son Solomon to achieve. But the promises to David appear to be regarded as of greater significance than all the achievements of Solomon.

It is significant, then, that the theology of God's covenant faithfulness and redemptive grace is predicated on David rather than Solomon. Again it is the promise in 2 Samuel 7:14 that is regarded as a covenant that explains God's saving acts. That David's name is used to identify 73 of the 150 psalms is noteworthy. Psalm 72:20 ends Book Two of the Psalms with, 'The prayers of David, the son of Jesse, are ended.' Psalm 78:68–72 describes how the waywardness of Israel is dealt with by the choice of David to be the shepherd of God's people. Psalm 89 is a celebration of the Davidic covenant:

> You have said, 'I have made a covenant with my chosen one;
>   I have sworn to David my servant:
> "I will establish your offspring forever,
>   and build your throne for all generations."'
> (Ps. 89:3–4)

The psalm goes on to extol the throne of God:

> Righteousness and justice are the foundation of your throne;
>   steadfast love and faithfulness go before you.
> (Ps. 89:14)

It then returns to the anointing of David. The psalm thus connects the throne of God with the throne of David. God reigns through his chosen and anointed one:

I have found David, my servant;
  with my holy oil I have anointed him,
so that my hand shall be established with him;
  my arm also shall strengthen him.
(Ps. 89:20–21)

He shall cry to me, 'You are my Father,
  my God, and the Rock of my salvation.'
And I will make him the firstborn,
  the highest of the kings of the earth.
My steadfast love I will keep for him forever,
  and my covenant will stand firm for him.
I will establish his offspring forever
  and his throne as the days of the heavens.
(Ps. 89:26–29)

Psalm 132 also reflects on the faithfulness of God to the covenant that he swore to David. Such expressions as these are surely foundational for the eschatology that will develop around the election of David and his dynasty.

Jerusalem and Zion
Zion is the name given to Jerusalem when the old Jebusite city comes to be the focal point of the purposes of God for Israel's salvation. Its possible link with Abraham lies in the identification of the mount on which it stands as Moriah (2 Chr. 3:1). Chronicles, however, does not mention it as the Moriah where Abraham was to offer up Isaac (Gen. 22:2). There are also grounds for identifying the city with the Salem where Abraham paid tithes to Melchizedek (Gen. 14:17–20). Zion, as the city of David and the city of God, comes into prominence from the time David captures the city and brings the Ark of the Covenant into it (2 Sam. 5:6–10; 6:1–15). Zion seems to replace Sinai in the theological reflections of Israel, but this is not to take away from the significance of the Torah throughout the life of Israel.

Solomon and the temple
The books of Kings begin with part of the so-called Succession Narrative, which is a brutal portrayal of how Solomon comes to succeed David as king.[13]

---

13. The Succession Narrative is understood to include 2 Sam. 9 – 20 and 1 Kgs 1 – 2. See R. N. Whybray, *The Succession Narrative*, SBT, Second Series 9 (London: SCM, 1968).

Though he is not David's oldest son, Solomon is nevertheless declared by the dying David to be his successor. Zadok the priest and Nathan the prophet anoint Solomon as king (1 Kgs 1:34–40). The pericope of Solomon's wisdom (1 Kgs 3 – 10) presents the king in a glowing light, yet not without the hint of ambiguity: 'Solomon loved the LORD, walking in the statutes of David his father, only he sacrificed and made offerings at the high places' (1 Kgs 3:3). 1 Kings 3 and 1 Kings 10 provide a wisdom 'bookend' or inclusio around the narrative of the glory of Solomon's kingdom and court and, above all, the building of the temple. It is reasonable to suggest that we are intended to understand all that lies between the granting of wisdom (ch. 3) and the manifestation of wisdom to the Gentile queen (ch. 10) as expressions of Solomon's wisdom. It is interesting that the builders of the tabernacle were endowed with wisdom (Exod. 28:3; 31:6; 36:1–2, where ḥokmâ [wisdom] is translated in ESV and other English versions as 'skill' or 'ability').[14] Hiram of Tyre, the man Solomon brings to cast bronze for the temple, is said to be filled with wisdom, understanding and skill (1 Kgs 7:13–14). Wisdom does appear to be especially connected to the ability to construct God's sanctuary. This being the case, it reflects the wisdom of God in creating his original sanctuary in Eden.

If there is ambiguity in Solomon as one who uses political intrigue to achieve the throne, and who worships Yahweh at suspicious-sounding high places, there is outright contradiction in his subsequent behaviour. We can hardly imagine a more praiseworthy situation than that of the visit to Solomon of the Queen of Sheba (1 Kgs 10). But in 1 Kings 11 Solomon is suddenly portrayed as a covenant-breaker, a philanderer, a political opportunist and an idolater. Whatever happened to his wisdom and the fear of the Lord? Was it that he began to think his wise thoughts outside the box of the fear of Yahweh? Solomon's reversal becomes the trigger for all the subsequent national acts of renewed idolatry and rebellion against God. Thus the supremely tragic irony of Solomon is that he who glorified Zion by building the temple became the architect of its ultimate destruction. This must surely be one important reason for Solomon's being all but ignored in the New Testament.

The temple is a central theme in biblical theology. As God's sanctuary it is the place above all where he meets his people. Those biblical theologians who see Eden as the original sanctuary are, in my opinion, absolutely

---

14. Commentators recognize that ḥokmâ is a word that seems to include skill beyond mental prowess and thus includes that of the craftsman. I believe it is significant that specifically the building of the tabernacle requires such wisdom. It supports the view that Solomon's building of the temple is an aspect of his wisdom.

correct.[15] The thematic progression, then, is Eden, Promised Land (denied in Egypt, then achieved), the land focused on the tabernacle and then on the temple in Jerusalem. Attaching to the temple is the demonstration of God's presence often described as his glory. The glory of the Lord appears to the Israelites after the exodus (Exod. 16:10–12). Moses encounters the glory on Sinai (Exod. 24:15–18). The glory of the Lord fills the tabernacle (Exod. 40:34–35). It appears to the people as God's fire consumes the burnt offering at the tent (Lev. 9:23–24). The promise that 'all the earth shall be filled with the glory of the LORD' (Num. 14:21), which is delivered alongside a word of judgment, hints at the time when the whole world will again become the sanctuary of God. The tragedy of Ichabod ('there is no glory' or 'the glory has departed', 1 Sam. 4:21–22) is that his name signified the capture of the centrepiece of the sanctuary, the Ark of the Covenant. When Solomon brings the Ark of the Covenant into the newly built temple the glory of the Lord fills the house (1 Kgs 8:10–11). Concerning the destruction of the temple in 586 BC Ezekiel's visions show the glory rising up from its place, settling on the threshold of the temple, and then moving from the east gate to the mountain east of the city (Ezek. 1:28; 3:12, 23; 9:3; 10:4, 18–19; 11:23). We must presume that the glory goes to be with the faithful remnant in Babylon but, if not, it certainly does not remain in the corrupted temple in Jerusalem.

Wisdom

As noted above, the narratives of 1 Kings provide the historical basis for the traditions concerning Solomon as the one who gave impetus to the wisdom movement in Israel. This includes his name being used in the title of Proverbs. However, it is also to be noted that David must be included in this development. David's counsellors show the way that wisdom becomes part of the fabric of the kingdom. Nor was this a new dimension with David, for the Lord had directed Moses to appoint seventy elders who would be endowed with the Spirit of Moses (Num. 11:16–17). In fact wisdom is a common notion in all cultures as peoples learn from experience and, within the framework of their world views, express ways of dealing with life. As Derek Kidner succinctly remarks:

> Incalculable as was Solomon's part in this cultural explosion, he was not starting from an intellectual void. Israel, like any other people, had its store of native wit: its sage

---

15. See, for example, T. Desmond Alexander, *From Eden to the New Jerusalem: Exploring God's Plan for Life on Earth* (Nottingham: IVP, 2008).

old characters and clever young men; its sharp sayings and its more elaborate and oblique ones.[16]

Joshua was 'full of the spirit of wisdom, for Moses had laid his hands on him' (Deut. 34:9). We cannot overlook the role of the Law of Sinai as central to the wisdom that guided the leaders of Israel in the period of the development of the kingdom. It would, however, be a mistake to treat books like Proverbs as a collection of reflections on the Law or as the fine print to the Sinai covenant. David's appointing of counsellors appears to coincide with the lessening of direct divine guidance. We may surmise that the Law and prophetic revelation become the major platforms of guidance. There can be little doubt that Israel's wisdom as the gathering of knowledge and the formation of precepts for right acting is as old as civilization itself. Wisdom traditions in Egypt and Mesopotamia go back at least a thousand years before Moses. The fear of Yahweh is linked to wisdom in Deuteronomy 4:6 in that the nations would perceive Israel's wisdom as a law-observing people. Two wise women impinge on David's life (2 Sam. 14:1–24; 20:16–22). Later he established the role of counsellor in a way that moves towards the institutionalizing of wisdom.

Given the fact that wisdom is partly the accumulation of life's experiences within any culture and according to a particular world view, why do we find the emphasis on wisdom particularly in connection with Solomon? I believe it is due to the relation that was perceived between empirical wisdom gained through experience and the revelation of God. Our survey of the structure of revelation has shown that the pattern of the kingdom and of the redemptive path into it reaches its climax with David and Solomon. From here on there can only be the reaching of perfection that prophetic eschatology will begin to trace, and there will be decline as the historical reality. It is no surprise, then, that the flowering of Israelite wisdom is portrayed as coinciding with this completed pattern of redemption and the kingdom. As Proverbs 1:7 and 9:10 indicate, the fear of Yahweh is the beginning of knowledge and wisdom. Such fear is a reverential submission to the revealed truth of God, which focuses on the covenant and redemption. Godly wisdom in Israel is based on life's experiences, which ideally are steered by the redemptive revelation of God. Wisdom seeks to understand the world and our place in it in the light of the world view revealed by God. The flowering of wisdom under Solomon

---

16. Derek Kidner, *Wisdom to Live by: An Introduction to the Old Testament's Wisdom Books of Proverbs, Job and Ecclesiastes* (Leicester: IVP, 1985), p. 15.

constitutes further evidence that he was seen as climaxing the whole epoch of Israel's history from Abraham onwards. When the pattern of salvation is complete, wisdom flourishes.

The down side of all this is that wisdom can go astray. In the context of Israel's covenant faith, wisdom goes astray when it ceases to reflect the fear of Yahweh and becomes mere worldly sagacity. The prophets take a number of swipes at the wise men who appear to have developed into a recognizable group of functionaries within Israelite society. Their wisdom comes to reflect the corruption of Solomon's wisdom and is marked out as a wisdom that will perish (Isa. 29:14–16; Jer. 8:8–9).

The exile and return

This is far too big a subject to analyse in detail here. However, I have noted above that the theology of exile begins in Genesis 3. Israel's history is one of exile seasoned with the promise of a new Eden in the land of their inheritance. Many events testify to the tenacity of exile: Abraham's existence as an alien in the Promised Land; the need for Jacob's sons to find food in Egypt and the subsequent captivity; the wilderness wanderings; the constant threat to the integrity of Israel's possession of Canaan; the two-stage exile to Assyria and Babylon; and the failure of the return and reconstruction to meet expectations of renewal. N. T. Wright comments that while Israel clung to the promise that God's glory would again return, 'Nowhere in second temple literature is it asserted that this has happened: therefore it still remains in the future. The exile is not yet really over.'[17] The strength of this assertion is seen in the way the exile theme is taken up in the New Testament in terms of the new exodus and redemption in Christ. The tension of exile is resolved in Christ's saving work.

The books of Kings describe the constant decline of Israel's fortunes particularly beginning with the reign of Rehoboam, Solomon's son. By contrast with the books of Chronicles, which confine themselves to the history of David's dynasty, the books of Kings provide an account of the division of the nation into two rival kingdoms, and the attempts to rival Zion and its temple by false cultic practices in the north. The ministries of Elijah and Elisha, and then those of Amos and Hosea, cannot prevent the spiritual decline leading to the destruction of the northern kingdom by the Assyrians in 722 BC. In the south the prophetic challenges of Elijah and Elisha barely prevent total national apostasy. Although the main place of their ministry was in the

---

17. N. T. Wright, *The New Testament and the People of God* (London: SPCK, 1992), p. 269.

north, they were also influential in the south (2 Chr. 21:12).[18] The reforms
of Hezekiah and Josiah are too little and too late to stop the slippery slide to
destruction that is completed by the Babylonians in 586 BC.

There are many places in the Old Testament that reflect on the events and
the significance of the exile. Both exilic prophets, Jeremiah and Ezekiel, are full
of condemnation for the virtual apostasy of Israel that has led to this catastrophe. Jeremiah's counsel, in contrast to Isaiah's at the time of the Assyrian invasion, was that the people of Jerusalem should capitulate to the Babylonians.
Ezekiel's visions of unspeakable pagan rituals taking place in God's temple and
the withdrawal of the glory of God from Jerusalem leave no possible excuse
for the people of Judah. It is clear that all the sacraments of redemption in salvation history have not prevented this spiritual suicide of the nation.

And yet there is evidence of the faithful remnant: believers that go on
trusting the promises of God as they also express grief and repentance for the
covenant-breaking of the people of God. Jeremiah himself epitomizes this
grief in his laments (Jer. 4:19–24; 8:18 – 9:1). He also gives a chilling account
of the destruction of the city and the exile of the people (Jer. 52). The book
of Lamentations, which came to be attributed to Jeremiah, consists of five
poems reflecting on the horrors of the exile. Yet the writer has hope, for God
is faithful:

> The steadfast love of the LORD never ceases;
> his mercies never come to an end;
> they are new every morning;
> great is your faithfulness.
> 'The LORD is my portion,' says my soul,
> 'Therefore I will hope in him.'
> (Lam. 3:22–24)

The grief of the exile is reflected in certain psalms, not least in Psalm 137:

> By the waters of Babylon, there we sat down and wept,
> When we remembered Zion. . . .
> How shall we sing the LORD's song in a foreign land?
> (Ps. 137:1, 4)

---

18. The importance of Elijah is seen in the prophetic reference to his return before
    the Day of the Lord (Mal. 4:5–6), and his place with Moses on the mount of
    transfiguration.

Other psalms may well refer to the Babylonian exile but, if not, they certainly refer to the challenge to Israel's possession of the promises and especially of the land. Psalm 44 expresses hope in the midst of disaster. Psalm 74 begs God not to cast them off for ever but to remember Mount Zion, where he dwelt. So also Psalms 77, 79, 80, 82, 83, 85, 90 and 106 all express the problem as one in which God has rightly allowed his people to be oppressed and the hope that he will redeem his people.

The ministries and writings of the pre-exilic Latter Prophets provide a detailed account of the situation leading up to the exile. The exilic and post-exilic prophets shine a light on the period from the first exile (597 BC) to the end of the Old Testament period. All the Latter Prophets contribute three aspects, either directly, or by implication (as in Jonah and Obadiah): indictment for covenant-breaking; pronouncement of God's judgment; and assurance of God's covenant-faithfulness and the salvation of a faithful remnant.

Conclusions

The inspired writers of Israel reflected on their covenant history and noted the disparity between the covenant promises with their stipulations and the actual fortunes of the people. Realistically they could conclude only that they were a faithless and ungrateful people. Nevertheless faith and hope were constantly revived and directed back to reflect on the marvellous deeds of Yahweh. The prophetic reflections provide us with a sense of structure that goes all the way back to the creation but finds a point of new beginning with Abraham.

From the foregoing summary of the major persons, places and events in the biblical history it becomes evident, I believe, that it is more natural to the biblical accounts to understand the watershed in revelation to be David and Solomon, not Moses. Vos's and Clowney's epochs, as valid as they are, properly belong within a more basic and useful framework of narrative from creation and Fall, through a new beginning with Abraham, to the climax in David and his son's building of the temple. An epoch from Moses to Christ tends to overshadow this redemptive zenith.

7. LETTING THE OLD TESTAMENT SPEAK II: PROPHETIC ESCHATOLOGY

The pattern of prophetic eschatology

Prophetic eschatology focuses largely on the return from exile and the restoration of the nation in the Promised Land. The manner in which this is done provides us with an important clue to the structure of revelation in the Old Testament.[1] The key point is that the prophetic perspectives of the future restoration and ultimate salvation are based on, and follow the pattern of, the salvation history of the past. That no prophet gives a systematic review of salvation history does not, I believe, undermine the cumulative importance of this constant recapitulation of past events from creation to David and the temple. Each prophet responds in his own way to the contemporary events and situation so as to reflect the nation's condition as a covenant breaker. From a canonical point of view the overall message is the renewal of all things against the background of judgment and cleansing.

As I indicated in chapter 1, we can identify the major moments of creation

---

1. I have dealt with this aspect in detail in my *Gospel and Kingdom: A Christian Interpretation of the Old Testament* (Exeter: Paternoster, 1981), republished in Graeme Goldsworthy, *The Goldsworthy Trilogy* (Milton Keynes: Paternoster, 2000), ch. 8, and in my *According to Plan* (Leicester: IVP, 1991), ch. 20. See also chapter 1 above.

and salvation history as they occur in the biblical narrative. The foregoing examination (chapter 6) of the way Israel reflects on its past identifies key persons and the events surrounding them. When we come to the eschatology of the Latter Prophets we find that it is consistently given against the background of the national decline from the glories of David and Solomon to the point of the final destruction of Jerusalem and the exile of the people. Whatever the failures of Israel prior to Solomon's apostasy, this event is clearly the watershed for decline that even the ministries of Elijah and Elisha, or the reforms of Hezekiah and Josiah, could not avert. When we examine the eschatology of restoration, as distinct from the themes of judgment, it is noteworthy that the past moments relating to the blessings of God keep recurring as the pattern for the future. Whatever way we try to put together and amalgamate the collective witness of the prophets, the picture we get is one of a recapitulation of the key redemptive aspects of the salvation history of the past. The difference lies in the permanence and glory of the renewal to come. It is the sensitivity to this, so central to Robinson's schema, that seems to be missing from the works of Vos and Clowney but brought out to some extent by Dennis Johnson.[2]

If the prophetic perspective is that the decline of the nation is due to covenant-breaking and unfaithfulness, even to the point of idolatry and apostasy, does not the glorious kingdom of David and Solomon stand as the high point in revelation in Israel's history? Nor is it merely the magnificence of this kingdom that marks it out, for it clearly represents the reaching of a goal of fulfilment of the promises to Abraham. While there is much rebellion and many expressions of God's judgment prior to this, 1 Kings 11 marks the watershed and the beginning with Solomon of the final decline towards destruction and exile. But it is also clear that the subsequent return from exile under Cyrus the Persian, the rebuilding of Jerusalem and the restoration of the temple and its services never come anywhere near to the glory of the Solomonic kingdom. While there is a sense in which these post-exilic events are a partial fulfilment of much prophetic hope, they nevertheless fail even to approach the perfection and glory of that hope. The function of the three post-exilic prophets is to highlight the fact that the period after the return is still problematic, and to encourage hope for the future coming of the kingdom.

If we observe the way the Latter Prophets use the various great moments of past salvation history as the pattern of the future coming of God's kingdom,

---

2. Dennis E. Johnson, *Him We Proclaim: Preaching Christ from All the Scriptures* (Phillipsburg: Presbyterian & Reformed), pp. 223–226.

there can be little argument about the proposition that they see a future stage that recapitulates their history. Biblical history begins with creation and, after the Fall, has a new beginning with the call of Abraham and the covenant of grace that God makes with him. This covenant underpins the exodus from captivity in Egypt and the binding of the redeemed people to the covenant instruction given by Moses at Sinai. This, in turn, underpins the responsibility of the people of Israel towards their God as he brings them to the Promised Land, gives them possession of it, raises up a king and establishes Zion and its temple as the focal point representing God's presence among his people.

When we consider the nature of prophetic eschatology, *epoch* may be a misleading term to apply. Perhaps it is better to speak of stages in the revelation of God's kingdom. At least we must recognize that while the prophets are developing their distinctive eschatology, they are also commenting on the historical decline of the kingdom of David and Solomon. Thus the revelation of a future epoch or stage overlaps the ongoing history of Israel even as it is collapsing in ruins. It is also a truism that the prophetic eschatology has at least two perspectives: the one is the more immediate view that applies to the destruction and exile followed by the release from that exile and return to the land. The other perspective is of the more distant view of the Day of the Lord when God finally acts in a way that has ultimate significance for the coming of the kingdom of God. Although there are many prophetic oracles in which it is not clear that any such distinction is being made by the prophet, in hindsight we are able to see that the partial fulfilment of prophecy brought about by the return from exile can be regarded as foreshadowing the ultimate fulfilment. The post-exilic prophets perform the important task of showing that this distinction of the partial and the perfect fulfilments is real. For them, whatever the benefits of the return, the kingdom is yet to come.

The canonical shape

The canon of the Old Testament Scriptures made the significant divisions of *tôrâ* (Law or Instruction), *nĕbî'îm* (Former and Latter Prophets) and *kĕtûbîm* (Writings). Jesus endorsed this arrangement simply by referring to it when indicating the connection between the threefold canon and himself (Luke 24:27, 44). Although Moses was the definitive prophet, the promise of another prophet like him, as recorded in Deuteronomy 18:15, does not find fulfilment in Israel, a matter indicated by the epilogue to the Pentateuch in Deuteronomy 33 – 34. John Sailhamer suggests that Deuteronomy 34:10–12 is a later addition that surveys the entire range of Old Testament prophets, none of which fulfils the promise.[3] The canonical divisions further indicate that the Prophets, both Former and Latter, constitute an important and distinct part of the whole. If Sailhamer is correct, as I believe he is, the 'big picture' of the Pentateuch must be viewed from the perspective of the canonical corpus that reflects on the period from Moses to Malachi. To make Moses to Christ an epochal focus of interest highlights the continuity but tends to downplay the discontinuity. It also seems to overlook the purpose of the final author of the Pentateuch in writing almost seventy chapters before he ever gets to the Law.[4] It would seem that we must accommodate the idea that the broader perspective of the Latter Prophets shows that the main messianic promise of the Pentateuch, that of a prophet like Moses who is to come, is never realized in the succeeding age of the prophets.

The main foci in prophetic eschatology

Creation

The eschatology of creation is not confined to the Latter Prophets. Various psalms use the creation motif as part of their view of the coming of the Lord. The link between creation and the covenant activity of God is clearly significant. In some texts the expression of God's *ḥesed* (covenant faithfulness) is so strong that the redemption from Egypt is seen as Israel's creation. In other psalms the creation is closely involved in the judgment of God, which itself is good news because it brings the redemption of Israel and, by implication, of the creation itself. So Psalm 96:1–3, 11–13 links the new song of all the earth with the rejoicing of the heavens and the earth over the coming judgment. Psalm 98:7–9 refers to the joy of creation in a similar way.

The theme of new creation emerges most clearly in prophetic eschatology. The creation and redemption of Israel are closely linked, especially so in Isaiah. The opening part of Isaiah 40, which speaks of the imminent redemption of Israel from captivity, is followed by praise of God the creator. As he has shown his power in creation, so he will show it in redemption. Then Isaiah 43:1–2 beautifully sums up this link:

---

3. John Sailhamer, *The Meaning of the Pentateuch: Revelation, Composition and Interpretation* (Downers Grove: IVP Academic, 2009), p. 24.

4. Ibid., p. 21.

But now thus says the LORD,
he who created you, O Jacob,
  he who formed you, O Israel:
'Fear not, for I have redeemed you;
  I have called you by name, you are mine.
When you pass through the waters, I will be with you;
  and through the rivers, they shall not overwhelm you;
when you walk through fire you shall not be burned,
  and the flame shall not consume you.'

These passages show that the original creation is a paradigm of the later new creation of Israel, which, in turn, is the expression of God's faithfulness to his covenant with Abraham.

In the same manner creation is eschatologically synonymous with redemption, which, in undoing the results of the Fall, means that creation itself is renewed. It could never be a mere bystander or backdrop to the biblical drama. The restoration of Israel must involve the restoration of the fruitfulness of Eden that the Promised Land flowing with milk and honey represented. As Amos portrays the restoration of the booth of David, the land will be renewed with it (Amos 9:11–15). For Isaiah, the restoration of the Davidic dynasty will be the day when the harmony of nature is restored (Isa. 11:6–9). When God's Spirit is poured out on his people, 'the wilderness becomes a fruitful field' (Isa. 32:15). Wholeness of creation and wholeness of body will accompany the Lord's coming to save (Isa. 35:1–7; 55:12–13). Creation is used as a metaphor for the exodus redemption in Isaiah 51:9–11.

The most comprehensive expression of Isaiah for the renewal of creation is in Isaiah 65:17–25. It stands in line with all the passages that speak of the renewal of nature as the final expression of the Promised Land's return to the perfection of Eden. This vision of a new creation is basic to the whole biblical doctrine of regeneration, and the perspective of Isaiah should be a reminder that regeneration is far wider than the personal new birth that so often preoccupies evangelical piety.[5]

For behold, I create new heavens and a new earth,
and the former things shall not be remembered
  or come into mind.

---

5. See my article 'Regeneration', in *NDBT*, pp. 720–723.

But be glad and rejoice forever
   in that which I create;
for behold, I create Jerusalem to be a joy,
   and her people to be a gladness.
(Isa. 65:17–18)

As Eden and the people of God were created as the pinnacle of God's work on the sixth day (Gen. 1:26–28), so here the pinnacle of the new creation is Jerusalem and her people. Isaiah's vision clearly lies behind John's vision of the new heavens and earth and the new Jerusalem coming down out of heaven from God (Rev. 21:1–2).

Fall

The latter prophets are preoccupied with three main messages: the sin and covenant-breaking of Israel; the consequent judgment they are bringing, and have brought, on themselves; and the faithfulness of God to the covenant, which will mean that his ultimate goal for his people and his kingdom will be realized. The Fall, then, is everywhere the presupposition of the indictments of Israel brought by the prophets.

One twist in the creation theme is the 'uncreation' that judgment will bring. This was first seen in Genesis 3 in the thorns and thistles that plague human efforts to wrest sustenance from the earth. But it hearkens back to the primeval chaos of Genesis 1:2a. The theme of wilderness as a place of judgment looms large in the book of Numbers. The plagues in Egypt are a kind of undoing of the created order with which God had blessed the Egyptians. So also the curses of the covenant in Deuteronomy 28:15–24 are aimed at the blessings of creation. This experience of the outcome of faithlessness and disobedience is heavily underscored in Israel's traditions. Thus when Jeremiah 4:23–27 projects the coming judgment as a return to primeval chaos when the earth was formless and void (*tōhû wābōhû*),[6] the undoing of creation becomes synonymous with God's judgment:

I looked on the earth, and behold it was without form and void;
   and to the heavens, and they had no light.
I looked on the mountains, and behold, they were quaking,
   and all the hills moved to and fro.

------

6. These two adjectives are paired here as they are in Gen. 1:2a, and it is clear that the intention is to recall that primordial chaos.

I looked, and behold, there was no man,
and all the birds of the air had fled.
I looked, and behold, the fruitful land was a desert,
and all its cities were laid in ruins
before the LORD, before his fierce anger.
(Jer. 4:23–26)

This passage reminds us that the prophets understand the coming Day of the Lord as one that brings both the blessings and the curses of the covenant. It is a day of purifying as Malachi 3:1–4 puts it. Again 'the arrogant and all evildoers will be stubble. . . . But for you who fear my name, the sun of righteousness shall rise with healing in its wings' (Mal. 4:1–2).

The flood
The flood does not feature in prophetic eschatology in any explicit way. Theologically, of course, it links with all references to God's judgment on sin. The covenant with Noah (Gen. 9:9–17) links with the theology of renewal of the creation, and Noah's line, through Shem, becomes the focus of God's covenant purposes that feature so prominently in the prophetic view of restoration and blessing. Isaiah recalls the covenant with Noah and likens it to God's covenant of peace that guarantees he will not desert his people for ever (Isa. 54:7–10).

Abraham and the patriarchs
We have seen that, if anything indicates the unity of the various covenant expressions, it is the promise to Abraham 'To be God to you' that is at the heart of this relationship. This promise, in turn, becomes the national covenant summary: 'I . . . will be your God, and you shall be my people' (Lev. 26:12; Gen. 17:7–8). This summary links the Mosaic covenant with the Abrahamic and is one way that the prophets speak of the fulfilment to come. Thus, while the prophets do not contain many references to Abraham by name, the covenant is everywhere the presupposition for all the prophetic pronouncements of either blessing or judgment. The covenant summary is repeated, fully or in part, in a number of places by the prophets to express the outcome of God's redeeming grace. In Jeremiah 24:4–7 the covenant summary is interwoven with the promise of the return from the Babylonian exile, and with the giving of a new heart to the people to know 'that I am the LORD'. This latter statement also becomes a covenant-based refrain to describe the outcome of God's action both to save and to judge.

Jeremiah's promise of the new covenant (Jer. 31:31–34) may seem to focus more on the Mosaic covenant because of its references to the exodus. But the connection between the Sinai covenant and the Abrahamic covenant is clearly made. The exodus redemption was predicated on the Abrahamic covenant (Exod. 2:23–25). Thus Jeremiah's new covenant renews the Sinai covenant in that God will 'write it on their hearts. And I will be their God, and they shall be my people' (Jer. 31:33). By renewing Sinai the promises to Abraham will be fulfilled. Other passages in which the covenant promise and the release from exile are linked include Jeremiah 32:38; Ezekiel 11:20; 34:24; 37:23, 27; and Zechariah 8:8. Jeremiah refers to Abraham by name only once but, significantly, links him with David and the covenant made with the king as the basis of assurance that God 'will restore their fortunes and will have mercy on them' (Jer. 33:25–26).

Isaiah has four references to Abraham by name. In Isaiah 29 the threat of Assyrian invasion leads to words of assurance to the people of Jerusalem of a coming renewal. Its basis is given in verse 22: the redemption of Abraham their father. That God will not cast away 'Israel, my servant' is predicated on their election in Abraham, the friend of God (Isa. 41:8–10). Again God's comfort of Zion stems from their origins in Abraham who, in turn, is linked to the blessings of Eden:

> Listen to me, you who pursue righteousness,
> you who seek the LORD:
> look to the rock from which you were hewn,
>   and to the quarry from which you were dug.
> Look to Abraham your father
>   and to Sarah who bore you;
> for he was but one when I called him,
>   that I might bless him and multiply him.
> For the LORD comforts Zion;
>   he comforts all her waste places
> and makes her wilderness like Eden,
>   her desert like the garden of the LORD.
> (Isa. 51:1–3)

Such passages indicate the fabric of redemptive history as one woven richly with interconnecting themes. Creation, covenant people, Zion, Promised Land and Eden all join in the harmony of God's plan and purpose for the future restoration.

Moses and the exodus

The references to Moses outside the Pentateuch are mostly references to his authorship of the Law books. The Latter Prophets carry few references to him. Isaiah 63:11–12 refers to the past mercies of the Lord in delivering his people. The prophet is recalling the steadfast love of the Lord, his *ḥesed* or covenant faithfulness, and recalls how Moses led the people in the exodus through the sea. But this is no mere reminiscence, for, as Alec Motyer points out, Isaiah 63:7 begins a section that moves towards its climax in the new heaven and the new earth.[7] The past mercies of God are the grounds of assurance of final salvation.

There is no doubt that the exodus event and the escape from Egypt form a paradigm for redemption in Israel. This is nowhere clearer than in the second half of Isaiah, which focuses on the release from exile and the fullness of salvation. William Dumbrell comments:

> Isaiah 40:3–5 is a divine herald's summons for the preparation of a divine way
> through the wilderness by which the process of comfort will begin. Elsewhere in
> Isaiah 40–55 (42:16; 43:16–19; 49:9c–11; 51:10), the return from exile is depicted
> as a new exodus.[8]

There is, however, little to indicate that the prophets regarded the period of Moses as a new dispensation of the grace of God. It still all goes back to Abraham.

David

The Latter Prophets contain a number of important references to David that indicate the theological significance they place on him. Thus in Isaiah 9 we are told of the light that will shine on the oppressed people, and it will come through the birth of the Davidic prince:

> For to us a child is born,
> to us a son is given;
>   and the government shall be upon his shoulder,
>   and his name shall be called

---

7. J. Alec Motyer, *The Prophecy of Isaiah: An Introduction and Commentary* (Downers Grove: IVP, 1993), p. 512.

8. William Dumbrell, *The Search for Order: Biblical Eschatology in Focus* (Grand Rapids: Baker, 1994), p. 112.

Wonderful Counselor, Mighty God, Everlasting Father, Prince of Peace.
Of the increase of his government and of peace
    there will be no end,
on the throne of David and over his kingdom,
    to establish it and to uphold it
    with justice and with righteousness
    from this time forth and forevermore.
    The zeal of the LORD of hosts will do this.
(Isa. 9:6–7)

Isaiah 16:5, 37:35 and 55:3 all link the saving work of God for Israel to the promises made to David. Jeremiah also reflects on the Davidic covenant as the basis for God's redemptive works:

> Behold, the days are coming, declares the LORD, when I will raise up for David a righteous Branch, and he shall reign as king and deal wisely, and shall execute justice and righteousness in the land. In his days Judah will be saved, and Israel will dwell securely. And this is the name by which he will be called: 'The LORD is our righteousness.' (Jer. 23:5–6; see also 33:14–17)

> The word of the LORD came to Jeremiah: 'Thus says the LORD: If you can break my covenant with the day and my covenant with the night, so that day and night will not come at their appointed time, then also my covenant with David my servant may be broken, so that he shall not have a son to reign on his throne, and my covenant with the Levitical priests my ministers.' (Jer. 33:19–21; see also vv. 25–26)

Ezekiel contains some of the most important references to the messianic role of the Davidic prince. Speaking to the people in exile, Ezekiel is a messenger of restoration:

> For thus says the Lord GOD: 'Behold, I, I myself will search for my sheep and will seek them out. . . . I will rescue my flock; they shall no longer be a prey. And I will judge between sheep and sheep. And I will set up over them one shepherd, my servant David, and he shall feed them: he shall feed them and be their shepherd. And I, the LORD, will be their God, and my servant David shall be prince among them. I am the LORD; I have spoken.' (Ezek. 34:11, 22–24)

This significant passage shows us that God himself is the good shepherd, as is also David. This indicates that the coming David will be the mediator of divine rule and compassion. In chapter 37 Ezekiel uses the covenant summary that originated with Abraham in reference to the shepherd rule of David who is to come. It is unlikely that he is referring to David restored to life, though that possibility cannot be ruled out. It is more likely that he refers to the descendant of David that will fulfil the role spoken of in the Davidic covenant.

> [T]hey shall be my people, and I will be their God.
> My servant David shall be king over them, and they shall all have one shepherd. . . .
> They shall dwell in the land that I gave to my servant Jacob, where your fathers lived.
> They and their children and their children's children shall dwell there forever, and
> David my servant shall be their prince forever. (Ezek. 37:23c–24a, 25)

Amos, who preached in the northern kingdom of Israel, concludes his prophecies with a reference to God's intention to 'raise up the booth of David that is fallen' (Amos 9:11). As Dumbrell comments, this 'enigmatic reference' to the booth may be to Jerusalem.[9] Zechariah, writing after the return from the Babylonian exile conveys the saving plans of God thus:

> And the LORD will give salvation to the tents of Judah first, that the glory of the
> house of David and the glory of the inhabitants of Jerusalem may not surpass that
> of Judah. On that day the LORD will protect the inhabitants of Jerusalem, so that the
> feeblest among them on that day shall be like David, and the house of David shall
> be like God, like the angel of the LORD, going before them. . . .
> And I will pour out on the house of David and the inhabitants of Jerusalem a spirit
> of grace and pleas for mercy, so that, when they look on me, on him whom they have
> pierced, they shall mourn for him, as one mourns for an only child, and weep bitterly
> over him, as one weeps over a firstborn. (Zech. 12:7–8, 10)

> On that day there shall be a fountain opened for the house of David and the
> inhabitants of Jerusalem, to cleanse them from sin and uncleanness. (Zech. 13:1)

It is evident that, whatever the achievements of Solomon, the focus continues to be on the covenant with David as the basis upon which God will act to restore the glories of the kingdom.

The royal covenant with David, as reported in 2 Samuel 7 and 1 Chronicles

---

9. Ibid., p. 79. But Douglas Stuart, *Hosea–Jonah*, WBC 31 (Waco: Word, 1987), pp. 396, 398, reads *sukkat* as *Succoth* and takes it as the name of a city. There is no clear textual evidence to support this.

17, takes on eschatological significance in that it is understood to be irrevocable. Even though there is the provision for discipline that becomes significant in the history of the dynasty subsequent to 1 Kings 11, the expectation is that the Davidic kingship will continue. The other aspect to note is that it has very important connections with the Abrahamic covenant. As Paul Williamson notes:

> While continuing the trajectory of the national covenant established at Sinai, the Davidic covenant is most closely aligned with the ancestral promises. The chapter in which the establishment of the Davidic covenant is first described (i.e. 2 Sam. 7) is replete with allusions to the divine assurances given to Abraham.[10]

Jerusalem and Zion

The use of the name Zion springs into prominence in the Psalms and Latter Prophets.[11] The theology of Zion cannot be separated from the theological importance of David and God's covenant with him in 2 Samuel 7. We may not want to go all the way with those scholars who see David as establishing a royal festival of the kingship of God as there is no direct evidence for it. There can be little doubt, however, that David's kingship in Zion is seen as the mediation of God's kingship over Israel and the earth. Some references to Zion are simply using it as an alternate name to Jerusalem, but it would be fair to say that the name is mostly used as a theological label for the place of God's dwelling and the focus of all his purposes for his people.

One example of this is the use of Zion in Isaiah. Barry Webb has shown that the canonical book of Isaiah contains the theme of the transformation of Zion.[12] On this view Isaiah 1 – 2 summarizes the thesis of the book by taking us from Zion under judgment to the transformed and glorified Zion. But Zion is Jerusalem, and the city of David takes on eschatological significance as the place where God acts to restore his people to himself. When the righteous branch from the stump of Jesse appears (Isa. 11:1–9), then the harmony

---

10. Paul R. Williamson, *Sealed with an Oath: Covenant in God's Unfolding Purpose*, NSBT 23 (Nottingham: Apollos; Downers Grove: IVP, 2007), p. 144.

11. There are some 38 references to Zion in the Psalms, 47 in Isaiah, 17 in Jeremiah and about 30 in the Minor Prophets.

12. Barry G. Webb, *The Message of Isaiah*, BST (Leicester: IVP, 1996), p. 41; 'Zion in Transformation: A Literary Approach to Isaiah', in David J. A. Clines, Stephen E. Fowl and Stanley E. Porter (eds.), *The Bible in Three Dimensions*, JSOTSup 87 (Sheffield: JSOT Press, 1990), pp. 65–84.

of creation means '[t]hey shall not hurt or destroy in all my holy mountain (Zion).' The day will come when

> the ransomed of the LORD shall return and come to Zion with singing;
> everlasting joy shall be upon their heads.
> (Isa. 35:10)

Thus the new exodus theme in Isaiah 40 – 55 is closely linked with the return of the people to Jerusalem. This not only recapitulates salvation history but also compresses it: captivity, release, exodus, the way through the wilderness, and the restoration of the land and Jerusalem are all part of the one great saving event of the Day of the Lord.

Solomon and the temple

Solomon is mentioned by name only once in the Latter Prophets and that only as a reference to the Babylonians plundering the bronze pillars he made in the temple (Jer. 52:12, 20). No doubt Solomon's apostasy would have affected the way he was viewed by the prophets. The temple, however, is a different matter. Theologically it has come to occupy the place of the tabernacle, where God makes his name to dwell. It is the focal point of the Promised Land, which, in turn, reflects the significance of Eden as the place where God originally fellowshipped with his people. It is linked to the Davidic dynasty, which, despite Solomon's failures, continues to be the centre of God's purposes for the mediation of his rule in the kingdom.

The temple, then, is at the heart of much of the prophetic eschatology. We cannot separate the renewal of Zion from that of the temple. Thus Isaiah 2:1–4 looks forward to the establishment of 'the mountain of the house of the LORD' and all the blessings that follow. In Isaiah 4:2–6 the people (daughters) of Zion are cleansed and the glory days of the exodus are repeated:

> Then the LORD will create over the whole site of Mount Zion and over her assemblies a cloud by day, and smoke and the shining of a flaming fire by night; for over all the glory there will be a canopy. There will be a booth for shade by day from the heat, and for a refuge and a shelter from the storm and rain. (Isa. 4:5–6)

This eschatological cloud recalls the cloud that covered the Israelites by day in the exodus (Exod. 14:19–20) and later covered the tabernacle as the glory of the Lord filled it (Exod. 40:34).

We have followed Ezekiel's visions of the glory of the Lord leaving the temple prior to its destruction. When the temple is destroyed by the

Babylonians, Ezekiel receives visions of a new temple that will one day be built (Ezek. 40 – 47). The glory returns and fills the temple (Ezek. 43:1–5; 44:4). This same glory will one day fill the new temple who is the Word made flesh and who 'tabernacles'[13] among us: 'and we have seen his glory, glory as of the only Son from the Father, full of grace and truth' (John 1:14). Ezekiel's vision combines two great themes as he sees Eden's river of life flowing from under the threshold of the new temple (Ezek. 47:1–12).

Wisdom

We have seen that the wisdom traditions in Israel are closely tied to David and Solomon. To deal with wisdom as a separate entity is only to isolate a theme that is interwoven with other strands of the Old Testament. However, it is worth noting the place of wisdom in eschatology. While it is a commonplace to trace the themes of prophet, priest and king through to fulfilment in Jesus, the place of the office of wise man tends to be neglected in the Christological analysis. It begins in the historical development of wisdom, which in turn is picked up in some of the prophetic visions of the future restoration. One of the most obvious is the messianic figure in Isaiah:

> For to us a child is born,
>   to us a son is given;
>   and the government shall be upon his shoulder,
> and his name shall be called
> Wonderful Counsellor, Mighty God,
> Everlasting Father, Prince of Peace.
> (Isa. 9:6)

> There shall come forth a shoot from the stump of Jesse,
>   and a branch from his roots shall bear fruit.
> And the Spirit of the LORD shall rest upon him,
>   the Spirit of wisdom and understanding,
>   the Spirit of counsel and might,
>   the Spirit of knowledge and the fear of the LORD.
> (Isa. 11:1–2)

The counsellor is a figure that arises in the court of David as I noted in the previous chapter. This Isaiah passage describes the coming Davidic scion as

---

13. Gk. *eskēnōsen*, from the verb meaning 'to dwell in a tent'.

one filled with all the attributes of the wise man. It goes on to refer to his judgments in righteousness (Isa. 11:3–5), and then returns to the theme of the renewal of nature (Isa. 11:6–9). This passage is very similar to Proverbs 8:12–15 and uses a number of the same technical wisdom words found in that poem that personifies wisdom.[14] It is difficult to sort out the different nuances of the word *righteousness*, but it is surely more than an ethical and moral concept. In Proverbs we see *righteousness* as a virtual synonym for *wisdom*. Isaiah points to a time when a king will reign in righteousness (Isa. 32:1), a time when fools will no more be called noble (Isa. 32:5–6). Then God's Spirit is poured out from on high and justice and righteousness characterize the natural world (Isa. 32:15–18). Again the vision is of the Lord's righteous and wise rule:

> The LORD is exalted, for he dwells on high;
> he will fill Zion with justice and righteousness,
> and he will be the stability of your times,
> abundance of salvation, wisdom, and knowledge;
> the fear of the LORD is Zion's treasure.
> (Isa. 33:5–6)

There may not be a wide use of the technical wisdom words in prophetic eschatology, but the notion of righteousness and wisdom as the divine resource in creation is found in many places. The tendency of some scholars to make a theology of creation to be the presupposition of wisdom, and to regard it as if creation were not integral to the whole covenant and redemptive-historical structure of the Bible, is probably not helpful.

The exile and return

As we have recognized in Israel's reflections on her past, the theme of exile is intimately bound up with that of the original expulsion from Eden. The promise of the fruitful land indicates the purpose of God to undo the catastrophe of the Fall. And yet the actual experience of Israel was to live under the threat and, at times, the reality of the exile as a new expulsion that challenges the idea that God will restore a people to a new Eden. The Day of the Lord will be characterized by his gathering of the exiles from every land to which they have been driven (Isa. 43:5; Jer. 23:3–8; 29:10–14; 31:1–12; 32:36–41; Ezek. 11:16–17). The return from exile is necessary if the integrity of the covenant promises to Abraham is to be maintained. It is the day of Israel's

---

14. See my *Gospel and Wisdom*, in *Goldsworthy Trilogy*, p. 467.

regeneration and of the renewal of the land (Ezek. 11:17–20; 36:22–38). It is
here that the idea of the survivors, the faithful remnant that will inherit the
promises, comes into prominence (Isa. 1:9; 11:10–12, 16; 46:3–4; Jer. 23:1–4;
31:7–8; Joel 2:32; Mic. 2:12; 4:6–7; Zech. 8:11–13).

Conclusions

Some major aspects of prophetic eschatology as it recapitulates salvation
history can be summarized thus:

Table 3: Prophetic eschatology and the recapitulation of history

Israel's history	Prophetic future	Some representative texts
Creation	New creation	Isa. 11:1–9; 51:3; 65:17–21; Ezek. 36:33–36
Covenant	New covenant	Isa. 49:5–9; Jer. 31:31–34; 33:25–26; Ezek. 34:25–31; 36:24–28
Exodus	New exodus	Isa. 40:1–5; 43:1–7, 15–21; 48:20–21; 49:24–26; 51:9–11; Jer. 23:7–8
Entry and possession	New entry and possession of the new land	Isa. 32:14–20; 35:1–10; Jer. 23:7–8; 29:10–14; Ezek. 34:11–16
Jerusalem	New Jerusalem	Isa. 44:24–28; 46:13; 49:14–21; 51:3
Temple	New temple	Isa. 2:2–3; Ezek. 40 – 47; Zech. 4:6–9
Davidic king	New David	Isa. 9:2–7; 11:1–5; 16:5; 55:3–5; Jer. 23:1–6; Ezek. 34:20–24; 37:24–28; Amos 9:11

The matrix of revelation is clearly indicated by the way the later writers and
theological commentators in Israel recall the past. After the Fall creation has
a new beginning with the call of Abraham. The process that is set in motion
with that call and the covenant with Abraham comes to a brilliant climax with
David, Solomon, Zion and the temple. The apparent hiatus of the captivity in Egypt turns out to be in the plan of God as a means of revealing the
paradigm of the redemptive processes that are necessary if sinners are to be
saved by grace and to inherit the kingdom of God. The crucial point is this:
nothing happens after Solomon in the history of Israel to improve the glorious pattern of the
revealed kingdom and the way of salvation. Prophetic eschatology does not add to
the pattern; rather it removes all blemishes to that pattern. Meanwhile the

downward spiral of the nation demonstrates the salutary truth that God must punish rebellion and that only through such judgment will the true kingdom be revealed. Thus the prophets pronounce doom on the whole wayward history of Israel leading to Solomon and, at the same time, speak of the faithfulness of the God of grace to fulfil his promises and bring in his glorious kingdom.

This pattern of recapitulation is the one highlighted by Donald Robinson and Gabriel Hebert and that, in my opinion, provides a better understanding of the matrix of revelation than the pattern of epochs proposed by Vos, Murray and Clowney. Its superiority, I hope to demonstrate, lies in its being closer to what we find in the New Testament, in its better understanding of what constitutes typology, and in its potential to provide a more Christocentric hermeneutic that can drive the preaching of the Old Testament as truly Christian Scripture. By highlighting the way prophetic eschatology recapitulates the pattern of previous salvation history, Robinson's understanding of the three stages of revelation provides, in my opinion, a more flexible and more accurate basis for making the links between the Old Testament and its fulfilment in Christ. It gives clearer guidelines to the typological relationship of Old to New Testament such that the Christian significance of both is more accessible.

One other point needs to be made. If we follow the epochs suggested by Vos and Clowney, there are certain distinctions that remain muted. Principally the distinction between biblical history and prophetic eschatology is that of glory and permanence. This can be summed up in terms of the contrast between the fallen creation, which is the context of biblical history, and the new creation, which is the context of the eschatological future. Certain aspects of fulfilment remain under wraps until the eschaton. One example is the promise of blessing to the nations (Gen. 12:3). A biblical theology of mission and the nations will show us that under the Law of Moses the emphasis is on Israel's need to remain separate from the nations. A few clues to the blessing are seen in the sporadic addition of a few individual Gentiles to the nation of Israel. But, only in the prophetic eschaton is Israel's exclusiveness changed to one in which the Gentiles come into the blessing by coming to Zion and the temple. The Robinson–Hebert perspective allows these distinctions to be given full play

8. LETTING THE NEW TESTAMENT SPEAK

Is the New Testament normative in the interpretation of the Old Testament?

The first question to be settled is that of the normative nature of the New Testament hermeneutic of the Old Testament. It could, of course, be argued that there is no single New Testament hermeneutic of the Old Testament. But even if there are a variety of ways the individual authors handle the matter, we are bound by the authority and unity of Scripture to say that such hermeneutic approaches are complementary and not contradictory. It is clear that the New Testament authors regard Jesus as the fulfiller of the Old Testament promises and expectations. In order to give expression to this they employ identifiable interpretative procedures. It is not an exaggeration to say that the New Testament is an interpretation, or series of interpretations, of the Old Testament in the light of the person and work of Jesus of Nazareth. The various authors of the New Testament documents were writing with their own focuses on the current situations that formed the contexts for their works. But, taking all that into account, can we doubt that the New Testament is the Spirit-inspired, true, reliable and sufficient testimony to the significance of the life, death and resurrection of Jesus as the fulfilment of the hope of Israel as revealed in the Old Testament?

The accurate contextualization of the New Testament documents is important both for our understanding and their contemporary application. It is one of the roles of biblical theology to enable us to see where the worldwide church in the twenty-first century fits into the salvation-historical drama of the whole of Scripture. I have already proposed that biblical salvation history embraces the whole of human history from creation to new creation. As we anticipate the climax of salvation history with the return of Jesus we find ourselves alongside the early Christians to whom, and among whom, the New Testament documents were written. But the various New Testament documents do not bear a uniform relationship to us in the present. This obvious fact can easily be overlooked or is often simply forgotten. Thus the words of Jesus to his disciples or to the Jews do not necessarily apply to us without qualification. In many situations the New Testament context is close enough to ours to allow us to 'read ourselves back' into the biblical context. We are able to do this in a fairly uninhibited way when dealing with the epistles. These, after all, are written to churches, or to individuals in churches, which is broadly the situation we are in. They are written to Christians who, as we do, look back to the events of the gospel, and look forward to the consummation at the return of Christ. We try to understand any differences that time and cultural changes might impose, but on the whole we feel justified in reading Ephesians or Philippians as if Paul wrote them for us. One matter that often seems to be overlooked by Christians is whether the opening addresses in James 1:1 and 1 Peter 1:1 indicate that the intended recipients of these epistles were Jewish Christians. It is widely accepted that the epistle to the Hebrews is addressed to Jewish Christians. If these letters are to Jews the terminology relating to the Old Testament promises to Israel may not simply be assumed to apply directly to Gentile Christians or to the Christian church as a whole in the same way they apply to Jewish believers.

If we move back a little in time from the epistles to the Acts of the Apostles we recognize that its narrative nature pins it down a little more closely to the historical context. But when we are considering the events at Pentecost the normative nature of these texts becomes a pressing hermeneutical issue. One of the most serious hermeneutical disagreements among Christians today is over the normative versus the essentially unrepeatable nature of at least some of these events. Even putting it like that does not really clarify the problem, for those who believe that Pentecost is unrepeatable do not dismiss it as irrelevant to us simply because it is seen as the once-for-all beginning of something new. Any normative aspect must be based on the theology of the event and not merely its historical occurrence. While the new situation of the Spirit indwelling the church continues, we can never again experience the transition from the old context (Jesus present in the flesh) to the new context (Jesus absent in the flesh but present by his Spirit). To be aware that this is *transition*, and not an ongoing event, does affect our hermeneutics and qualifies our application of the Pentecost narratives.

I do not want to labour the point. All the qualifications I have tried to express thus far do not, in my opinion, cancel out the assertion that the hermeneutics of the New Testament documents are in an important sense normative for us. A biblical theology of the New Testament will be greatly concerned to understand how Jesus, the apostles and all the New Testament authors understood the primary question of the relationship of the Old Testament to Christ. This, in turn, becomes for us the question of the relationship of the two Testaments of our canonical Scriptures. The final hermeneutical question is that of our own relationship to Christ since that will be the way to understand how the Old Testament relates to us. In other words, Jesus as the one mediator between God and Man (1 Tim. 2:5) is the mediator between us and the word of God in the Old Testament. Within the overall salvation history in the Bible our biblical-theological perspective on the New Testament as a whole should inform us of the nature and effects of our distance from any given text.

Does the New Testament exhibit a structure of revelation?

Our examination of the Old Testament has shown us that key moments in the salvation history of the people of God were reflected upon as providing a structure to the way God has acted and revealed himself and his purposes. I have suggested that both the narrative of biblical history and the prophetic interpretation of that history showed an overwhelming concern with the promises to Abraham and the subsequent events that in some sense fulfilled these promises. The climax came with David and Solomon. The ensuing decline and fall of Israel provided the backdrop to the eschatology of the prophets. This involved a recapitulation of the great moments of salvation history that were seen as fulfilling the promises to Abraham. The question before us concerns the extent to which the New Testament writers bear testimony to the same pattern or matrix of revelation in the course of their exposition of the fulfilment of the promises of God in the person and work of Jesus Christ.

Creation
Creation is an important concern in some New Testament documents. It is the opening focus of John in his Gospel. Creation in Genesis was through

the agent of God's word, 'Let there be . . .' This word is now personified by John:

> In the beginning was the Word, and the Word was with God, and the Word was God. He was in the beginning with God. All things were made through him, and without him was not any thing made that was made. . . .
>
> And the Word became flesh and dwelt among us, and we have seen his glory, glory as of the only Son from the Father, full of grace and truth. (John 1:1–3, 14)

That he dwells (tabernacles) among us and displays God's glory is John's introduction to his theology of the new temple that is emphasized in John 2:13–22. Paul also reflects on the creative role of the Son:

> He is the image of the invisible God, the firstborn of all creation. For by[1] him all things were created, in heaven and on earth, visible and invisible, whether thrones or dominions or rulers or authorities – all things were created through him and for him. And he is before all things, and in him all things hold together. (Col. 1:15–17)

In Hebrews Jesus is also the divine word, this time as the final and true prophet of God. It is significant the writer links this word of God immediately both with his creative role and his role as the true image of God who brings salvation:

> Long ago, at many times and in many ways, God spoke to our fathers by the prophets, but in these last days he has spoken to us by his Son, whom he appointed the heir of all things, through whom also he created the world. He is the radiance of

---

1. Paul here uses the preposition *en*, which has a certain ambiguity. ESV has the dative use of agency (or instrumentality), 'by him,' as does NIV. NRSV has 'in him' but includes 'by him' in a marginal note. Peter O'Brien, *Colossians, Philemon*, WBC (Waco: Word, 1982), p. 45, comments, 'Quite clearly the point about Christ as the Mediator of creation includes the notion of instrumentality. But is the phrase stating something more than this, going beyond even 1 Corinthians 8:6 and John 1:3. . . . According to Haupt the phrase "in him" has the same force as in Ephesians 1:4; God's creation, like his election, takes place "in Christ" and not apart from him.'

   Of course, even Eph. 1:4 is not without its problems concerning what being chosen 'in him' means. I suspect Eph. 1:10 presents us with a similar dilemma. See the discussion of macro-typology below.

the glory of God and the exact imprint of his nature, and he upholds the universe by the word of his power. After making purification for sins, he sat down at the right hand of the Majesty on high. (Heb. 1:1–3)

Perhaps less directly connected to creation is the way Luke's Gospel clarifies the baptismal designation of Jesus as the Son of God by inserting the genealogy of Jesus immediately after the account of his baptism. The genealogy picks up on 'You are my beloved Son; with you I am well pleased' (Luke 3:22) and follows the family tree back through Joseph's line all the way to 'Adam, the son of God' (v. 38). The implication is clearly that, by referring to Jesus as 'my beloved Son', the Father designates him as the true Adam and the true Israel (see Exod. 4:22; Hos. 11:1). As Adam was the pinnacle of the original creation, so Jesus' humanity is the pinnacle of the new creation.

Fall

The sin of Adam is not mentioned specifically very often but, as in the Old Testament, it is clearly presupposed in the whole New Testament account of the sin of humanity and the need for redemption. Paul provides us with the classic examples of the reversal typology of Adam–Christ, namely that what Adam perpetrated as the federal head of a sinful race, Christ redresses as the federal head of the redeemed race (Rom. 5:12–21; 1 Cor. 15:20–22, 45–49).[2] We do not need to pursue here any further the New Testament doctrine of sin since the doctrine of redemption everywhere presupposes it. The doctrines of redemption and sin are interdependent in that sin requires redemption, and the radical nature of redemption shows the seriousness of the rebellion of sin. In other words, what God needed to do in order to fix the problem indicates the nature and seriousness of the problem.

In the understanding of the radical nature of the Fall as recorded in the Old Testament we have several important and related themes in the New Testament. '[I]n the day that you eat of it you shall surely die' (Gen. 2:17) is the original sanction. It must be taken seriously, and various ways of describing the outcome have commonly been used. One approach is to say that Adam and Eve died spiritually when they disobeyed. This is true enough provided we also recognize that their death also involved the body: they came from the dust and were condemned to return to it (Gen. 3:19). Both New and Old

---

2. To refer to this as 'reversal' typology is only to highlight the fact that Adam's sinful act is the antithesis of Christ's righteous act. The typology is direct when we focus on the federal headship of each over their respective races.

Testament understand death as belonging to the fallen order of things. The Fall means that we have died with Adam (1 Cor. 15:21–22) and are dead in our trespasses and sins (Eph. 2:1). Consequently we must be made alive in Christ in order to experience resurrection from the dead with him (Eph. 2:5). Even more central to the matter is the cost to God in his dealing with the problem of this death due to sin. Nothing less than the death of the sinless Son of God can achieve a redress of the situation. The seriousness of death and hell can really only be gauged by the death of Christ, and by the necessity for us to be united with him in his death and resurrection.

Related to death is the existential impotence of the sinner. Thus the doctrines of original sin, sovereign grace and election are part of the dynamics of salvation. The Fall, then, is a catastrophe from which we are totally powerless to recover ourselves. The doctrine of God's predestination of his people reinforces the seriousness of sin. Without it none would be saved, because dead people cannot get up and go out to the front at an evangelistic meeting unless they are being made alive together with Christ by the Holy Spirit.

The flood

Noah's flood is referred to or implied in only a few of places in the New Testament. As in the Old Testament the flood is seen as an instrument of God's judgment. The imagery of a flood, which may or may not be intended to recall Noah's, occurs in some forecasts of ultimate judgment (Matt. 24:36–39; Luke 17:26–27; 2 Pet. 2:5; 3:5–7). Noah is also referred to as one of the heroes of faith (Heb. 11:7). But in this he is the instrument of salvation. Peter also draws the analogy between the salvation of Noah and his family, and the salvation now expressed in Christian baptism (1 Pet. 3:18–22). The flood does not feature as significantly in the New Testament as an epoch-making event.

Abraham

Abraham is referred to explicitly more than seventy times in the New Testament. We saw how Abraham is emphasized in the Old Testament as the one through whom God brings a new beginning for his people. Though he is preceded by a stylized description of the line of antecedents from Seth, through Noah and Shem, to Terah, his father, Abraham still marks a new beginning. It would be tedious to try to examine every New Testament reference to the patriarch, but we can consider some of those places where Abraham is regarded as the beginning of the salvation-historical story.

First, we note the genealogy of Jesus according to Matthew. Matthew's Gospel begins by identifying itself as 'The book of the genealogy of Jesus Christ, the son of David, the son of Abraham' (Matt. 1:1). Matthew thus indicates that his book is somehow driven, even structured, by this genealogy. The structure of what follows is summed up in Matthew 1:17 thus:

> So all the generations from Abraham to David were fourteen generations, and from David to the deportation to Babylon fourteen generations, and from the deportation to Babylon to the Christ fourteen generations.

While we recognize the deliberately stylized nature of the genealogy into three groups of fourteen generations, the significant feature is that it emphasizes four pivotal points that identify the Christ: Abraham, David, the exile and Jesus Christ. Matthew is also concerned to portray the Christ as the fulfiller of prophecy. He emphasizes the antitypical role of Jesus by drawing clear analogies between the sons of Abraham in the Old Testament and the son of Abraham who has now come. So the child is born according to promise (Matt. 1:20–23) and is exiled in Egypt, from whence he emerges as the Son of God (Matt. 2:13–15). In his baptism Jesus represents Israel who, through the water of the Red Sea, and again at the Jordan, is designated as the people of God, the son of God (Matt. 3:11–17).[3] As the Son of God he is tempted in the wilderness for forty days, which recalls the forty years of Israel's wanderings and temptations. The Sermon on the Mount (Matt. 5 – 7) presents Jesus as the new and greater Moses who fulfils the law and the prophets (Matt. 5:17), and whose prophetic word structures the life of the redeemed. All these recollections are of Old Testament events that are part of the fulfilment of the Abrahamic covenant.

Matthew's structure may well serve to indicate that Jesus is the one greater than Moses as a way of asserting that Jewish Christianity is greater than its chief rival in Pharisaism. Thus the Sermon on the Mount pulls the rug out from under those who plead a righteousness based on observing the Law. If the five blocks of Jesus' teaching Matthew presents are intended to show a new 'Pentateuch', a suggestion that may well be stretching the evidence, it would be a way of defending Christianity as the true way for Israel. There is no doubt that Matthew's attitude to the Gentiles is somewhat ambivalent, except for the important events at the beginning and end of Jesus' life here on earth. The coming of the Gentile magi to the king of the Jews (Matt. 2:1–12) seems

---

3. Israel's crossing of the Red Sea and the next generation's crossing of the Jordan may be seen as a new beginning. John's baptism at the Jordan would seem to indicate the need for Israel to start over again with repentance for its sins. Jesus' baptism indicates that he personifies the new obedient Israel.

to reflect the coming of the Gentile Queen of Sheba to Solomon (1 Kgs 10), and both events reflect the promise to Abraham that his descendants will bring blessing to the nations (Gen. 12:3). At the end of Matthew's Gospel the so-called Great Commission indicates that the promise to Abraham is now activated in the command to make disciples of all nations (Matt. 28:18–20). In between these two Gentile references Matthew emphasizes Jesus as the fulfiller of the promises to Israel. He chooses his Jewish apostles, telling them, 'Go nowhere among the Gentiles and enter no town of the Samaritans, but go rather to the lost sheep of the house of Israel' (Matt. 10:5–6). Jesus' apparent rejection of the Canaanite woman who pleads for healing for her daughter (Matt. 15:21–28) reinforces the primary fact that his ministry is to the 'lost sheep of the house of Israel'. That he relents and heals the girl shows the established order in salvation: Israel first, but the Gentiles are not excluded.

While Mark makes only one reference to Abraham (Mark 12:26),[4] Luke is much more centred on the patriarch. Luke is clearly concerned to structure the birth narrative within the theology of the temple. Thus the annunciation by the angel Gabriel puts the coming event in the context of the promises to David concerning his throne (Luke 1:30–32; 2 Sam. 7:12–16). Mary's response to this is her Magnificat (Luke 1:46–55), which extols the saving work of God and concludes with these significant words:

> He has helped his servant Israel,
>> in remembrance of his mercy,
>> as he spoke to our fathers,
>> to Abraham and to his offspring forever.
> (Luke 1:54–55)

The song of Zechariah is no less significant in linking the coming saviour to the promises made both to David and to Abraham:

> Blessed be the Lord God of Israel,
> for he has visited and redeemed his people,
> and has raised up a horn of salvation for us,
>> in the house of his servant David,
> as he spoke by the mouth of his holy prophets from of old,
> that we should be saved from our enemies

---

4. The point being made is that, in being the God of Abraham, Isaac and Jacob, God is the God of the living and not of the dead.

and from the hand of all who hate us;
    to show the mercy promised to our fathers
and to remember his holy covenant,
    the oath that he swore to our father Abraham,
to grant us that we, being delivered from the hand of our enemies,
might serve him without fear,
    in holiness and righteousness before him all our days.
(Luke 1:68–75)

It would seem, then, that Luke's theological framework consists in the covenant with Abraham, the promises to David and the fulfilment of the role of the temple as the context of the coming of the Christ. John the Baptist also emphasizes this new event as he prepares the way for the Lord's coming. His pointed remark to the 'brood of vipers' is that they are not the true children of Abraham and that 'God is able from these stones to raise up children for Abraham' (Luke 3:8).

The Acts of the Apostles gives us the account of the growing mission of the original body of Jewish believers towards the world of the Gentiles. Peter's sermon after the healing of the lame man is an occasion for the proclamation of what God has done in Jesus. Peter concludes with a reference to the covenant with Abraham as the foundation for all that has happened in the coming of the Saviour (Acts 3:11–26).

I do not think we can overestimate the importance of Stephen's *apologia* in Acts 7. It is one of the lengthiest salvation-historical recitals in the New Testament and, significantly, begins with Abraham. The quite detailed account of Abraham and his descendants (Acts 7:2–17) would appear to be intended to emphasize the need to move out to a new beginning. Abraham answered the call of God and left Mesopotamia. His descendants, led by Moses, moved out from slavery in Egypt (Acts 7:18–43). Now, declares Stephen by implication, it is time to move on again to embrace the Righteous One, but these Israelites have rejected him. He emphasizes the need to leave the temple made with hands and to move on to Christ (Acts 7:44–50). The testimony of the false witnesses would appear to have some substance, as he does indeed declare the temple made with hands to be redundant (Acts 6:13–14). Thus the parameters of Stephen's *apologia* are Abraham and the temple of Solomon and, by implication, Christ.

Paul's two detailed accounts of Abraham are foundational for his understanding of justification by faith. In both Romans 4 and Galatians 3 Abraham is set forth as the one who provides the paradigm of the Christian gospel. In Romans Paul points to the fact that Abraham 'believed God, and it was counted to him as righteousness', and that this occurred before he was circumcised (Rom. 4:3, 9–13). He was thus justified outside the Law. The same principle holds for us who believe (Rom. 4:23–25). In Galatians 3 Paul asserts that the true descendants of Abraham are those who are of faith. The promises made to Abraham are described as the gospel that was preached beforehand to him. The dynamics of this lie in the fact that the promise concerning Abraham's offspring finds its fulfilment in Christ. So 'if you are Christ's, then you are Abraham's offspring, heirs according to promise' (Gal. 3:29). Within this economy of the promise to Abraham the Law of Moses forms a temporary provision, which now must pass away (Gal. 3:19). For Paul, spiritual permanence springs from the promises to Abraham, not from the Law.

The reference to Abraham in Hebrews 7:1–9 is primarily concerned with Melchizedek and the high priesthood of Jesus. Other references to Abraham (Jas 2:21–23; 1 Pet. 3:6) do not really concern us here. James seeks to show that faith without works is dead. There is no conflict here with the Pauline doctrine of justification apart from the works of the law (Rom. 3:21).

Moses and the exodus

Our investigations in the Old Testament have shown that the ministry of Moses and the Law of Sinai are founded upon the promises given to Abraham. The exodus and the instruction given to the redeemed people are expressions of the covenant faithfulness of the God of Abraham, Isaac and Jacob. It is for this reason that the Law features so much in the salvation history of the Old Testament. The vocation of Israel is to be the people of God, and the characteristics of this vocation are revealed in the Law. To break the Law is to transgress the covenant, which, in turn, is to despise the promises to Abraham. The New Testament contains two broad types of reference to the Law of Moses: those which indicate that there is an abiding significance for the Law and those that indicate the fulfilment of the Law in Christ.

I am concerned here only to try to understand the manner in which the New Testament regards Moses and the Law as epoch-making. Our task is not to consider the overall New Testament teaching on the Law, for we have already assessed the role of Jesus as the fulfiller. It is clear from Paul's treatment of the Law in Galatians that the significance of the Jewish observance of the Law relates to their status as children of Abraham. In other words Paul is at one with the emphases in the Old Testament that Moses and Sinai are subsumed under the covenant promises to Abraham. It is also clear in Galatians that the Law was an interim measure (Gal. 3:19), which does not diminish its importance, but throws the focus more on Abraham.

I have indicated above that Matthew's Gospel is suggestive of the ministry of Moses, but in such a way as to proclaim Jesus as the one who fulfils the Mosaic role and, thus in a real sense, supersedes him. The three Synoptic Gospels recount the transfiguration of Jesus. Peter, James and John witness this preview of Jesus' glory as he converses with Moses and Elijah. These two Old Testament figures are the definitive prophets who summoned Israel to faith. Jesus is here the ultimate prophet, God's 'beloved Son' to whom the disciples must listen (Matt. 17:5; Mark 9:7; Luke 9:35). Luke also records that Jesus converses with the two prophets about 'his departure (Gk. *exodos*), which he was about to accomplish at Jerusalem' (Luke 9:31).

I do not want to understate the importance given to Moses in the New Testament. That would be to engage in special pleading. But Peter's address in Solomon's portico refers to Moses only once to indicate that Jesus is the prophet whom Moses predicted in Deuteronomy 18:15 (Acts 3:22). The focus is on the covenant promises to Abraham (Acts 3:13, 25). Stephen's speech concentrates a good deal on Moses but as the one who mediates the promise made to Abraham (Acts 7:17–38). Paul's sermon in Antioch reaches a climax in the proclamation that what could not be achieved through the Law of Moses has now come through Jesus (Acts 13:38–39). Paul makes only a few references to Moses. In Romans 5:14 he speaks of death reigning from Adam to Moses. Thus, while Moses was God's lawgiver, the law itself did not affect the fact that death came with sin, and sin came with Adam. In Romans 10:5–10 Paul contrasts the Law-righteousness that Moses wrote of with the faith-righteousness that Christ brings. In 2 Corinthians 3:12–18 Moses stands for the Torah, which unbelieving Jews read with veiled hearts since only Christ can remove the veil. The epistle to the Hebrews, of all the New Testament epistles, contains the most references to Moses. The majority are in chapter 3, where Jesus is proclaimed as superior to Moses in every respect. In Hebrews 10:29 the writer makes a 'how much greater' argument: if punishment under the Law was severe, how much worse is that deserved by one who spurns the Son of God and profanes the blood of the covenant? In Hebrews 11:23–28 Moses is numbered among the heroes of faith. The only reference to Moses in the book of Revelation is to the song of Moses, the servant of God, and the song of the Lamb (Rev. 15:3–4). This is the song of those who have conquered the beast and it builds on the idea that the salvation the Lamb achieves is a true exodus.

David

There is no question that a vital aspect of New Testament Christology revolves around the relationship of Jesus to the person of David and the promises made to him. Jesus is frequently referred to as the Son of David in the Gospels, especially in Matthew. It is also true that a certain ambivalence seems to exist in the New Testament with regard to Jesus as the Son of David. Alan Richardson comments, 'It is truly astonishing, in view of the weight of OT prophecy concerning the Davidic Messiah, how little the NT makes of the matter.'[5] Some suggest that this reticence was due to the political expectations and overtones that Judaism attached to the idea of the kingly rule of the Davidic Messiah. Goppelt points out that it is only Matthew who places emphasis on the title 'Son of David'.[6] But he also points out that the use of the designation 'Messiah' is Davidic and widespread in the New Testament. Although the Hebrew form is rare in the New Testament, the Greek equivalent 'Christ' is in constant use.[7]

Paul's gospel summary in Romans 1:1–4 is instructive. He defines his gospel with four propositions: it is God's gospel; it is the gospel promised by the Old Testament prophets; it concerns God's Son, who is descended from David according to the flesh; and it concerns the One who is declared to be the Son of God through his resurrection from the dead. Thus the Son of God is also the son of David, and is demonstrably so because of his resurrection. Paul's perspective here agrees with Peter's Pentecost sermon, which links the fulfilment of the Davidic covenant to the resurrection (Acts 2:29–31). Paul's salvation-historical perspective in his sermon in Pisidian Antioch takes us from the election of Israel, the exodus and possession of Canaan to David. Concerning David he remarks (Acts 13:23), 'Of this man's offspring God has brought to Israel a Saviour, Jesus, as he promised.' Jesus is thus identified as the Son of David in a way that emphasizes the theological significance of both. The resurrection is the fulfilling of the promises to David, as Paul declares (Acts 13:34), 'And as for the fact that he raised him from the dead, no more to return to corruption, he has spoken in this way, "I will give you the holy and sure blessings of David."' Paul's references to David in his epistles are few. Goppelt's point about 'Messiah' being synonymous with *ben-dāwîd* in the synagogue may have some value in considering the Gospel's accounts that refer to Jesus as 'Christ' (Messiah). Some may argue that the constant references to

---

5. Alan Richardson, *An Introduction to the Theology of the New Testament* (London: SCM, 1958), p. 126.

6. Leonhard Goppelt, *Theology of the New Testament*, vol. 1: *The Ministry of Jesus in its Theological Significance* (Grand Rapids: Eerdmans, 1981), p. 168. He refers to Matt. 1:1; 9:27; 12:23; 15:22; 21:9, 15.

7. According to Goppelt, ibid., 'Messiah' was synonymous with *ben-dāwîd* in the synagogue.

'Christ' in Paul's letters can hardly be said to represent deliberate references to Jesus as Son of David. But they surely do spring from his Christology, which, as we have seen, he links with David in more than one place.

Zion

The New Testament contains some seven references to Sion or Zion, most of them as quotes from the Old Testament. Zechariah 9:9 is quoted in Matthew 21:5 and John 12:15 with regard to Jesus' entry into Jerusalem on a donkey. In Romans 9:33 Paul quotes Isaiah 28:16 interwoven with Isaiah 8:14. The purpose is to explain the unbelief of the Jews of his time. In Romans 11:26–27, quoting Isaiah 59:20 and Jeremiah 31:34, he speaks of the eventual salvation of Israel. Isaiah 28:16 is also quoted in 1 Peter 2:6 and followed by Psalm 118:22 and Isaiah 8:14, which focus on the disaster that comes to the unbelievers. In Hebrews Zion is referred to as the present defining locus of the believing Jews who are being addressed in the epistle:

> But you have come to Mount Zion and to the city of the living God, the heavenly Jerusalem, and to innumerable angels in festal gathering, and to the assembly of the firstborn who are enrolled in heaven, and to God, the judge of all, and to the spirits of the righteous made perfect, and to Jesus, the mediator of a new covenant, and to the sprinkled blood that speaks a better word than the blood of Abel. (Heb. 12:22–24)

This is in contrast to the situation of the Israelites under the old covenant gathered before Moses at Sinai. A similar perspective is given in Revelation 14:1, which records John's vision of the 144,000 gathered before God on Mount Zion.

References to Zion, or Sion, in the New Testament are driven by the theological significance that the respective writers understand as attaching to Jerusalem as the holy city of God and the place in which he meets his people. Common to all the New Testament references is the Christological significance that now attaches to the city. This means that Zion is the place in which the Christ of God is revealed. It is significant that narrative references to Jerusalem include those passages in which the destruction of the city is foretold. The only references to a subsequently renewed Jerusalem are those that move beyond the actual city of Jesus' time and focus on the new eschatological city of God. There is nothing in the New Testament that indicates that a literal fulfilment of Old Testament prophecy concerning the restoration of Jerusalem will take place. Thus, while some prophecies are fulfilled in a literal manner, the New Testament does not use a literalistic hermeneutic of the fulfilment of all prophecy.

Solomon and the temple

If Solomon marks the climax of the historic epoch or stage in Old Testament revelation, why does he feature so little in the New Testament? This question has arisen because of the significance of Solomon in the development of salvation history. Yet it is clear that Solomon is all but ignored in the New Testament. It is also clear that David is given the theological prominence so that, as in the Old Testament, Solomon is seen as wise man and temple builder in fulfilment of the promises to David. These Davidic promises are the primary focus in both Old and New Testament. Solomon's apostasy (1 Kgs 11) is an enigma and is probably one motive for the eclipse of Solomon in prophecy and in Christology. Solomon's significance is as the son of David. He achieves much but then squanders his position by leading his kingdom in the direction of destruction. Jesus, then, is identified, not as the true Solomon, but as the faithful Son of David. The only exceptions to the silence about Solomon are the cryptic statements of Jesus to the Pharisees 'Something greater than Solomon is here' (Matt. 12:42; Luke 11:31) and his assertion that even the lilies of the field have greater glory than Solomon (Luke 12:27). The focus of the New Testament is clearly on David and the temple.

Wisdom

Wisdom plays a significant part in New Testament Christology. Thus it focuses first on Jesus as the wise man. Perhaps one of the most important passages occurs at the end of the Sermon on the Mount (Matt. 7:24–29). Jesus' use of the parable of the wise man and the foolish man building their respective houses involves the classic contrast of wisdom and folly that so characterizes the book of Proverbs. The difference is that Jesus does not speak as the scribes, generally thought of as the wise men of Jesus' time. Scribal authority was coming more and more to reside in rabbinic opinions. Jesus' authority lies in the fact that he is the source of wisdom, for the wise person is the one who hears his words and does them. It thus astonished his hearers that he did not simply point to the storehouse of wisdom collected over the ages as a scribe might have done, but that he asserted his own authority. Jesus' use of proverbs and parables shows that he was well versed in the idioms of the wisdom literature, but he used them to proclaim his own mission to bring in God's kingdom. His parable of the wise and foolish virgins (Matt. 25:1–13) highlights the wisdom of being prepared for the Lord's coming.

The same contrast is carried on in the epistles, especially by Paul in 1 Corinthians. Here the Christology of wisdom is given full expression. Jesus again is not simply the source of wisdom but embodies true wisdom. This contrasts with the folly that the world perversely calls 'wisdom' (1 Cor.

1:18–30). Both Jews and Gentiles have rejected the wisdom of God in Christ but, to those who are called, the wisdom of God and the power of God is Christ. The climax to Paul's argument is that God has made Jesus Christ to be our wisdom. The fear of the Lord as the beginning of knowledge and wisdom in the Old Testament is here shown to be allegiance to Christ. Although Paul does not specifically mention the connection, the Christology of wisdom in the New Testament is sufficiently clear to enable us to see the parallels with the Old Testament situation. There it was the glory of the kingdom of David and Solomon and the temple that saw the flowering of wisdom. In the New Testament it is the new temple and the fulfilment of the covenant with David in Jesus that sees the true wisdom found in the person and work of Christ.

The mission to the Gentiles

In my writing about the book of Revelation I commented on the two per-spectives of the gathered people portrayed in Revelation 7. I suggested that the 144,000 'sealed from every tribe of the sons of Israel' (Rev. 7:4) and the 'great multitude that no one could number, from every nation, from all tribes and peoples and languages, standing before the throne and before the Lamb' (Rev. 7:9) were one and the same. The one perspective was on the perfect number of the elect, the other on the multitude of the saved.[8] For some time now I have felt that this is an unsafe exegesis. In this I have been spurred on by the writings of Donald Robinson who has written a number of articles in which he cogently argues that the distinction between Jew and Gentile is not lost in the New Testament.[9] That is, although Jew and Gentile believers are made into one new man in Christ (Eph. 2:15), this unity does not remove all distinctions until its final eschatological fulfilment. Paul still maintains that the gospel is 'to the Jew first' (Rom. 1:16; 2:9–10). His whole argument regarding his hope for the salvation of the Jew in Romans 9 – 11 hinges on this distinc-tion. Galatians 3:28 does not remove this distinction any more than it removes the ongoing distinctions between male and female. Oneness in Christ does not mean that all differences are removed. A consequence of this is that I now favour a different interpretation of Revelation 7, namely that the 144,000 symbolizes the perfect number of the saved of Israel, and the great multitude

---

8. *The Gospel in Revelation: Gospel and Apocalypse* (Exeter: Paternoster, 1984), in Graeme Goldsworthy, *The Goldsworthy Trilogy* (Milton Keynes: Paternoster, 2000), p. 194. This would seem to be a commonly held view.
9. See Peter G. Bolt and Mark D. Thompson (eds.), *Donald Robinson Selected Works*, vol. 1: *Assembling God's People*, pt. 1, 'Jew and Gentile in the Purposes of God'.

represents the Gentiles saved as a result of Israel's servant status to be a light to the Gentiles.

Given the importance of the covenant promises to Abraham relating to the blessing to all the nations (Gen. 12:3), and the perpetuation of this perspective in the Old Testament with regard to the salvation of the Gentiles, it seems unlikely that such a significant distinction would simply disappear in the New Testament. Certainly the apostolic experience in Acts shows how vital it was for the early church to get the relationship of Jew and Gentile right. They could not ignore the constant emphasis in the Old Testament that Israel was called as God's servant to be a light to the Gentiles. While Israel was not given an active evangelistic task in Old Testament times, the prophetic picture was one of an eschatological event in which Israel's mission would flourish. The effect of the Law of Sinai was to establish the exclusiveness of Israel in separation from the nations round about. This was a necessary move in view of the propensity of the people to absorb, and even convert to, the polytheism of the nations. It would require the ultimate saving act of God on the Day of the Lord for the great Jewish mission and the ingathering of the nations to take place.

The Abraham–David/Solomon axis and the fulfilment of prophecy

It is important to remember that Christianity began as a Jewish phenomenon. It may seem unnecessary to stress that Jesus and the apostles were Jews and that the first church at Pentecost was Jewish. The fact is that the modern Christian church, being almost entirely non-Jewish, tends to view the events of the day of Christ and the apostles as if it represented a sudden break with all things Jewish. Such is not the case. Thus the primitive history of Christianity as set out in the Acts of the Apostles is a history of the beginning of the fulfilment of the covenant promises to Abraham as these are developed in Old Testament prophetic eschatology. The promises involve the children of Abraham through whom all nations will be blessed. It is as Jesus told the woman of Samaria, 'salvation is from the Jews' (John 4:22). Thus salvation comes to Israel first, and only then are the Gentiles included.

Acts 1 provides an instructive narrative. The apostles have apparently recovered from the trauma that Luke recounts in the final chapter of his Gospel, and now have proof of their Lord's resurrection. Yet their mindset still seems fixed on an immediate political solution to the present situation, which is dominated by the presence of the Roman occupiers. 'Lord, will you at this time restore the kingdom to Israel?' they ask (Acts 1:6). Jesus' answer is not a diversion but is directed as an answer to the question. They are to wait in

Jerusalem until the outpouring of God's Spirit, when they will witness within Jewry and beyond to the Gentiles. On both accounts they are to experience the fulfilment of the prophecies and promises that stem from as far back as Abraham (Acts 1:7–8).

The event Jesus foretells is, of course, that which takes place on the Day of Pentecost (Acts 2). The baptism with the Holy Spirit promised by Jesus in Acts 1:5 is effected by their being filled with the Spirit (Acts 2:4), which is poured out upon them (Acts 2:33). Peter's sermon is instructive, especially as it is the first sermon preached under this new dispensation of the Spirit. After denying that the phenomena that accompany the giving of the Spirit are the result of drunkenness (Acts 2:15), he goes on to expound them as the fulfil-ment of Joel's prophecy of the Day of the Lord (Acts 2:16–21, quoting Joel 2:28–32). It is clear from this that Peter regards the end times to have arrived and the great eschatological age to be upon them. This is the day of Israel's salvation and of the beginning of the ingathering of the nations.

The structure of the sermon that follows Peter's announcement of his text is crucial for its emphases. The mighty works, wonders and signs of Jesus were a further indication that this is the eschaton. But the subsequent lawless killing of Jesus was followed by the resurrection, which is also a fulfilment (Acts 2:24–28, quoting Ps. 16:8–11). Peter then links the resurrection to the promise to David in 2 Samuel 7: 'Being therefore a prophet, and knowing that God had sworn with an oath to him that he would set one of his descendants on his throne, he foresaw and spoke of the resurrection of the Christ . . .' (Acts 2:30–31a). Thus Peter understands that within the ambit of Joel's prophecy is the resurrection as the fulfilment of the Davidic covenant. Jesus' resurrection is the enthronement of the Davidic messiah that was prophesied.

Peter's sermon in Solomon's porch at the temple follows his healing of the lame man (Acts 3:1–11). The parameters of this sermon (Acts 3:11–26) are Abraham, the patriarchs and Jesus, the servant of God. The link is important. Also, as we have noted above, Stephen's speech takes the salvation-historical story from Abraham, through the exodus, and climaxes in Solomon's build-ing of the temple (Acts 7:2–53). His quote of Isaiah 66:1–2 (vv. 49–50) gives the grounds of his final accusation of their resisting the Holy Spirit (Acts 7:51–53). As the enraged Jews stone Stephen he has a vision of the glory of God and Jesus at the right hand of God. This is Jesus in the true sanctuary of God of which Isaiah spoke, for that is where the glory of God is. This is the temple that these Jews refuse to acknowledge as they cling to the man-made Jerusalem temple.

To return to the sermon of Paul that he preached in the synagogue at Antioch of Pisidia (Acts 13:16–41) we again note his emphasis. Paul begins with reference to God's election of the fathers, which could be a reference to Abraham and the patriarchs or, as in 1 Corinthians 10:1, it could refer to their Hebrew ancestors in Egypt. Certainly Paul addresses them specifically as 'sons of the family of Abraham' (Acts 13:26), so there is no doubt as to the significance of Abraham in Paul's summary of salvation history here. His narrative takes in the exodus, the conquest and possession of Canaan, the judges, Samuel and Saul. His survey of their history comes to its climax with David, of whom God said, 'I have found in David the son of Jesse a man after my heart, who will do all my will' (Acts 13:22). At that point he proclaims, 'Of this man's offspring God has brought to Israel a Saviour, Jesus, as he promised' (Acts 13:23). His exposition of Jesus includes the significant point that he is not only the promised one, but that the Jews failed to recognize him as the fulfilment of the words of the prophets. The irony is that this failure led the Jews actually to fulfil the prophecies about Jesus by having him executed (Acts 13:27–29). The end point of the sermon is the resurrection of Jesus and Paul's important summary:

> And we bring you the good news that what God promised to the fathers, this he has fulfilled to us their children by raising Jesus, as also it is written in the second Psalm,
>> 'You are my Son,
>> today I have begotten you.'
> (Acts 13:32–33)

It is fair to say, then, that Paul here expounds the structure of revelation in a salvation history that stretches from Abraham to David and then to Christ. The note of prophetic promise is strong and its fulfilment focused. The resurrection of Jesus fulfils all that it means for Jesus to be the Son of God, which is interpreted in terms of the promises to Israel. This seems to be inclusive at both ends; all God's promises are fulfilled completely by the resurrection.

A comparison of approaches

Comparisons can indeed at times be odious or at least unprofitable. There are also times, however, when comparing one method or approach with another can draw out the best of both and show how they complement each other. Since I was so radically influenced by Donald Robinson's method I am naturally biased. I have tried in this study to overcome bias and to be fair to other approaches: the epochal approach represented by Vos and Clowney; the multiplex approaches of Greidanus and Scobie; and the narrative-drama schema of Bartholomew and Goheen. Two things above all should, I believe, shape our assessments of the respective methods: the one is its sustainability as representing what really is in the whole Bible; the other is its practical application as way of interpretation that informs our reading, teaching and preaching of the Bible.

It might well be asked whether there are any important distinctions between the two main approaches that seem to have most in common. These are the Vos–Clowney method and the Robinson–Hebert method. The similarities are many and significant:

1. Both understand the progressiveness of revelation and the fact that the progression is not a kind of gradual dawning of the light but something that happens in stages.
2. Both recognize that the Old Testament story is built mainly on the promise of salvation and the revelation of what this salvation means for the world of fallen humanity.
3. Both recognize that there is an important sense in which the Bible presents the person and work of Jesus of Nazareth as fulfilling all the promises and hopes of the Old Testament.
4. Both recognize the importance of understanding the structure or matrix of revelation as a key factor in hermeneutics.
5. Both are concerned to show the relevance of the Old Testament to Christians as a book about Christ.
6. Both recognize that typology rooted in salvation history is at the heart of the relationship between the two Testaments.
7. Both are based on presuppositions of the inspiration and authority of the Bible as the Word of God.[10]

The first and obvious point of distinction lies in the designation of epochs or stages. It has been my contention throughout this study that the Vos–Clowney designation of the epoch that runs from Moses to Christ is viable. It is also my contention that it contains at least four potential problems. The first

10. These concepts of inspiration and authority would mean for Hebert something different from Robinson's biblicism. Despite this, Hebert as a conservative Anglo-Catholic nevertheless had a high view of Scripture and a clear sense of the structure of revelation. See A. G. Hebert, *The Authority of the Old Testament* (London: Faber and Faber, 1947), and *Fundamentalism and the Church of God* (London: SCM, 1957). The latter contains some criticism of evangelical views of Scripture and provoked a response from James I. Packer, *'Fundamentalism' and the Word of God* (London: Inter-Varsity Fellowship, 1958).

is the tendency to see Moses and Sinai as a new beginning in a way that can separate it from the promises to Abraham. The second is the failure to give full significance to the glories of David and Solomon and to recognize that 1 Kings 3 – 10 is an important fulfilment of the promises to Abraham. The third is the downplaying of the role of prophetic eschatology and the way it recapitulates the progress of salvation history from the beginning to David's son and the temple in Zion. The fourth is that it does not, in my opinion, provide the best basis for a working typology.

If we grant that the overall timeline of the Bible from Genesis 1 to Revelation 21 – 22 contains the theme of creation to new creation, it is not surprising that the progressive revelation contains this theme of creation both in repetition and intensification. This is what typology is all about. The biblical pattern starts with the original order of creation that is disrupted by human rebellion and the Fall. The redemptive process, following the loss of both Eden and fellowship with God, has its main expression in the promise to Abraham of a land and restored fellowship with God. This climaxes in the glories of David and Solomon, Zion and the temple, but it is glory within the fallen world. The prophetic eschatology points towards the restoration of the pre-Fall situation in terms of the outworking of the promises to Abraham. This perspective includes the renewal of all things so that the new heaven and the new earth are foretold as the context of fulfilment. The new creation is first and foremost found in Jesus Christ whose life, death and resurrection are the redemptive means of that which belongs initially to Christ becoming also the possession of all God's people. The consummation of Christ's work is the new heavens and the new earth as the dwelling of God with his people. This is at the heart of the Robinson–Hebert perspective on biblical theology. It is, in my opinion, a better analysis of the dynamic and structure of biblical revelation than the alternatives that have been proposed.[11]

---

11. Perhaps it is not too far fetched to propose that the Vos–Clowney schema has been influenced to some degree by the connection of its adherents with the Westminster tradition. The Westminster Confession's teaching on the covenant of works with Adam, later given expression in the Decalogue, could well reinforce the parameters of Adam–Moses–Christ. By contrast, the adherents of the threefold schema, including Phythian-Adams, Hebert, Robinson and myself, all come from the Anglican tradition in which the Thirty-Nine Articles, by comparison to the Westminster Confession, are minimalist in their definition of the articles of our faith, and in particular in defining the significance of the Law. So, for example, the sabbatarianism of Westminster is completely absent from the Thirty-Nine Articles.

9. TYPOLOGY

Robinson's typology

At the heart of Donald Robinson's method of biblical theology lies his discernment of typology. In his lecture of 1996, after outlining the course in biblical theology that he originally devised and taught, he goes on to say:

> Based on the foregoing understanding of what the Bible is 'about', we enunciated a biblical 'typology' using the three stages in the outworking of God's promise to Abraham, that is, (a) the historical experience of the fulfilment of God's promise to Abraham through the exodus to the kingdom of David's son in the land of inheritance, (b) the projection of this fulfilment into the future of the day of the Lord, by the prophets, during the period of decline, fall, exile and return, and (c) the true fulfilment in Christ and the Spirit in Jesus' incarnation, death, resurrection, exaltation and in his parousia as judge and saviour in a new heaven and new earth.[1]

---

1. Donald W. B. Robinson, 'Origins and Unresolved Tensions', in Richard J. Gibson (ed.), *Interpreting God's Plan: Biblical Theology and the Pastor*, Explorations 11 (Adelaide: Open Book; Carlisle: Paternoster, 1997), p. 9. Although this passage is quoted in chapter 1, I thought it worth repeating here as a statement that is seminal to our subject.

The foregoing understanding of what the Bible is about involves his determination to engage in 'the study of the Bible *in its own terms*'.[2] Such an inductive approach is at the heart of biblical theology, but is done within the parameters of evangelical presuppositions about the nature of the Bible and its authority. As I have been at pains to demonstrate, the typological structure Robinson arrives at differs somewhat from the epochal structures determined by Vos and his disciples. It is clear that Robinson uses the word 'typology' in his own way by defining it in terms of the 'three stages' of revelation that he discerns in the Bible. These are not so much epochs as modes of revelation. *Epoch*, however, is not an entirely inappropriate term in that these stages are sequential though with some overlap of the first two.

I have already discussed the fact that Robinson's designation of the first stage in terms of 'the historical experience of the fulfilment of God's promise to Abraham through the exodus to the kingdom of David's son in the land of inheritance' in no way separates it from the first eleven chapters of Genesis, nor, for that matter, from the history subsequent to the heyday of the reigns of David and Solomon. The history of Israel's decline and subsequent exile constitute an overall reversal of the blessings of the period from Abraham to Solomon. This reversal is contemporary with the revelation in Robinson's second stage, which is constituted by the eschatology of the Latter Prophets. Prophetic eschatology includes a projection of the decline of the nation towards its destruction and the exile. Destruction and restoration are perceived in both more immediate and more distant terms. Robinson's treatment allows for the overlap of the stages, which, in turn, makes for more subtle nuances in the understanding of the revelation of redemption than are allowed by Clowney's single epoch from Moses to Christ. The non-fulfilment of the promises to Abraham during the period from 1 Kings 11 through to the end of the Old Testament is thus complemented and answered by 'the projection of this fulfilment into the future of the day of the Lord, by the prophets, during the period of decline, fall, exile and return'.[3] The prophetic perspective on judgment does not override the gracious promises of God. The recapitulation of Israel's history in prophetic eschatology not only recalls the promises to Abraham, but extends the purview right back to creation itself.

When we come to Robinson's third mode of revelation we have the antitype of the typology within both Old Testament history and prophetic eschatology. But we note that he again states it in such a way that we are

---

2. Ibid., p. 7, italics mine.
3. Ibid., p. 9.

forced to come to terms with the internal structures of the New Testament. The statement itself is deceptively brief as it involves 'the true fulfilment in Christ and the Spirit in Jesus' incarnation, death, resurrection, exaltation and in his parousia as judge and saviour in a new heaven and new earth'.[4] Here the antitype is found in three further stages: fulfilment in the incarnate Christ, fulfilment in the Spirit (the corollary of Jesus' exaltation) and fulfilment in the parousia. Christ indeed fulfilled the promises when he came in the flesh, lived, died, rose and ascended. The Spirit is involved in all of this, but is further involved in making those events real to those who participate in union with Christ by faith. Promise always involves tension between the 'now' and the 'not yet' (Rom. 8:24–25). It was so for Abraham and the believing Israelites. It was so for all those who clung to the promises of the prophets about the coming salvation in the Day of the Lord. And it has always been so for Christian believers who walk by faith and not by sight and hold fast to the promises of God that Jesus will return to consummate all his promises. The present age of the church is the age of the Holy Spirit's work in connecting the world of sinners with the redeeming word of Christ.

In *Faith's Framework* Robinson raises the question of the origin of the notion of the kingdom of God, which is most frequently referred to in the Synoptic Gospels.[5] It clearly has its roots in the kingdom concept in the Old Testament. In both Testaments the concept of God's rule is both present and future. In reviewing the experience of God's people in the Old Testament he shows that there is first the historical experience of God's rule in the blessing of Jacob and his sons, which leads to the kingdoms of David and Solomon 'with all the benefits of security, plenty and peace'.[6] The second phase is

> the prophetic reflection on God's rule, when the kingdom of David was no more, the nation divided and scattered, and the symbols of God's presence and blessing – the land, Jerusalem, and the temple – either ruined or possessed ambiguously to only a very small degree by a segment of the people or a few survivors.[7]

It is during this phase and further to the prophetic reflection on the disaster that has befallen them, that their message of hope is enunciated.

---

4. Ibid.

5. Donald W. B. Robinson, *Faith's Framework: The Structure of New Testament Theology* (Exeter: Paternoster; Sutherland, NSW: Albatross, 1985), pp. 72–75.

6. Ibid., p. 74.

7. Ibid., p. 75.

Yet to this second period belong the great prophecies of the establishment or re-establishment of God's kingdom in the land and over all nations: another exodus, another possession of Canaan, another Jerusalem and Temple, the reappearance of David the king to reign in righteousness, a new covenant.[8]

This, Robinson says, is the core of the promise to Abraham. It is this Old Testament prefigurement or preparation for the kingdom of Christ in the New Testament that constitutes typology. Typology is a way of describing the comprehensive nature of this prefigurement of the fulfilment in Christ.

That this typological framework informed Robinson's thinking and writing more generally is seen in his short work on eschatology, *The Hope of Christ's Coming*.[9] In order to understand the eschatological hope of the New Testament he examines its antecedents in the Old Testament in a chapter on 'The Day of the Lord'. The following quotation shows with absolute clarity the importance Robinson places on the notion of the recapitulation of Israel's earlier history and history in the prophetic eschatology. This is seen as the basis for the New Testament proclamation of fulfilment in Christ:

> The blessings of God's End-time are described in the Old Testament for the most part in terms drawn from Israel's past history. The day of the Lord would be Israel's history all over again, but new with the newness of God. There would be a new Exodus, a new redemption from slavery and a new entry into the land of promise (Jer. 16:14, 15); a new covenant and a new law (Jer. 31:31–34). No foe would invade the promised inheritance, 'but they shall sit every man under his vine and under his fig tree; and none shall make them afraid' (Micah 4:4). There would be a new Jerusalem (Isa. 26:1, Ez. 40) and a new David to be God's shepherd over Israel (Jer. 23:5, Ez. 34:23, 24) and a new Temple where perfect worship would be offered and from which a perfect law would go forth (Isa. 2:2–4, Ez. 40–46). It would not be too much to say that Israel's history, imperfectly experienced in the past, would find its perfect fulfilment 'in that day.'[10]

---

8. Ibid.
9. Donald W. B. Robinson, *The Hope of Christ's Coming* (Beecroft, NSW: Evangelical Tracts and Publications, 1958). In the foreword Robinson indicates that the material was first given as studies at the 1954 Clergy School of the Anglican Diocese of Sydney. In the rewriting for publication he acknowledges the criticisms and suggestions of his colleague at Moore College, Dr Broughton Knox and, once again, of his friend A. G. Hebert of St Michael's House, Adelaide.
10. Ibid., p. 13.

Robinson's typology is wider than the repetition of Israel's history in that it sees the End as transcending and fulfilling the whole history of creation. 'Indeed, nothing less than a new creation, a new heaven and a new earth, could contain all that God has in store for the End (Isa. 65:17).'[11] There is, of course, nothing particularly original in this understanding of the Old Testament prophetic eschatology. The important thing for this discussion is the way these perspectives inform Robinson's understanding of the New Testament. Unlike some other Reformed biblical theologians he has, in my opinion, understood the way both the universalism of creation and new creation, and the particularism of Abraham and his descendants, all feature in the theology of the New Testament. This is a matter we shall examine in more detail in the next chapter.

Approaches to typology

Different approaches have been taken to the study of typology understood as a property of Scripture. One method has been to investigate the occurrences of *typos* and its cognates in the LXX and the New Testament.[12] There is, of course, some value in trying to understand if this set of vocables yield a consistent understanding of some dynamic within the text of the Bible, especially as the word *typology* has become part of the vocabulary of biblical studies with a fair consensus as to its meaning. However, as David Baker points out, the semantic field of *typos* words is not unlike, for example, words that relate to *deigma* (specimen, example) and its cognates.[13] The dangers inherent in word studies are now too well known for us to need to linger here.

Another approach is to study inductively the dynamics of the larger canonical corpora with regard to patterns of repetition or recapitulation. This of necessity means going beyond the instances of *typos* words, found mainly in the New Testament, and the matters they refer to. The common feature in these instances appears to be that of some kind of prefigurement by the type of what comes later. The idea that *typology* is a term that must be reserved only for the explicit cases in the New Testament that are described

---

11. Ibid.

12. So David L. Baker, *Two Testaments, One Bible: The Theological Relationship Between the Old and New Testaments*, 3rd ed. (Nottingham: Apollos; Downers Grove: IVP, 2010), ch. 7.

13. Ibid., pp. 175–176.

as types or typical is too restrictive and is not followed in the majority of discussions. What we find, rather, is that a notion of typology has emerged that does attract a certain consensus, namely (1) that it is based on historical (or narrated) events including persons, institutions and ceremonies; (2) that it involves some kind of intensification from the type to its antitype; and (3) that it involves some kind of eschatological perspective.

That typology involves an interpretation of history confronts us with the matter of the nature of biblical history. For some scholars the type, as a pattern in the biblical history, does not necessarily mean that it expresses a divine design in the process of revelation, but only that it was so understood by the faithful and by the writers of the relevant documents. Even more sceptical is the assessment that the typological patterns are literary ploys, largely in the construction of antitypes, which do not reflect reality. An evangelical approach, however, treats such patterns in Scripture as reliable expressions of the sovereign work of God. The notion of salvation history examined in chapter 3 is relevant to this discussion. We recognize that *Heilsgeschichte* (biblical faith-claims to historical fact and God's control over it) and *Historie* (established historical facts) are not totally disparate notions of what actually happened in the past. The fact that biblical-historical narrative does not necessarily follow the same rules as modern historiography does not mean that we cannot have confidence in the biblical retelling of events as historical.[14]

Leonhard Goppelt

The modern discussion of typology gained momentum with Leonhard Goppelt's monograph of 1939, *Typos*.[15] But as E. Earle Ellis states in his preface to the English edition, 'a typological understanding of Scripture governed the interpretation of NT writers and continued to be followed, more or less closely, by Irenaeus of Lyon (ca. A.D. 125–195) and by the

---

14. See my discussion of this matter in my *Gospel-Centred Hermeneutics* (Nottingham: Apollos; Downers Grove: IVP, 2006), ch. 15. The matter is discussed more fully in V. Philips Long, *The Art of Biblical History*, Foundations of Contemporary Interpretation, vol. 5 (Grand Rapids: Zondervan, 1994).

15. Leonhard Goppelt, *Typos: Die typologische Deutung des Alten Testaments im Neuen* (Darmstadt: Wissenschaftliche Buchgesellschaft, 1973), first published in 1939 by C. Bertelsmann. English translation, *Typos: The Typological Interpretation of the Old Testament in the New* (Grand Rapids: Eerdmans, 1982). References hereafter to the English edition.

patristic school of Antioch'.[16] Ellis gives a further very useful brief analysis thus:

> Unlike allegorical exposition, the typology of the NT writers represents the
> OT not as a book of metaphors hiding a deeper meaning but as an account of
> historical events and teachings from which the meaning of the text arises. Unlike
> a Judaizing hermeneutic, typology views the relationship of OT events to those in
> the new dispensation not as a 'one-to-one' equation or correspondence, in which
> the old is repeated or continued, but rather in terms of two principles, historical
> correspondence and escalation.[17]

Goppelt's analysis of Hellenistic Judaism focuses first on the allegorizing of Philo. He understands Philo's method to be driven by Platonism so that it does not take seriously God working in history.[18] By contrast, Goppelt speaks approvingly of J. Gerhard's definition: 'Typology consists in the comparison of facts. Allegory is not concerned with the facts but with the words from which it draws out useful and hidden doctrine.'[19] He defines his task thus:

> The concept of typology with which we begin may be defined and distinguished
> from other methods of interpretation as follows: Only historical facts – persons,
> actions, events, and institutions – are material for typological interpretation; words
> and narratives can be utilized only insofar as they deal with such matters. These
> things are to be interpreted typologically only if they are considered to be divinely
> ordained representations or types of future realities that will be even greater and
> more complete.[20]

Goppelt thus places his understanding of typology in the general area of salvation history, and as embracing the idea of the escalation of the historical facts. 'Typology demonstrates not only the nature of the new in comparison with the old, but also shows that the new is founded directly and solely on redemptive history.'[21]

In dealing with the use of the Old Testament in the Synoptic Gospels he

---

16. E. E. Ellis, forward to English translation of Goppelt's *Typos*, p. ix.

17. Ibid., p. x.

18. Ibid., p. 52.

19. Ibid., p. 7.

20. Ibid., p. 17.

21. Ibid., p. 152.

claims, 'The way in which the OT passages are introduced suggests that theirs is a typological approach which looks for similarity in essentials, not simply for the fulfillment of external features.'[22] He also sees the actuality of the type emerging when the significance of Jesus is apprehended:

> The full meaning that the NT finds for Jesus Christ in his typological relationship to the OT can be appreciated only when we consider how Christ was viewed by his church, the ones for whom his ministry, as well as his suffering, death, and resurrection, were intended.[23]

But this is not a one-way affair with the New Testament giving the definitive meaning of the Old as the typology emerges. In speaking of Paul's understanding of the veil being removed from Jewish readings of Scripture only when there is knowledge of Christ (2 Cor. 3:15–16) he goes on to state, 'There is a dialectical interplay in this because Christ opens the meaning of Scripture, and Scripture reveals the significance of Christ.'[24]

Hebrews is especially significant for its extended use of typology. Goppelt concludes the following from his study of Hebrews:

> These terms indicate that typology is a comparative relationship and is arranged qualitatively rather than quantitatively. The type is not essentially a miniature version of the antitype, but is a prefiguration in a different stage of redemptive history that indicates the outline of essential features (σκιά, παραβολή–εἰκών) of the future reality and that loses its own significance when that reality appears.[25]

But that significance is real in the type:

> A type is not the mechanically reduced prototype of something greater; rather, it presents some basic element in the relationship between God and man that was not fulfilled in the Old Covenant, but is fulfilled in Christ.[26]

---

22. Ibid., p. 103.

23. Ibid., p. 106.

24. Ibid., p. 128. This is similar to Vischer's assertion that whereas the Old Testament tells us what the Christ is, the New Testament tells us who he is (Wilhelm Vischer, *The Witness of the Old Testament to Christ*, tr. A. B. Crabtree [London: Lutterworth, 1949], p. 7).

25. *Typos*, p. 177.

26. Ibid., p. 176.

Goppelt's approach is closely integrated with a view of redemptive history that allows him to avoid being confined to explicit New Testament quotations of Old Testament texts. Indeed most of the references to Scripture are by allusion.[27] The centrality of redemptive history means that the New Testament writers 'are convinced that there is continuity between OT history and Jesus Christ in the sense of preparation and fulfillment'.[28] The integrity of typology rests in the fact that the New Testament writers are not simply reading salvation back into the Scripture. 'The OT type retains its own independent status as something God has ordained, and this is why it can serve as a true type.'[29]

Is typology, then, a way of understanding the Old Testament, or of expounding the message of the New? In the light of this discussion it must be seen as both. Goppelt leaves no doubt that he understands the priority in the exposition of Christ. Of typology he says as follows:

> The NT does not regard it as a formal hermeneutical technique . . . It is simply an indication of the relationship that results from the fact that salvation is a present reality in the NT. . . . The results of typological exegesis are primarily statements about NT salvation, not statements about the OT. The typological heightening indicates that something new is breaking in and shows the importance of this event. . . . Typology helps faith to recognize the greatness of Jesus. He who by his word and action is greater than any of the OT heralds of salvation is the Christ of God.[30]

This would seem to be saying that it is the nature of the gospel as that which not only occurs within redemptive history, but is its climax, that makes typology not merely possible but necessary. Typology is thus never fortuitous but is ruled by the sovereignty of God. It also asserts that the continuity between the Testaments includes the fact that it is the same God who acts in both. The fullness of the antitype never makes consideration of the type superfluous. Thus viewed, it underlines the assertion that the true believers of the Old Testament were saved through faith in Christ: by grasping the type by faith they truly grasped the antitype.

---

27. Ibid., p. 198.
28. Ibid., p. 199.
29. Ibid.
30. Ibid., pp. 200–201.

Gerhard von Rad and Walther Eichrodt

Two other German theologians of significance, von Rad and Eichrodt, should be noted. Gerhard von Rad's important essay on typology was originally published in 1952. For von Rad typology is not a specifically theological concern but 'an elementary function of all human thought and interpretation'.[31] 'It rises out of man's universal effort to understand the phenomena about him on the basis of concrete analogies.'[32] It is simply a way of recognizing regularity and order in relationships. Nevertheless 'The Old Testament . . . is dominated by an essentially different form of typological thinking, namely, that of the eschatological correspondence between beginning and end (*Urzeit und Endzeit*).'[33] The issue of the events and their later interpretation emerges as von Rad focuses on the analogical thinking in the New Testament. Nevertheless he asserts that the Old Testament is a history book.[34] But it is a history of faith:

> Clearly a *credendum* has here been projected into history. That is to say, the redemptive activity of God toward Israel has been portrayed as the unity that it was believed to be; a *doxa* is heaped on the event which reaches far beyond what actually occurred, for what is believed in is placed on view as something already effectuated in history.[35]

It seems that von Rad regards the theological interpretation as imposed by means of shaping the record of events. But, leaving aside the dispute over whether or not *Historie* and *Heilsgeschichte* are essentially the same or widely separated, we can understand the seriousness with which von Rad views typological interpretation as a way that the New Testament understands the Old. It provides a unity for the canon in that 'the same God who revealed himself in Christ has also left his footprints in the history of the Old Testament covenant people'.[36] Significantly von Rad recognizes that typology cannot be confined

---

31. Gerhard von Rad, 'Typological Interpretation of the Old Testament', tr. John Bright, in Claus Westermann (ed.), *Essays on Old Testament Hermeneutics* (Richmond, Va.: John Knox, 1964), p. 17.

32. Gerhard von Rad, *Old Testament Theology*, vol. 2: *The Theology of Israel's Prophetic Traditions*, tr. D. M. G. Stalker (Edinburgh: Oliver & Boyd, 1965), p. 364.

33. Von Rad, 'Typological Interpretation', p. 19.

34. Ibid., p. 25.

35. Ibid., p. 34.

36. Ibid., p. 36.

to a few explicitly designated correspondences: there is no limit to the types in the Old Testament.

> [T]ypological interpretation has to do with the entire Old Testament. . . . Wherever one of God's dealings with his people, or with an individual, is witnessed to, the possibility exists of seeing in this a shadow of the New Testament revelation of Christ. The number of Old Testament types is unlimited.[37]

In agreement with the general run of views on typology, von Rad recognizes the essence of typology is in its kerygmatic content and in the way the antitype completes the type by removing its limitations. In the end he is content to speak of the Old Testament witness to Christ.[38]

Walther Eichrodt's *Theology of the Old Testament* was first published in German in 1933.[39] His essay on typology appeared in the Westermann volume in 1960.[40] Typology is for Eichrodt a view of history, but the types do not gain significance only from the New Testament events:

> On the contrary, these are quite concrete things taken from the historical narratives of the Old Testament, which, precisely because of their real historical function, appear as valuable testimony to the divine governance of history.[41]

Thus it is not mere analogy that makes them types, but

> their religious and theological significance in the historical revelation of the Old Testament gives to them their significance as divinely established prerepresentations of important elements in the salvation manifested in Christ.[42]

This contrasts with allegory, which depreciates history. Eichrodt conceives of typology as a means by which the Christian community understands both the

---

37. Ibid.

38. Ibid. p. 39.

39. Walther Eichrodt, *Theology of the Old Testament* (London: SCM, 1961). English version tr. John Baker from the 6th ed. of the German.

40. Walther Eichrodt, 'Is Typological Exegesis an Appropriated Method?', in Claus Westermann (ed.), *Essays on Old Testament Hermeneutics*, English version edited by James Luther Mays (Richmond: John Knox, 1964), pp. 224–245.

41. 'Typological Exegesis', p. 226.

42. Ibid., p. 227.

termination of the history of salvation and its continuity so that the following occurs:

> On the other side, like its own Lord, Jesus Christ himself, the community feels
> the forces and gifts of this history of salvation to be so living and so directly active
> in its own existence that it takes this book right into its own life, completely
> avoiding any rational opposition to the law, and, full of joy and amazement, provides
> witness in it to its own possession of salvation and thus finds that this possession
> has been planned and prepared from long beforehand by the faithfulness of
> God.[43]

This significant statement is, however, qualified by Eichrodt's assertion that our view of history that is now formed by historical criticism means that we cannot read the historical testimony of the Old Testament in the pre-critical fashion of the New Testament.[44] Nevertheless he does not abandon typology, since it is integral to the Old Testament itself:

> Thus typology belongs in principle to prophecy; it is extremely closely connected with
> the eschatological hope and must be explained from the same fundamental forces
> as the latter. This suggestion is confirmed by the fact that even in Old Testament
> prophecy itself typology is already playing a part.[45]

Eichrodt has a parting shot at von Rad's views on the matter: 'One would not be able . . . to make the whole exposition of the Old Testament into typo-logical exegesis, as von Rad proposes in his well-known essay.'[46] According to Rolf Rendtorff, however, von Rad's position is not to be confused with that of Wilhelm Vischer.[47] Vischer is interesting and significant because of his attempts to rescue the Old Testament, not only in the face of the German anti-Semitism of the 1930s, but also from the prevailing biblical scholarship that reduced biblical theology to the history of religion. On examining some examples of Vischer's exegesis, Rendtorff suggests that

---

43. Ibid., p. 230.
44. Ibid., p. 232.
45. Ibid., p. 234.
46. Ibid., p. 244.
47. Rolf Rendtorff, *Canon and Theology: Overtures to an Old Testament Theology*, tr. Margaret Kohl (Minneapolis: Fortress, 1993), ch. 8.

the exegetical scholar is frequently faced with the question whether he is not led by mere associations, which are not merely unsupported by the exegesis of the text but are also incapable of contributing anything to the theological understanding of it.[48]

Rendtorff notes von Rad's criticism of Vischer as that of reducing the Old Testament utterances in every case to the greatest possible generality, or common denominator. Thus 'The choir of voices that witness to God's judgment and salvation is infinitely more varied than Vischer describes it as being.'[49] It would appear that von Rad's objection was not that Vischer engaged in a Christological interpretation of the Old Testament, but that he fragmented the text in his attempt to make the links with the New Testament.[50] Thus, Rendtorff comments, 'This too is an important hermeneutical viewpoint: not to split up the texts into small units, but to ask about the wider contexts and to seek in these above all the essential theological utterances.'[51]

The differently perceived distinctions between the historical events (*Historie*) and the interpretation of the events in the Old Testament texts (*Heilsgeschichte*) mean that the assessments of typology differ accordingly. For von Rad the reality of typology lies more in the textual presentation of the saving history of God than in the actual events. Similarly John Breck, writing from his position in Eastern Orthodoxy, can say, 'The type, then, consists of *interpreted events* whose historicity is of secondary importance. . . . Yet this should not be construed to imply that "history doesn't matter," that it is immaterial whether the Exodus occurred or not.'[52] Thus 'The interpretation has priority over the event in the sense that the antitype is perceived only in the light of that interpretation.'[53] Typology, on Breck's view, is more what happens in the textual interpretations of events than what is inherent in the events themselves. From an evangelical point of view this would appear to reduce the value of the antitype since it is understood in the light of something that is not quite what it purports to be. Yet Breck prefaces his remarks on typology by asserting his presuppositions of the absolute sovereignty of God, his govern-

---

48. Ibid., pp. 81–82.

49. Ibid., p. 83.

50. Ibid., p. 84.

51. Ibid.

52. John Breck, *Scripture in Tradition: The Bible and its Interpretation in the Orthodox Church* (Crestwood, N.Y.: St Vladimir's Seminary Press, 2001), p. 28, italics his.

53. Ibid.

ance of all events in history, and the ordering of salvation history in terms of promise and fulfilment.[54] It is difficult to see how this squares with his assertion that the historicity of the interpreted events is of secondary importance.

Some issues in the debate

The foregoing discussions by a number of important biblical scholars suggest that there are some significant points of convergence among them as well as significant points of disagreement. Some definitions of typology limit its scope; others broaden it. There is a general consensus that typology exists, and that it involves events, people and institutions in the Old Testament that prefigure aspects of the New Testament's teaching about Jesus Christ. For some biblical theologians typology exists as little more than literary fictional devices to make religious points. For others typology exists as God-given revelations that are a part of real history and foreshadow the central event of real world history. There is a general recognition that the antitype represents some kind of significant correspondence to the type in theological meaning, and some kind of intensification so that the antitype renders the type in some way redundant. It is never completely redundant, since without the type we could not fully understand the antitype for what it is. If antitype and fulfilment are perspicuous without their respective type and promise, this would also seem to render the whole Old Testament superfluous to Christian theology.

The purpose of the foregoing survey is not to give a comprehensive summary of views on typology and the ongoing debate, but rather to show the broad lines of agreement of the notion that enable us to place Robinson's typological theory and method well within this consensus. There is, however, one area in his thinking that I regard as worthy of special note. It seems to me that the implications of his brief exposition of the subject put him more in agreement with von Rad's view that there is no limit to types. This derestriction follows from von Rad's view that typology 'rises out of man's universal effort to understand the phenomena about him on the basis of concrete analogies'.[55] It is simply a way of recognizing regularity and order in relationships. For Robinson, typology expresses itself in the full range of significant dimensions to the biblical story stretching from creation itself to the glories of the

---

54. Ibid., p. 21.

55. Gerhard von Rad, *Old Testament Theology*, vol. 2: *The Theology of Israel's Prophetic Traditions*, tr. D. M. G. Stalker (Edinburgh: Oliver & Boyd, 1965), p. 364.

kingdom in Jerusalem with its Davidic kingship and the temple. Elsewhere I have indicated my view that New Testament Christology includes a comprehensive summing up in the person and work of Christ of all the biblical elements.[56]

Macro-typology

The macro-typology I propose is a way of showing the comprehensive nature of the fulfilment of God's promises in Christ. I regard this notion as being at the heart of Robinson's typology. When we allow the Old Testament categories to expand to their full potential, antitype is shown to be broader than the mere fulfilment of certain explicit types and promises. Biblical theological study of the events, people and institutions provides us with a comprehensive view of reality and God's part in it. On this view, typology has regard for the full scope of God's redemptive work in that salvation means that he restores everything that was lost or marred by the Fall. According to Paul's take on Genesis 3, this involves the entire creation (Rom. 8:18–23). It was also Paul who declared the resurrection to be the locus of fulfilment of all God's promises (Acts 13:32–33). Paul's cosmic Christology, especially in Colossians 1:15–20[57] and in Ephesians 1:10, would appear to present a view that God has drawn all things together in Christ, through whom and for whom all things were created.

In my *Gospel-Centred Hermeneutics*[58] I have outlined my view of the way Jesus sums up for us the whole of reality. It is also my contention that Ephesians 1:10 should not be confined to the eschatological consummation. Paul's reference to God's making known the mystery of his will, 'according to his purpose, which he set forth in Christ as a plan for the fullness of time, to unite all things in him, things in heaven and things on earth', is significant. The idea of the fullness of time lies behind Jesus' announcement of the gospel in Mark 1:15 that '[t]he time is fulfilled'.[59] Paul also refers to the fullness of time as the moment of the incarnation (Gal. 4:4). It is not that Ephesians 1:10 does not refer to the time of Christ's return in glory, but that the structure of New

---

56. *Gospel-Centred Hermeneutics*, ch. 16.

57. See above chapter 8, pp. 152–153.

58. *Gospel-Centred Hermeneutics*, pp. 248–257.

59. The impact of which is seriously weakened in the NIV's translation as 'the time has come'.

Testament eschatology requires that we at least consider that it is both fulfilled now in the incarnation and awaiting its consummation at Christ's return. That is, what happened in Jesus' first advent as fulfiller of all God's promises is the paradigm of what will happen at his parousia. Everything was fulfilled in him representatively at his first coming, and everything will be fulfilled in a universal consummation at his return.

The summing up of all things in Christ (Eph. 1:10) is, in my view, integral to typology. I hasten to add that I am unaware of any exposition of typology by Robinson that explicitly takes this logical further step from his schema of typology. Nevertheless I believe the seeds of it are there in what he proposes. As I understand the quotation above from Robinson's own exposition of his method,[60] he is in fact proposing that the three stages of revelation are, first, the type in the biblical history; secondly, the confirmation of the type in the way the prophets look forward to a recapitulation in a perfected eschatological form of the events of redemptive history; and thirdly, the antitype in the fulfilment in Christ. The antitype in Christ involves the events from the incarnation and ministry of Jesus through to the parousia. In *The Hope of Christ's Coming* Robinson refers to the fact that the end has been inaugurated in the earth, but is yet to be consummated.[61] The point I wish to stress is that Robinson's typology is consistent with the macro-typology I propose, and that his threefold schema is what drives it. That is, typology is not restricted to certain key people, events and institutions that are prominent in the salvation history of the Bible, but rather the whole first stage is typological of the coming of Christ. The whole prophetic perspective of the Day of the Lord is also typological and confirms the typology of the revelation in biblical history. Thus I suggest that Robinson's typology allows that there is no limit to types in Scripture other than Scripture itself, which embraces the whole of reality.

Coupled with this is the understanding of the incarnation that allows it to be the 'summing up of all things in him'. Our Christology aids us here. The union of God and Man in Jesus is the bringing together in perfect harmony of all the dimensions of reality: God, humanity and the created order. Adam was made from the dust and, theologically, is the pinnacle of creation, so that Adam's fall involves the fall of the whole creation (Gen. 3). The revealing of the sons of God in Christ will in like manner bring about the restoration of the whole created order (Rom. 8:19–24). Robinson's typology, then, enables us to

---

60. See p. 170 above.

61. *Hope of Christ's Coming*, p. 17.

take a comprehensive view of the biblical exposition of reality as that which is restored in Christ to what it was intended to be by the Creator. Reality is expressed in the doctrine of creation and of God's relationship to his creation. There is no aspect of reality that is not included in this biblical view. *There is no aspect of reality that is not involved in the person and work of Christ.*

Once we step outside the merely literary consideration of *typos* words we can ask what constitutes legitimate typology. Greidanus has pointed to one significant contribution of Genesis being the establishment of 'a world view that is assumed but not necessarily taught by later Scriptures'. A world view, he says, 'consists of the knowledge of three entities and their interrelationship: God, the cosmos, and human beings'. [62] This analysis is not new as, for example, it is used by Vriezen to structure his Old Testament Theology.[63] It has also been my own chosen approach to biblical theology.[64] It may seem to state the obvious, but the implications are important for typology. This threefold world view of the Bible encompasses all of reality. The only element not explicitly included is that of the angelic beings. These, however, do belong to what is created and thus are a part of the cosmos and impinge on the world. The reason for distinguishing humanity from the rest of creation is simply that the Bible makes this distinction because the destiny of all creation is bound up with the destiny of humanity. But this is not to separate these two parts of creation. I suggest that our world view and our Christology make it necessary to enlarge the idea of typology to encompass everything found in the Old Testament, indeed in all reality *when stated in biblical categories.*

To express this broad view of a macro-typology is not to throw caution to the wind. The removal of limits to typology does not mean that anything goes, or that we take a cavalier attitude to finding types of Christ in every little detail on the basis of some association of ideas.[65] The pomegranates on the

---

62. Sidney Greidanus, *Preaching Christ from Genesis: Foundations for Expository Sermons* (Grand Rapids: Eerdmans, 2007), p. 7.

63. Th. C. Vriezen, *An Outline of Old Testament Theology* (Oxford: Blackwell, 1958).

64. God's people in God's place under God's rule is my characterization of the kingdom of God in Graeme Goldsworthy, *Gospel and Kingdom: A Christian Interpretation of the Old Testament*, Exeter: Paternoster, republished in *The Goldsworthy Trilogy* (Milton Keynes: Paternoster, 2000), and God, humanity and world (*kosmos*) in Graeme Goldsworthy, *According to Plan: The Unfolding Revelation of God in the Bible* (Leicester: IVP, 1991; Downers Grove: IVP, 2002).

65. What Greidanus rejects as typologizing, *Preaching Christ from Genesis*, p. 9.

robes of the Israelite priest are not types of the fruits of the Spirit. The circular hole for the priest's head in his robe is not a type of Christ's eternal nature. The redness of Rahab's cord is not a type of Jesus' blood.[66] Such is the use of fanciful, non-contextual associations that avoid the real theology behind these things. The context of typology is the entire stage of revelation in which it occurs. The typological value of a person, event or institution is governed by the role that each plays in the theology of the redemptive revelation within the stage of revelation in which it occurs.

The viability of this approach to typology hinges on the fact that God is concerned with all that is real. The Creator established the whole of creation in relationship to himself. One of the great contributions of the wisdom literature is the way it highlights the orderliness that God established and the common grace by which he maintains, even in a fallen creation, an order within which it is possible for us to live.[67] The redemptive work of Christ is to retrieve the orderliness of creation, including humanity, in its intended relationship with God. God sums up all things in Christ (Eph. 1:10); that is, he first puts the order back together *in* Christ who is true God and true man. To do this he must also deal with the fractured relationships that human sin has wrought. The cross becomes the place where this is done, as, 'For our sake he made him to be sin who knew no sin, so that in him we might become the righteousness of God' (2 Cor. 5:21). Well did Hans H. Schmid describe righteousness as world order.[68]

Figure 4 overleaf represents reality before the Fall. All things and people are in right relationship to the Creator. Humanity is part of the created order and is its pinnacle. Thus the fall of Adam brings with it the fall of all creation. All relationships between God and the created order, and all relationships within the created order, are adversely affected as they come under God's judgment on Adam's rebellion. In like manner, the restoration of all things in Christ as the New Creation (Figure 5 overleaf) results in the restoration of the created order. Put simply, first God restores all relationships in the person of the incarnated Jesus; then he begins the process of uniting his people to this Christ by faith in his reconciling work on the cross, and the Holy Spirit (the progress of the gospel in the world); and finally, at Christ's return, all things will be perfectly restored to their proper order.

---

66. If there is typology here it lies in the significance of an easily seen signal that people of faith are there and should be saved.

67. See my *Gospel and Wisdom*, in *Goldsworthy Trilogy*, pp. 329–550.

68. Hans H. Schmid, *Gerechtigkeit als Weltordnung* (Tübingen: J. C. B. Mohr, 1968).

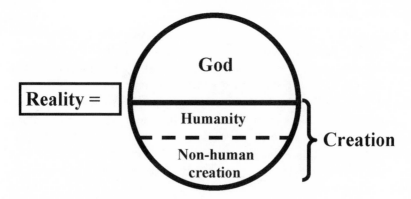

Figure 4: The biblical view of pre-Fall reality

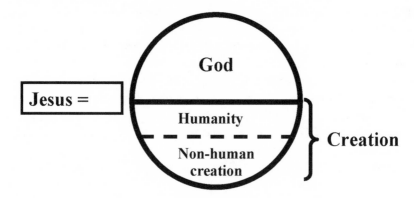

Figure 5: The biblical view of all things summed up in Christ

It is, then, not without value to be able to say that there is a typological link between every aspect of the Old Testament and the person of Jesus Christ. The exegetical and homiletic values of each individual link will depend on the significance of the person, event or institution within its context of redemptive revelation. At the very broadest level of typology, there are two kinds of created order: perfect (pre-Fall creation) and fallen. There are likewise two kinds of people: sinless or fallen. Other than Eden as the prototype sanctuary of God, where he has fellowship with his creatures, there are only imperfectly managed institutions that foreshadow the truth in the antitype. In other words, the great offices that are typological of Christ's ministry (prophet, priest, king and wise man) are exercised by sinful human beings until the antitype comes. That is why Hebrews can draw such a contrast between the priesthood of Israel and that of Christ (Heb. 8:1–7; 9:1–14, 24–26; 10:11–14).

I do not doubt for a moment that there is much value in the distinctions Greidanus makes between the various roads through the Old Testament to Christ. The link between, say, promise and fulfilment is different from other links such as typological events or analogies. But the promises are couched in terms that are typological of the ultimate fulfilment. Rather than following Griedanus's approach in making typology one of a number of 'roads' from Old to New Testament, I would propose an understanding of typology that embraces all of his valid distinctions and shows the underlying unity that exists between them. This lays bare the underlying structure or matrix of Scripture that generates the variety of connections. If we understand the substructure, we have a comprehensive basis for tracing the way that every text in the Old Testament is a testimony to Christ.

When we understand a typology that sees whole stages of revelation as typological, as Robinson's schema proposes, we are in a better position to find lateral interconnections within themes that otherwise might be restricted by distinguishing the varieties of connections between the Testaments. Thus when Greidanus asserts, in his treatment of Genesis 1:1 – 2:3 that there is no promise of Christ or typology in this passage, from his narrower definition of these categories of Old Testament to New Testament connections he is probably correct.[69] But, if God is summing up all things in Christ (Eph. 1:10), if Christ is the locus of the new creation (2 Cor. 5:17), and if the goal of Christ's person and work is the new heavens and new earth (Isa. 65:17; 2 Pet. 3:13), then it seems to me that the creation is broadly typological of the new creation and, therefore, of Christ who, in himself, is the representative new creation and the basis for the consummated new creation. This surely has potential for preaching the Old Testament as God's testimony to Christ.

---

69. *Preaching Christ from Genesis*, p. 50.

10. THE ROBINSON LEGACY

Robinson's typology and method in biblical theology

The first thing that needs to be reiterated here is that my debt to Donald Robinson, as the one who inspired me to do biblical theology along the lines of his thinking on the matter, is a debt that goes much further than to one man. Some would call this the Robinson–Hebert approach. Because I have written more extensively on the matter, it has sometimes even been identified as my own approach.[1] It has also, rather inaccurately, been spoken of as the Moore College approach to biblical theology.[2] What I owe to Donald

---

1. While this is personally gratifying to me, I hasten to say that this has come about because of my writings in which I have consistently expressed my gratitude to Donald Robinson. I also owe much to those who have enabled me to have my books published, especially Paternoster, IVP, Eerdmans, and those publishers that have produced translations in Korean, Chinese, Spanish, French and other languages.

2. Though Robinson developed his biblical theology at Moore College, and I taught along these lines at Moore for a number of years, it cannot be said that the members of the Moore faculty have followed some party line, or that there is some official Moore position on biblical theology. I believe there would be some broad

Robinson I also owe in part to Gabriel Hebert and, through them both, to many others.

Robinson's brief exposition of the structure of biblical revelation, which I referred to at the outset in this book, was given to a class of probably close to fifty theological students. I know how radically that exposition affected me. But I have no real knowledge of whether other students picked it up in the way I did, nor of what may have come from the fact that most of this class went on to ordination and active ministry. I can only suppose that Robinson dealt with the matter so briefly towards the end of our course in Old Testament because he was already expounding his biblical theology to the students in their first year.[3] Many Moore students would have benefited from Robinson's insights. The practical benefit of these insights lay in their application especially to the Old Testament. Most Christians are aware that the use of the Old Testament and its application to us is problematic. This has been my constant concern in practically all my writings and in my lecturing and preaching. What Robinson did for me was to awaken a sense of the need to go carefully into the whole subject of how we use the Old Testament, a subject that involves us in a close examination of how the New Testament understands and applies the Old Testament. Having said that, I am fully aware that the relationship of the two Testaments and, in particular, the way we use the Old Testament is full of difficulties. Although I have spent over fifty years reading, thinking, talking and writing about this matter, I still find preaching from the Old Testament often does not come easily.

To sum up the Robinson legacy in this matter I shall specify the following:

1. Donald Robinson gave me a sense of the unity of the Bible without discounting its diversity.
2. He opened up the Old Testament to me in a new and exciting way.
3. He helped me understand the whole Bible as Christian Scripture.
4. He gave me an understanding of the structure of revelation that is broad enough to embrace typology and all the other dimensions that make up the multifaceted relationship of the two Testaments.

---

consensus about a redemptive-historical approach to biblical theology. Beyond that I would not want to go.

3. The first-year course was a preliminary to the two-year ordination course. For reasons I will not go into here, I entered college in the ordination course and did not have the benefit of the preliminary year. This structure of the Moore College curriculum has long since ceased to exist.

5. He, among others, helped me develop the exegetical and hermeneutical tools for dealing with biblical texts so that the practical issues of preaching and teaching can be addressed.

6. He showed me that thematic studies are much broader than word studies and are capable of being approached with the method of biblical theology.

7. He demonstrated that evangelicals need to be in touch with non-evangelicals and their thinking.

8. He impressed me with the importance of biblical theology in the academy and in the ministry of the local church.

9. Perhaps more peripheral to the concerns of this book, but not unrelated, is that Robinson is what is sometimes referred to as a 'churchman'. He clearly loves Anglicanism, its traditions and its formularies. He is in many respects very conservative in these matters. One highlight for me as a student was the course of lectures he gave in 'Prayer Book' (Anglican Liturgy), which I found engrossing in that it gave me an appreciation of the role of liturgy and the genius of the Anglican Reformers. He also tutored us students in church music and psalmody in weekly periods spent in the College chapel.

The unity and diversity of the Bible

It is universally recognized that the Bible is characterized by both unity and diversity. Some see the unity as fairly slim and emphasize the diversity. Those who recognize a significant unity, however, are not without a sense of diversity.[4] Robinson's theology is consistent with his Reformed position in which both the continuity and discontinuity between the Testaments are taken into account. It is well expressed by Vern Poythress that a Christocentric approach means that 'Christ's climactic salvation includes within itself continuity and discontinuity in harmony'.[5] This thoroughly

---

4. In the important conservative study John S. Feinberg (ed.), *Continuity and Discontinuity: Perspectives on the Relationship Between the Old and New Testaments. Essays in Honor of S. Lewis Johnson, Jr.* (Westchester, Ill.: Crossway, 1988), each of the major subjects is treated in turn by a scholar who stresses continuity between the two Testaments and one who stresses discontinuity. Almost without exception the various authors point out that it is never either one *or* the other, either continuity or discontinuity, but rather a matter of emphasis.

5. Vern S. Poythress, *The Shadow of Christ in the Law of Moses* (Brentwood, Tenn.: Wolgemuth & Hyatt, 1991), p. 285.

Chalcedonian perspective of harmony of dimensions, which are so often treated as being in conflict, informs the Reformed hermeneutic and enables the apparent problem of unity and diversity to be dealt with.[6] There can be no discord between the dimensions of unity and distinction within the word of God who, as Trinity, is unity and distinction within himself. The trinitarian reality of God and the unity-distinction of the union of the two natures of Christ become a key hermeneutic principle in dealing with the biblical text.[7]

Robinson's system of typology, as in the case of any typological approach, recognizes the distinctions drawn between the type and the antitype. For me, the insights I gained from biblical theology meant that I could try to avoid two prevailing but opposite problematic approaches in some evangelical treatments of the Old Testament. The one simply assumes a unity that allows the Christian to read the Old Testament as if it were originally written especially for us and directed immediately to us as Christians. This encourages moralizing and legalism through an overemphasis on an exemplary view of the characters and events in the narrative, and through a more direct application of the Law. The other avoids this direct application but has little to offer in its place. The result is often an implied canon within the canon as the reader or preacher concentrates on the few selected texts he or she feels comfortable with as pointing to Christ or the Christian life.

The relevance of the Old Testament

One could not listen to Robinson's lectures on the Old Testament and remain oblivious to its vitality, inherent beauty and purpose. But, of course, it is his biblical theology that shows powerfully that the Old Testament Scriptures are

---

6. The Council of Chalcedon, AD 451, established a formula for expressing the reality of Christ's incarnation as being a union of God and man that neither fuses nor separates the two natures (J. Stevenson [ed.], *Creeds, Councils, and Controversies: Documents Illustrative of the History of the Church A.D. 337–461* [London: SPCK, 1975], p. 337).

7. Particularly in Chalcedonian theology, the *hypostatic union* was a technical term used to designate the union of the two natures of Christ as personal and resulting in one indivisible person. Thus, as Calvin states, '[W]e affirm his divinity so joined and united with his humanity that each retains its distinctive nature unimpaired, and yet these two natures constitute one Christ' (*Institutes of the Christian Religion*, tr. Ford Lewis Battles, LCC 20–21 [Philadelphia: Westminster; London: SCM, 1960], 2.14.1).

essential to the understanding of the Christ as the fulfiller. Once again we are confronted by the interdependence of the two Testaments and the fact that the New Testament exposition of Jesus and his mission is in terms of the fulfilment of the promises of the Old Testament. We have rehearsed this at length and it need not detain us here any further.

The whole Bible as Christian Scripture

Not long after Robinson's exposition of the biblical-theological perspective to our Old Testament class, the majority of us who had completed the ordination course were made deacons in the Anglican Church, most of us in Sydney. With a weekend parish appointment I continued at Moore College in order to finish off an external degree from London University. I was given some teaching assignments as a Junior Tutor in Hebrew and Old Testament at Moore. The latter task forced me to think through issues of biblical theology as I was asked to lecture on the prophet Joel. Over fifty years on and I still have the handwritten notes I worked from for these lectures. I am gratified to see references to what I regard as a result of Robinson's teaching in Old Testament and biblical theology. The notes show, however inadequately, my concern to exegete the text in its Old Testament canonical context and then to explore its necessary links with the New Testament.

Since those beginnings I have regarded the task of the Old Testament exegete unfinished until the passage in question is related to its fulfilment in Christ. The presupposition to this is the fact of the New Testament's witness to the Christ as the one who fulfils the Old Testament in every respect. As a preacher I have always felt it necessary to treat an Old Testament passage first and foremost as that which testifies to Christ. As a theological lecturer I was never happy to deal with the Old Testament only from the perspective of its historical, cultural and exegetical dimensions. I looked upon the students as men and women who, as student ministers or youth leaders, were already engaged in teaching the Scriptures to those under their care. I wanted them to be able exegetes of the text and to become effective pastors to people who were in the process of growing to be more like Jesus. I regarded it as my sacred duty to help them form adequate and biblical hermeneutical procedures so that they could, without distorting the text, show the Old Testament as what it is: Christian Scripture.

We cannot take up the matter of the Bible as Scripture without touching on the question of its authority. Mark Thompson has commented on the role of Robinson's biblical theology in the way he dealt with the issues of the authority of the Bible and, in particular, how we understand it as both infallible and inerrant.[8] It is not only his understanding of the narrative substructure of the Bible that points to the trustworthiness of Scripture, but also the dimension of promise, the promise of a God who is trustworthy.

Understanding the structure of revelation

In this book I have been concerned mainly to open up the structural map of Robinson's biblical theology and to show its congruence with the biblical evidence. One of the principal benefits of the 'big picture' approach of a unified biblical theology is that it, in effect, gives a road map that links every text with every other text. You may have heard the story of the traveller in Ireland who asked a farmer how to get to a particular town. The farmer replied, 'If I was going there I wouldn't leave from here at all.' Several years ago my wife and I were in Ireland and wanted to find the house in which my mother had been born. It was in a small village in County Wexford, but that village did not appear on any of the maps I had managed to get hold of, and no longer seemed to exist. Many years before, we had been there and had successfully found the place, so I knew generally in which direction to go. We eventually found it with the help of a farmer who assured us that we could 'get there from here!' Biblical theology helps us to avoid such problems in finding our way around the biblical text even when the road is sometimes less travelled. The unity of the Bible is of such a kind that every text bears some discoverable relationship to every other text.[9] We should be able to leave from anywhere and arrive at our destination. Our destination, however, is not a matter of chance since Jesus has already shown us that he is not only to be our goal but that he started out with us on our journey.

What we lacked in our Irish travels was a sufficiently detailed map that included the village of my mother's birth. We made up for it when we were lost by asking locals. With the Bible, however, all we have is the text as it stands along with such background information that we can muster. This makes some kind of conceptual map showing the structure of revelation imperative. Of course, this again presupposes a unity that allows such a

---

8. Mark D. Thompson, 'What Have We Done to the Bible? Or Lessons We Should Have Learned From Donald Robinson on the Authority of Holy Scripture', in Peter G. Bolt and Mark D. Thompson (eds.), *Donald Robinson: Selected Works. Appreciation* (Camperdown, NSW: Australian Church Record; Newtown, NSW: Moore College, 2008), pp. 181–187.

9. I would emphasize that by *text* I do not mean a few words or perhaps a single verse, but a meaningful literary unit.

coherent representation to be possible. I have spent much of the foregoing discussion giving my reasons for believing that this presupposition is well founded. Robinson's threefold structure has served me well. In turn I have found its acceptance through my teaching and writing has clearly involved a revelation for many people. I do not bow to those who think it simplistic, as I believe that all the textual detail anyone can muster can be incorporated into it without distortion. It refuses to follow those who want to find Jesus in every detail, nook and cranny of the Old Testament. Instead it seeks only the theologically sustainable links between the Testaments. Yet it is simple enough to make it comprehensible to the most unskilled and untutored. To continue the road-map analogy, such an outline of structure can be presented in so basic a way as to include only the main highways between key places. But it can also be detailed enough to fill in the gaps so that all roads we travel to all places are included. How much detail a teacher gives is a matter of the pedagogic strategy required in any given situation. Whatever the strategy, Christ remains the starting point and the goal.

Exegetical and hermeneutical proficiency

Robinson's academic training included the study of classical Greek at Sydney University. He refers to the importance of this in an article published in 1989.[10] Rory Shiner, in his masterly essay, mentions this article, which quotes Robinson concerning his training under Professor G. P. Shipp:

> From Shipp I learned a little about how to assess the actual semantic value of words as they are used by the individual writers and in particular contexts, without simply importing a dictionary meaning into them with a heavy hand. I began to find a Greek concordance of more use than a lexicon: the lexicon tells you what a word might mean, while the concordance encourages you to consider how it is actually used.[11]

Robinson's careful exegesis was a hallmark of his scholarship. That, with his sense of a biblical theology, led him to explore in new and often quite courageous ways some matters about which evangelicals had often made assumptions that really did not stand the test of rigid examination. I shall refer to some of these subjects later in this chapter.

An early monograph of Robinson's, *Josiah's Reform and the Book of the Law*,

---

10. 'The Church Revisited: An Autobiographical Fragment', *RTR* 48.1 (1989), pp. 4–14; repr. in Bolt and Thompson, *Donald Robinson*, vol. 1, pp. 259–271.

11. Rory Shiner, 'Appreciation', in Bolt and Thompson, *Robinson: Appreciation*, p. 12.

illustrates his skill in exegesis and critical appraisal of current opinions of Old Testament scholarship.[12] At the time of his writing this study there had been considerable scholarly discussion as to what the Book of the Law found during the time of Josiah was and that, according to some, led to his reforms (2 Kgs 22 – 23; 2 Chr. 34 – 35). One problem lay in the need to square the Kings account with that in Chronicles. Critical scholarship tended to cast some suspicion over the historicity of one or both accounts. Robinson seeks from the biblical evidence to unravel what book was discovered, and when Josiah's reforms actually began. It is a careful and meticulous examination of the texts including evidence from contemporaries such as Zephaniah.

Other than the ones he writes about, there must have been many influences on Donald Robinson's theological method. He has pointed to his training in classical Greek and to his theological studies in Cambridge under men like C. H. Dodd and C. F. D. Moule.[13] He acknowledges the impact of the writings of many other theologians and biblical scholars from different traditions. But one cannot ignore his upbringing as a son of the Rectory. His father, Archdeacon R. B. Robinson, was a prominent evangelical clergyman of the Diocese of Sydney, and I have no doubt that both parents played an important role in the young Donald's spiritual development and love for the Scriptures. Other influences were the Crusader Union at school and the evangelical student ministries in both the Sydney University Evangelical Union and the Cambridge Intercollegiate Christian Union (both affiliates of the International Fellowship of Evangelical Students).

The exegetical tradition of Cambridge enabled Robinson to build on his

---

12. Donald W. B. Robinson, *Josiah's Reform and the Book of the Law* (London: Tyndale, 1951).

13. Robinson went to Queens College, Cambridge, in 1947 and studied for the Theological Tripos. It was my privilege to be accepted into Clare College, Cambridge, in 1959 to study Part III of the Theological Tripos in Old Testament. My Hebrew Tutor was Henry St J. Hart, Dean of Queens College, who had also tutored Don Robinson. Hart was a meticulous Hebraist with an encyclopedic knowledge of word usage. As I had not previously graduated at Cambridge, I needed to attend lectures in a couple of non-Old Testament subjects to qualify for entrance. One of these was Charlie Moule's course in New Testament Theology. Moule was a Fellow of Clare and kindly offered to tutor me privately in New Testament Greek, an offer I gladly accepted. I thus had the opportunity to follow Don Robinson to Cambridge and to experience some of his teachers as well as the general ethos of that great university.

own experience of semantic studies in classical Greek. It is a hallmark of his published articles that he would follow the text wherever it took him. This is not to say that he did not have his own well thought-out hermeneutical guidelines, but he would never set these in concrete or allow them to divert him from what the text said. But he did not veer from his convictions, which he described as being 'a cover to cover man' when it came to the Scriptures. His exegetical rigour, along with his sense of textual relatedness, is referred to in the comment of Donald Cameron:

> He would not allow his students to fall unchecked into the common evangelical aberration of importing extraneous ideas into the passage being expounded just because these ideas seemed pious and helpful and were able to be connected by some word or phrase to the passage. In this he taught his students to expound the text honestly and not add to it ideas of their own. At the same time, he was able to associate other passages of Scripture, the connection of which may not have been seen before, and thereby build up a more complete and integrated understanding of what God is saying to us in his Word.[14]

This rigour is everywhere to be seen in the many articles and monographs Robinson published. Although he has not to my knowledge written specifically on hermeneutics, his hermeneutical method is evident in its dependence not only on his doctrine of Scripture but on his biblical theology.

Thematic studies

Robinson was fully aware of the problems of word studies. He undertook them when necessary, as we shall see below. This would be to establish the semantics of a particular word and its cognates. He never assumed that a word was always used in the same way throughout Scripture. On the other hand he found some thematic studies involved him in both words and concepts. His development of a biblical theology while teaching at Moore College stemmed largely from the need to investigate the concept of *church*, which in turn led him into a wider study of the theme of the *people of God*.

Some thematic studies tapped into key biblical concepts. Robinson's study

---

14. Donald Cameron, 'Appreciation', in David Peterson and John Pryor (eds.), *In the Fullness of Time: Biblical Studies in Honour of Archbishop Donald Robinson* (Homebush West, NSW: Lancer, 1992), p. xii. Cameron was a student of Robinson's, was ordained in the Diocese of Sydney, and later served with Archbishop Robinson as an assistant bishop.

of the theme of the people of God was an essential adjunct to his considerable output on the church and on the Jew–Gentile relationship in the church.
The first volume of Robinson's *Selected Works* contains fourteen studies on
the church. Some of these relate to the broader biblical-theological study of
the people of God. Others were stimulated, as Robinson himself tells us, by
two issues facing Anglicanism. One of these was the idea, largely espoused by
the World Council of Churches, of the need for denominational amalgam-
ation or, as it was incorrectly termed, Church Union. Robinson, along with
his friend and colleague David Broughton Knox, was concerned to work out
a thoroughly biblical doctrine of the church since neither he nor Knox could
accept that Church and Denomination are coterminous. The other was the
domestic matter of the need for a constitution for the Anglican Church in
Australia, which up to the mid-twentieth century was a part of the Church of
England and carried its name.[15] The second half of the century saw a number
of moves towards Denominational Union. One of these resulted in a union in
Australia of Presbyterian, Methodist and Congregational churches. That many
resisted this theologically compromising move meant that instead of three
denominations we now really had four.[16] Both Knox and Robinson were
fearless when it came to putting forward what they believed was the biblical
position. This sometimes involved a quite radical departure from views held
within the Anglican Church, though, I rather think they would have argued
strongly that their view was both biblical and in accord with Anglican formularies.

Eclecticism
Donald Robinson's conservative approach to the Bible did not mean that he
did not value the work of others who differed from him in their understanding of biblical authority. His friendship with Gabriel Hebert was not soured
by the fact that the latter had strongly criticised IVP's *New Bible Commentary*,
to which Robinson had been a contributor.[17] Nor did it stop these two men
from discussing their view of biblical theology and from being prepared

---

15. The Church of England in Australia.
16. Some few scattered congregations of both Methodist and Congregationalist
    convictions remain. The main split was among Presbyterians. Many orthodox
    Presbyterians along with some who seemed culturally bound to their Scottish
    roots remained apart from the new Uniting Church.
17. Richard J. Gibson (ed.), *Interpreting God's Plan: Biblical Theology and the Pastor*,
    Explorations 11 (Adelaide: Open Book; Carlisle: Paternoster, 1997), p. 6.

to learn from each other. I have already referred to the influences of non-evangelical scholars on Robinson during his time in Cambridge and to the literature he refers to as having helped to mould his views. His strong evangelical convictions were not dampened by his eclecticism and willingness to learn from whomever he could. I have already noted his own testimony to the influence of Dodd, Moule and Cullmann.

Biblical theology in the academy and the local church

Donald Robinson was completely committed to the relationship of academia to the local church. Theological training was never for its own sake but for preparing pastors to be effective in their ministries in the local church. The ability to exegete a passage of Scripture was a means to an end: the clear teaching of the Bible and the proclamation of its message. I imagine he would approve of the way some of the Reformed Seminaries in the United States teach biblical theology within the departments of Practical Theology. My own contribution to the Robinson Festschrift, which honoured him on his seventieth birthday, was an essay entitled 'The Pastoral Application of Biblical Theology'.[18] There were eighteen essays in the volume and mine was number eighteen. I was pleased to receive his handwritten note of thanks, which includes the following revealing, and most gratifying, remarks:

> I'm afraid it has taken me a while to cover all the ground, but I do want to thank you formally for being part of the septuagintal offering presented to me recently. (The time lag is due to your being the last essayist in the book!) I am sorry you were not *first* in the book, as you set out, tho' in few words, the significance of having a *biblical* theology at all. . . . I have always thought we needed many more people to be doing what you are doing, and it is good to have an account of it from you.[19]

For him, then, the ultimate significance of having a biblical theology was its pastoral application. To that end it needed to be an intentional part of the theological curriculum for preparing men and women for Christian ministry.

---

18. In Peterson and Pryor, *Fullness*, pp. 301–317.

19. 'What you are doing' refers to the fact that at the time of publication of this Festschrift (1992) I was engaged in ministry in a local church in Brisbane and endeavouring to find ways and means of applying biblical theology and also of teaching it to members of the church.

Israel and the church

Of all the biblical subjects that exercised Donald Robinson's thinking none was more important than his concern to understand the relationship of Israel and the church and the Jew–Gentile distinction in the New Testament. All his skills were marshalled in this endeavour, including his biblical theology and his fearless exegetical method. If we take as our starting point the Robinson schema of biblical theology, where should we expect it to lead us in a quest for the biblical understanding of the people of God? If we consider this question carefully we shall, I believe, find that it leads us to important conclusions. Robinson is convinced that many Christians have got it wrong. His opening shot in *Faith's Framework* is this:

> The significance of early Jewish Christianity is that it fulfilled the Old Testament promise of God to restore the tabernacle of David that had fallen and then to use the restored remnant of Israel as an instrument to save the Gentiles. The popular view that God rejected the Jews and that the gospel became a wholly Gentile matter is so far at variance with the New Testament as well as with the expectation of the Old Testament that a complete reappraisal of the New Testament is called for.[20]

Robinson's interest in the meaning of *ekklēsia* in the New Testament and his concern for its relationship to Israel go hand in hand. Though stimulated by an article by Jim Packer on *the covenant*, he came to favour as a more comprehensive way into biblical theology the idea of promise and fulfilment. In recalling these beginnings he comments, 'But I rejected the conventional view that "Israel" was fulfilled in "the Church."'[21]

The progression of events that embrace the people of God begins with the creation of Adam and Eve in the garden. The Fall takes us to the events involving a rebellious and sinful humanity within which the grace of God is already at work. We have noted the importance Robinson places on the promises to Abraham in Genesis 12, which include the significant guarantee that it will be through the descendants of Abraham that blessing will come to all nations. The focus on the universal humanity has shifted to the representative elect man who is the object of God's grace and to whom specific promises

---

20. Donald W. B. Robinson, *Faith's Framework: The Structure of New Testament Theology* (Exeter: Paternoster; Sutherland, NSW: Albatross, 1985), p. 97.

21. Donald W. B. Robinson, '"The Church" Revisited: An Autobiographical Fragment', in Bolt and Thompson, *Donald Robinson*, vol. 1, p. 283.

are given. First and foremost in the pattern of redemption the elect people of God have their head in Abraham. We might infer that 'in you all the families of the earth shall be blessed' (v. 3), means that the same blessings promised to Abraham will spread from the representative to all.[22] But redemption is the means of gaining the kingdom while creation is the presupposition of redemption. The story of God's people begins with Adam, and it is to be expected that it will conclude in some way with a new Adam.

As we follow the progression into the developing history of the sons of Abraham the focus shifts to Isaac, then to Jacob (Israel) and then to the twelve sons of Israel who are the progenitors of the tribes of the nation of Israel. Distinctions that go back to the beginnings of the 'outside Eden' humanity in Genesis 4 are now focused on the distinction between Israel and the Gentile world beyond. The stronger emphasis at first is the need for Israel to remain separate and untainted by the idolatry of the Gentile nations that surround them. Little by little another element appears, namely that of the inclusion of a few Gentiles into the people of God. But such inclusion is always achieved by the proselytizing of the person in question so that he or she comes to share the blessings of the nation that gathers in the presence of Israel's God. The 'sojourner who is within your gates' (Exod. 20:10) is under the same obligations as Israelites but is not thereby an Israelite; he or she is still a sojourner. This distinction has remained in perpetuity in Judaism. Paul, in the synagogue in Pisidian Antioch, addressed himself to both Israelites and (Gentile) God-fearers (Acts 13:16).

When the history of the people of God reaches a high point in the dedication of the Jerusalem temple of Solomon, David's dynastic son, two things of note occur. The first is the flowering of wisdom in the context of Solomon's kingship with the splendour of his royal court and the building of the temple as major aspects of this wisdom. The second is the fact that Gentiles flock to hear the wisdom of Solomon (1 Kgs 4:34; 10:1–9). Apart from the occasional individual Gentile coming into the life of Israel, there is neither a great programme of evangelism driving Israel nor a consequent mass conversion of Gentiles. When the Gentiles oppress Israel and ultimately destroy the nation, its kingship, Jerusalem and the temple, a new understanding of the people of God has emerged through the prophetic proclamation. The eschatological promise of the renewal of all the things that have been promised to Abraham's people brings with it the specific promise that on that great day, the Day of

---

22. Donald W. B. Robinson, 'Israel and the Gentiles in the New Testament', ibid., pp. 12–18.

the Lord, nations will come to the new temple in a restored Jerusalem and find blessing from the God of Israel. That is, the Gentiles will come to experience blessing through Israel. The Gentiles are not seen as replacing Israel or, it would seem, as ceasing to be Gentiles. Israel will be a light to lighten the Gentiles. Israel, the priestly nation, becomes the means through which Gentiles can become God's people along with Israel.

Such an eschatological ingathering of the nations to the new temple did not occur in the subsequent history of Israel. Even after the restoration from the Babylonian exile the Day of the Lord, with all its promises, remained aloof. If we accept the general proposition that the resolution to this non-fulfilment is found in the person and work of Jesus of Nazareth, what would we expect to be the pattern of such fulfilment? The Old Testament pattern is that of the covenant made to Abraham and the role of his descendants in mediating God's blessings to all the nations of the world. Why should we expect that pattern now to be superseded in the New Testament? At most we might suppose that the ingathering of the Gentiles results in their simply being, to all intents and purposes, Jews: Israel. But there are no grounds in the Old Testament for supposing that the Gentiles would one day replace Israel as the people of God.

It is significant that the editors of the Robinson *Selected Works* have placed the thirteen essays and lectures dealing with the Jew–Gentile relationship in the New Testament as the first part of volume 1. It is also noteworthy that Robinson's 1961 lecture, the earliest of this group, shows that even at that point his views on the matter had crystallized.[23] In many respects Robinson's later contributions to this subject developed some of the finer points and sought to answer many of the objections to the general position taken in this early paper. In the 1961 lecture he contrasts the dispensational view and the 'other view'.

> The Scofield [dispensational] position rightly denies that the distinctive Jewish promises – apart that is from the spiritual promises of the Abrahamic covenant – are inherited by Christians generally. The other view, however, rightly denies that God's promises to Israel have to wait for the millennium or later to be fulfilled. What neither position allows for, but what I believe to be the teaching of the New Testament, is that God's distinctive promises to Israel are in the New Testament fulfilled, not to all believers, but to Jewish believers who constitute the restored

---

23. 'Jew and Greek: Unity and Division in the Early Church', originally delivered as the (Australian) InterVarsity Fellowship Annual Lecture, 1961, ibid., pp. 79–109.

remnant of Israel; and that Gentile believers are the inheritors of other promises altogether, that is, the promises made in the Old Testament to the nations who should come to Israel's light. These two sets of promises, though distinct, are closely related, and are both finally transfigured by a new disclosure of God's purposes, namely that both Israel and the Gentiles should lose all their distinctiveness in the one new man which will be the end-product of the salvation of God in Christ.[24]

The distinction between Jew and Gentile is not erased by the Gentile believers becoming a new Israel, or by the church being the new Israel, but by both Jew and Gentile believers ultimately becoming the new Adam in Christ.

Thus, in the New Testament, Gentile believers are not, in fact, represented as spiritual Israelites, or as forming part of the renewed Israel of prophecy. Certainly they are represented as coming to Israel's light, eating the children's bread, coming to worship God at Jerusalem and receiving a rightful place in God's Temple. All this is foreseen in the Old Testament. Yet beyond these pictures lies another, in which Israel and the Gentiles are completely at one, and in which both groups, not merely one of them, lose their identity. This is the new body of Christ, not a new Israel, but a new mankind, the church in its spiritual and heavenly reality. Only here do we go beyond the categories of Old Testament promise, for this is a unity not previously revealed to the sons of men.[25]

These assertions also emerge as germane to Robinson's other focus: the doctrine and nature of the church. Both his biblical theology and understanding of eschatology play important roles in this:

The church, then, in the Ephesians (and less probably Hebrews) sense is a reality related to creation, redemption, and the restoration of all things. To explain why the term *ekklesia* should be used to express the final transcendent reality of the new man in Christ it was necessary to turn to the history of salvation . . . [T]he doctrine of the church in the New Testament could not be understood apart from the history of Israel and of God's purpose for salvation through Israel to the Gentiles.[26]

This position of maintaining the distinction of the new Israel and the church is contentious but is amply dealt with exegetically by Robinson in his various

---

24. Ibid., p. 81.
25. Ibid., p. 85.
26. "'The Church' Revisited', in Bolt and Thompson, *Donald Robinson*, vol. 1, p. 269.

articles on the matter. The presenting problem is the tension between those statements in the New Testament that speak of the eschatological reality in which all distinctions disappear in the one new man in Christ, and the concern of New Testament writers to maintain a real distinction between Jew and Gentile. It would be wrong to suppose that Robinson has simply capitulated to the Dispensationalists' view, which keeps Israel and the church separate – for distinction is not the same as separation. Only by maintaining the distinction can we accommodate Jesus' claim that 'salvation is from the Jews' (John 4:22), or Paul's insistence that the gospel brings salvation 'to the Jew first and also to the Greek' (Rom. 1:16; 2:10).

There are two questions implied by Robinson's position: the one is whether it is exegetically sustainable; the other is that of the practical significance of the distinction if it is sustainable. In my own review of *Faith's Framework* I have stated the problem thus:

> The assumption that the church is the new Israel is ably disproved on exegetical grounds. It is demonstrated that Paul's concept of the unity of the body is based on the new humanity rather than the new Israel. What is not clear is how these exegetical gains affect the meaning of Hebrews, 1 Peter, James and Jude for us Gentile Christians. The author seems to me to be saying that the effect is not great since we share in the inheritance of Israel.[27]

However, two Jewish Christians, Martin Pakula and Jeff Read, have spoken more positively of the importance of Robinson's position. Understandably both see one of the significances of this perspective in the attitude of Gentiles to Jews and the mission to Jews.[28] For Pakula, Robinson's emphasis highlights the two missions in the New Testament: one to Jews and the other to Gentiles. He believes that this distinction is necessary for a sound biblical theology of the New Testament. For Read, neither Jew nor Gentile can be conceited given God's marvellous plan. The Jew should be told that God still saves Jews; Gentiles should see their task to make Jews envious of their salvation. It is understandable that, as Jewish Christians now both in the ministry, these two men should feel some satisfaction in the recognition of what it means to be members of spiritual Israel. The Tongan theologian Ma'afu Palu

---

27. Graeme Goldsworthy, Review of *Faith's Framework*, RTR 45.1, p. 1986.

28. Martin Pakula, 'A Biblical Theology of Israel in the New Testament', in Bolt and Thompson, *Donald Robinson: Appreciation*, pp. 105–112; Jeff Read, '"That You May Not Be Conceited"', ibid., pp. 113–123.

relates the matter to a better understanding of the issues of contextualization. This is a major concern for cultures to which Christianity has come in more recent times. Missionaries have worked hard to contextualize the message for the cultures of Africa, Asia and the Pacific. Palu notes the 'contrived attempt to "transport" the gospel from its supposedly biblical "culture" or, in the case of the Pacific, from the western culture of the missionaries, to the "local culture"'.[29]

> The importance of maintaining the Jew–Gentile distinction . . . is . . . that it clearly identifies the Gentiles in a vantage point outside the sphere of God's salvation influence depicted in the Bible. On a personal level, it means that as a Gentile 'in the flesh', one necessarily approaches the Bible, whose central message concerns the blessings promised to the forefathers of Israel, as an 'outsider'.[30]

This leaves the Gentile just one recourse: to enter into the blessings promised to Abraham by faith through the cross of Christ.

Eschatology

It is not surprising that Robinson's biblical theology led him to contribute to the study of some aspects of eschatology. It is so characteristic of him that what many would consider a significant contribution to theological discussion emerged rather low key and for lay consumption. A good example of this is the little pamphlet on eschatology *The Hope of Christ's Coming*.[31] The most pertinent comment I can make about this tract of thirty-two pages is that it shows clearly the role of biblical theology in the hermeneutics of eschatological texts in the Bible. The significance of this work is far greater than its brevity might suggest.

Although he does not refer in detail to his biblical-theological analysis of the structure of revelation, one can see it as the basis upon which he comes to the conclusions he does. I have referred to this in the previous chapter. It will suffice, therefore, to note that the understanding of Christ as fulfiller of

---

29. Ma'afu Palu, 'The Significance of the Jew–Gentile Distinction for Theological Contextualization', ibid., p. 141.
30. Ibid., p. 144.
31. Donald W. B. Robinson, *The Hope of Christ's Coming* (Beecroft, NSW: Evangelical Tracts and Publications, 1958).

the Old Testament prophetic promise is basic to Robinson's eschatology. It is consistent with his biblical theology that he finds no grounds for imposing on the New Testament the hermeneutics of Premillennialism. He finds no evidence in the New Testament of this doctrine. In the previous chapter I referred to this work in conjunction with the typological approach so central to Robinson's biblical theology. The passage quoted enumerates the prophetically proclaimed aspects of the 'blessings of God's End-time'.[32] Significantly this passage continues with a reference to the new creation:

> Not only would the End transcend Israel's past history; it would transcend and fulfil the whole history of creation. The harmony of paradise would be restored. . . . Indeed, nothing less that a new creation, a new heaven and a new earth, could contain all that God has in store for the End. . . . The Old Testament believers did not regard the day of the Lord as indefinitely remote in time. It seemed to them very close indeed. It hung, like some vision in the clouds, over many of the stirring events through which their nation passed. To the prophets especially, the day of the Lord seemed to stand alongside each successive crisis, so that each event was assessed and measured in the light of the End.[33]

Chapter 3 of this Robinson work ends with a reference to the fact that Israel's return from the Babylonian exile, however promising, turned out to be a disappointment: 'The End had not yet come.' Chapter 4 is headed, 'The End Has Come'. Then follows an exposition of the way the New Testament carries the message 'that with the appearance of Jesus Christ the End has arrived':[34]

> We must not miss the point of all this. It was not simply that the kingdom of God had come, but that the kingdom had come in Jesus Christ. It was in Him – in his ministry, death, resurrection and ascension – and not otherwise, that the End had come, and with it the fulfilment of all the promises. . . . Two experiences set this truth beyond all doubt for the apostles, (1) **God poured out His Spirit** on them in an unmistakable way – a sure mark of the day of the Lord. (2) **The gentiles came to the light**.[35]

He goes on to indicate two New Testament truths about the End: it is wholly compassed by the person and work of Jesus and, though the End has been

---

32. Ibid., p. 13.

33. Ibid., pp. 13–14.

34. Ibid., p. 15.

35. Ibid., p. 16. Bold type original.

inaugurated on earth, it has yet to reach its consummation. It seems that
Robinson does not subscribe to the distinction that some make between prophecies of the first coming and those of the second coming of Christ. The distinction is rather between the fulfilment of all prophecy in Christ's first coming, and
the consummation of all prophecy that is yet to come at his parousia.

In the light of this perspective the next chapter of this work looks at 'The
Coming of Jesus Christ'.[36] He asks, 'What does a Christian now look forward
to?' The logic of his exposition would seem to rest on his biblical-theological
perspective that all the promises of God have been fulfilled in Christ. If he is
the locus of fulfilment, its solid reality, we cannot contemplate the consummation as a return to the shadows of prophetic typology in the way proposed
by a literalist interpretation of prophecy. Thus the return of Christ to earth
will bring human history to an end. The End will be marked by bodily resurrection and the transformation of the entire universe. In asking the question
'When will this be?' Robinson returns to one of his most cherished themes:
the interval during which we wait for his return 'is so that the fullness of the
Gentiles may come in and all Israel be saved (Rom. 11:25, 26)'.[37] This view
of Christ's coming, his parousia, is exactly what we would expect Robinson's
biblical theology to lead us to.

Baptism

In dealing with the subject of baptism Robinson, like his colleague Broughton
Knox, was prepared to go where the Scriptures took him. It is not an exaggeration to say that much of the literature on baptism starts with the assumptions
and already formed convictions of the writers, either baptistic or paedobap-
tistic, as to what needs to be defended against the alternate view. Both Knox
and Robinson have written on baptism in ways that are remarkable for their
lack of assumptions beyond those of the authority and clarity of Scripture.[38]
Of course, none of us is completely free of assumptions and even prejudices,
but both these men were fearless in reaching conclusions about baptism that
many would see as being way out on a limb.

---

36. Ibid., ch. 5, pp. 20–25.
37. Ibid., p. 29.
38. Knox's latest contribution was 'New Testament Baptism', in David Broughton
    Knox, *Selected Works*, vol. 2: *Church and Ministry* (Kingsford, NSW: Matthias Media,
    2003), pp. 263–315.

A significant contribution to New Testament theology was published originally as a brief tract, *The Meaning of Baptism*.[39] Here Robinson shows the effect of both his semantic sensibilities and his understanding of a biblical theology. He refuses to travel with those who exhaust themselves, and their readers, with etymological excursions into root meanings of *baptizein* and its cognates. In examining these words he does so for their usage in the literature rather than for possible root meanings. In effect he concludes that *baptizein* means to perform the rite of baptism, and it tells us nothing about the mode of baptism: 'Arguments in favour of immersion as the original form of Christian baptism which are based on the meaning of the word have no substance. The word points to the meaning of the rite rather than to its mode.'[40]

Robinson called into question many of the assumptions often made about the subject of baptism. He challenges the assertions of the great New Testament scholar F. F. Bruce that the recipients of Paul's letters would think of their own baptism in water whenever they read the word 'baptism', 'unless the context made it quite clear, that another baptism was meant'.[41] Robinson challenges this as reflecting an unsustainable bias. 'In the first place we are not in a position to assert how general might have been the incidence of Christian water-baptism in New Testament times until we have resolved the question of what passages, especially of the Epistles, refer to it.'[42] That refusal to accept water baptism as the necessary primary reference, when allied with his training in semantics, led him to some startling conclusions. In the article just referred to, published in 1975, he begins, 'A persistent difficulty in determining the meaning of baptism in the New Testament is largely unobserved. It is the linguistic difficulty of distinguishing literal from metaphorical use of *baptizō*, *baptisma*, and *baptismos*.'[43] This distinction between literal and metaphorical uses of baptism words in the New Testament is crucial for Robinson's position. Some would say that his reliance on semantics and biblical theology showed

---

39. Donald W. B. Robinson, *The Meaning of Baptism* (Beecroft, NSW: Evangelical Tracts and Publications, 1956). It is gratifying to see this work reprinted in Bolt and Thompson, *Donald Robinson*, vol. 2, pp. 227–251.

40. Ibid., p. 25.

41. 'Towards a Definition of Baptism', ibid., p. 252. A quote from F. F. Bruce, *The Epistle to the Ephesians* (London: Pickering & Inglis, 1981), pp. 79–80. The article was first published in *RTR* 34.1 (1975), pp. 1–15.

42. 'Towards a Definition of Baptism', in Bolt and Thompson, *Donald Robinson*, vol. 2, p. 252.

43. Ibid.

a lack of regard for systematic theology. I doubt this. And this certainly could not have been the case for Broughton Knox, whose lectures to my class in Christian doctrine remain for me one of the highlights of my time as a student.[44] Don Robinson wrote a number of important articles on baptism, some of which related to the domestic issues of Anglicanism.

In a lengthy monograph of 1965, but unpublished until it was included in the *Selected Works*, Robinson shows again his semantic expertise in surveying the various uses of the *baptism* words in the New Testament. He distinguishes ten different uses of the term that are not necessarily all unrelated:[45]

1. Jewish ritual washings.
2. The baptism of John the Baptist.
3. Baptism performed by the disciples of Jesus.
4. Jesus' death as his baptism.
5. Baptism with the Holy Spirit.
6. Baptism with fire.
7. Baptism with water in the name of Jesus.
8. Israel's baptism in the exodus from Egypt.
9. Baptism for the dead.
10. Noah's flood as a type of baptism.

By this simple survey it is clear that blanket assertions such as that *baptizein* means 'to dip', or that of F. F. Bruce noted above, are simplistic and largely unhelpful.

The important question of how early Christians would perceive the matter of baptism is a key issue for Robinson. In an excellent essay Robert Doyle has summarized some significant conclusions in Robinson's investigations.[46]

---

44. Knox followed the set syllabus for ordination examinations in Christian Doctrine but his lectures were an amalgam of biblical, systematic and historical theology. The greater part consisted in expositions of the Scriptures relating to the topic in view. Some would say it was a weakness that he paid little attention to contemporary theologians, preferring rather to go to the early Fathers and the Reformers. In my view it was a decided strength. Beyond the lecture room our energies were directed to the reading of Calvin rather than Barth and Tillich.

45. 'Baptised Into Christ: The Nature of Christian Initiation', in Bolt and Thompson, *Donald Robinson*, vol. 2, pp. 278–280.

46. Robert Doyle, 'Suppressed Truth: Donald Robinson's Contribution to Understanding Baptism', in Bolt and Thompson, *Donald Robinson: Appreciation*, pp. 205–224.

While recognizing differences among Christians of frequently held assumptions concerning baptism he says,

> the commonalities are sufficient to have produced an almost uniform understanding of the meaning of Christian baptism: it is a mandatory water rite which effects the grace it signifies, forgiveness of sins and initiation into the community of the church. . . . Donald Robinson fundamentally challenges these assumptions.[47]

While Robinson pointed to the difficulty in resolving the ambiguities in the use of the baptism words in the epistles, and therefore in knowing exactly how a first-century Christian would understand references to baptism, there was no such problem in Mark's Gospel. Doyle comments:

> In sharp contrast to the Epistles, the meaning in Mark is unambiguous, which allows the possibility of moving from the known to the unknown.
> The reader of Mark is introduced to four different baptisms:
>   1. in Jewish custom, of both persons and utensils (Mark 7:1–5);
>   2. the baptism of John . . . (Mark 1:4–5);
>   3. a predicted baptism of the Holy Spirit . . . (Mark 1:8);
>   4. the baptism of Jesus on the cross (Mark 10:38–39).[48]

Doyle indicates that for the Christian reader the Jewish baptisms were downplayed by Jesus, and John's baptism was seen to be eclipsed, if not wholly superseded, by the baptism of the Spirit. Jesus' baptism of suffering was central to his mission and is shared by his followers. Thus the two most significant baptisms for the Christian have nothing whatever to do with water.

As my purpose is to try to show how his understanding of biblical theology affected his contributions to biblical studies, I shall leave the consideration of the details of Robinson's views on baptism. One of the clear effects of a biblical theology is the recognition of a dynamic to Scripture that is often overlooked in topical studies. It means that we look for, among other things, those elements in the biblical story that mark transitions from the old to the new and for the unique and possibly unrepeatable. The following points can be made concerning Robinson's position:

---

47. Ibid., pp. 205–206.
48. Ibid., p. 209.

1. In the Old Testament, beyond the various cleansing rituals, there is little evidence of anything that approaches John's baptism.

2. The references to John's baptism of repentance are the only places the New Testament points to such a rite performed in the Jordan (Mark 1:4; Luke 3:3; John 1:28).

3. The baptism of repentance at Pentecost is the only indication of such an event in Jerusalem (Acts 2:38–41).

4. Paul's downplaying of baptism in Corinth indicates that he did not see it as central to the apostolic mission (1 Cor. 1:13–17). It could even be argued that Paul regarded it as divisive.

It seems to me that the dynamics of his biblical theology have enabled Robinson to pursue his careful exegetical approach with an understanding of the progression from Jewish ritual cleansings, through the metaphorical usages of baptism words in the LXX, to the baptism of John the Baptist in which Israel was called to repentance at the advent of the Messiah, who brings in the promised kingdom. John then points to the greater baptism that Jesus himself will administer: a baptism of the Holy Spirit (Mark 1:8). Jesus speaks of his own baptism of suffering and death, which his disciples will share (Mark 10:38–39). The baptism of Jews at Pentecost brings the repentance of Israel to the gospel event through which the Spirit is given. Robinson's conclusion is this:

> Thus, in the undisputed evidence we have examined for the incidence and meaning of water-baptism in the New Testament, we have found no clear ground for expecting that such a baptism among Christians should signify anything other than what it signified in John's mission – a gesture of repentance on the part of an Israelite turning to his God, in hope of forgiveness and the fulfilment of the blessings of the covenant.[49]

John's baptism was for repenting Jews. There is no suggestion at any point that baptism was considered an initiation into the church. Robinson concludes, somewhat controversially, the following:

> To this we must add the evidence of Paul, that although he had baptized a handful of people at Corinth, he did not consider baptism to be part of his essential apostolic

---

49. 'Towards a Definition of Baptism', in Bolt and Thompson, *Donald Robinson*, vol. 2, p. 267.

mission to the Gentiles. I can see no reason why we should not accept this as indication that Paul regarded water-baptism as ultimately an *adiaphoron*, a matter of indifference. This would be consistent with everything he says about the non-essential character of ordinances of the flesh. He did not regard the bestowal of the Spirit through his preaching as a matter of indifference (e.g. Gal. 3:2), and he regarded fellowship in the sufferings of Christ as the absolute hall-mark of being a true Christian. . . . Whatever value he put on water-baptism . . . there is little or no reason for thinking that it was for him the focus of the fundamental truth of being crucified with Christ, and thus of being baptized into Christ's death.[50]

Robinson has not completely revised his Reformed thinking on baptism. He sees it as related closely to the covenant and agrees that, if we are going to practice water baptism, it is perfectly in keeping with its covenant connections that it be applied to the children of believers. This is the connection that Peter expresses at Pentecost: the rationale for baptism is the promise of God (Acts 2:38). While repentance and faith are necessarily related to baptism the benefits it points to are those of the promises to Abraham.

Assessment

I have concluded my reflections on Donald Robinson's legacy to the church with reference to the three topics Israel and the church, Eschatology and Baptism for a specific reason. In each of these matters as Robinson expounds them, I believe the influence of his biblical-theological perspective is evident. In Israel and the church and in his treatment of eschatology it is more explicit than it is in the treatment of baptism. One reason for this is that baptism is not an Old Testament theme and its links to the faith of Israel are inferential from the use of baptism words in the LXX and from certain New Testament texts. The application of biblical theology in these concerns is important, but each case illustrates the point that biblical theology is never an end in itself. I think we may in principle concur with Charles Scobie's view that it serves 'as a bridge discipline situated between the historical study of Scripture on the one hand and its use by the church in its faith and life on the other'.[51]

---

50. Ibid., pp. 267–268.

51. Charles H. H. Scobie, *The Ways of Our God: An Approach to Biblical Theology* (Grand Rapids: Eerdmans, 2003), p. 46. Scobie notes my own use of the bridge metaphor in *Gospel and Kingdom*.

In my view, Robinson's studies reviewed in this chapter, along with his contributions to the debates on the church and ecumenism, on ministry and the role of women within it, and his practical pastoral concerns as a bishop in the Anglican Church illustrate the fact that his threefold schema of biblical theology is for him a useful and indeed a powerful structural framework to be employed in our quest to understand what the Bible says to the church today.

11. HOW TO DO BIBLICAL THEOLOGY[1]

Is there a future for biblical theology?

It should be obvious by now that I recognize that there are various ways of doing biblical theology, but also that I follow the path I do with a certain confidence that others may regard as misplaced. But while we may develop our own concepts of the structure or pattern of revelation in the Bible as a whole, there is no one stereotype that should completely control our doing of biblical theology. Biblical theology is not a matter of a fixed number of predetermined procedures. I think the four Gospels are ample demonstration that one can take different standpoints and concentrate on different perspectives and still uncover the truth that is within Scripture.

It is evident from the discussions and debates over the nature and method of biblical theology that have taken place over the last century or so that there are a number of different approaches to the task depending on what we want to achieve, and how we understand the structure of the biblical message. I

---

1. This title is borrowed from the book by renowned Tübingen biblical scholar, Peter Stuhlmacher, *How to Do Biblical Theology*, Princeton Theological Monograph Series 38 (Allison Park, Pa.: Pickwick, 1995). In this chapter, however, I follow a rather different approach from Stuhlmacher's.

have been at pains to set out what I understand to be the essential structure of revelation that is relevant to any of the tasks we might wish to undertake in biblical theology. We must first of all be true to the nature of the biblical text in the way we conduct our exegesis. Secondly, we should be prepared, with the overarching control of exegesis, to exercise imagination and creativity as we seek to uncover both the obvious and the more obscure relationships within Scripture. To do this we need to be able to link any particular text to the theological significance of the people, institutions and events that constitute its wider context. In this way we can sometimes find spiritual or theological links that were not immediately obvious because of our unfamiliarity with the textual idioms, or because of our distance from the original events, language and culture. Using imagination and being creative does not mean an open season on the text to invent connections that are not there. Rather we should be bold in suggesting possibilities, but also ruthless in discarding those that do not stand up to close scrutiny.

The proposals of overall structure and the possibilities for designating key themes or even a theological centre of the Bible emerge from readings of the texts within the canon. The hermeneutical spiral operates on different levels. First, we are open to understanding texts within their structural contexts, yet such structures have emerged from our readings of the text. The hermeneutical spiral also operates at the level of the relationship of systematic theology to biblical theology, and of the relationship of both of these to historical theology.

The foregoing investigations in this book lead me to make the following proposals:

1. The Reformed and evangelical presuppositions regarding the unity of Scripture, the uniqueness of the canon, and the central role of Jesus Christ in the message of the Bible are sustainable and to be preferred for sound and productive biblical theology.

2. The concept of epochs that control the biblical theologies of Vos, Clowney and others is a valid and useful aspect to the analysis of the structure of biblical revelation. It has the disadvantage of lacking the flexibility necessary to best appreciate the relationships between any text and the person and work of Christ.

3. The caution about a centre to biblical theology and the preference for a multiplex approach to the discipline, as indicated in the works of Hasel, Greidanus and Scobie, is a needed and timely warning against simplistic approaches. Nevertheless I regard these men as being overcautious in this matter. Somewhere along the line we have to ask what gives the Scriptures their unity.

4. The Robinson–Hebert schema allows for the full appreciation of epochs or stages and allows full play to the valid identification of various *roads* (to use Greidanus's term) in the way the Old Testament is linked to the New.

5. The idea of a centre to biblical theology is distinct from the question of how one can organize the writing of a biblical theology of the whole canon.

6. Typology can be regarded in more narrow terms as one, and only one of the ways that the New Testament finds its links with the Old. On the other hand, we can conceive of typology in terms of the recapitulation, not only of key people, events and institutions, but of entire stages of revelation.

7. The Robinson–Hebert schema provides an approach that, in my view, is the most accommodating of the actual emphases given in both Old and New Testaments with regard to the structure of salvation history and the revelation of God's plan and purposes.

Biblical theology not only has a future, but it should be approached with confidence that this future will be robust and productive. It is, after all, a name we give to the divine imperative to the church to listen to God's Word and to live in submission to its authority.

Possibilities for biblical theology

With regard to how to do biblical theology, I think we have established at least these three things. *First*, we must identify and own our presuppositions concerning Scripture. *Secondly*, what we want to achieve will govern our approach. *Thirdly*, the kind of matrix of revelation we have discerned will affect the way we relate different parts of Scripture to each other and, above all, to Jesus Christ. Given our evangelical presupposition of the unity of Scripture with its central focus on Christ, we should expect that the different acceptable approaches will reflect that unity. A consideration of what the Bible is, and of surveys of the various kinds of study regarded as exercises in biblical theology, show that we can distinguish at least the four following ways of engaging in biblical theological studies.

Thematic and word studies
In this kind of exercise there is an ever-present danger, especially in word studies. If you are not of the generation that was around when James Barr

demolished a particular approach to word studies,[2] perhaps you will have
seen Don Carson's timely warnings about exegetical fallacies.[3] The following
points can be made:

1. The best aids to word studies are concordances of the Hebrew and
   Greek texts. Usage in particular texts is always of more significance than
   root meanings of words since meanings of words can and do change.
2. A study of a particular word in the English (or other modern language)
   text may be a study of a phrase in the original, and vice versa.
3. It should never be assumed that the same word (or phrase) is always
   used with the same meaning, even by the same author.
4. Since biblical theology is concerned with theological concepts, otherwise
   completely unrelated words may be participants in the common
   semantic field relevant to the concept being studied.
5. Some theological concepts come to be largely represented by a particular
   technical term that invites study of its history and development in
   progressive revelation.
6. Word or concept studies can be confined to particular books or
   corpora, or may by pursued as longitudinal studies that are guided by the
   connectedness and unity within the canon.

I believe that pretty well any subject that is of concern to Christians can
be examined from the viewpoint of biblical theology. Thematic studies can
be enormously helpful in showing the dynamic of progressive redemptive
revelation. It can hardly be doubted that there are many important themes
in the Bible that are developed even from the earliest stages of redemptive
history. The kind of unity we find in the Bible will affect the way we perceive
such developments. Furthermore how we determine a theme is important. I
have expressed elsewhere that the theme of the *kingdom of God* is a fruitful one
to pursue throughout the whole of Scripture even though the actual term is
found mainly in the Synoptic Gospels. The theological idea of God's rule is
everywhere in Scripture and is not confined to any one word or phrase.

The fact that a theological idea or theme is not necessarily tied to the same

---

2. James Barr's critiques of certain aspects of the word studies in the earlier volumes
   of *TDNT* are too well known to require repeating. See his *The Semantics of Biblical
   Language* (Oxford: Oxford University Press, 1961).
3. D. A. Carson, *Exegetical Fallacies*, 2nd ed. (Grand Rapids: Baker, 1996), has a section
   that deals with 'Word-study fallacies'.

word or group of words requires word studies to be pursued with caution. The fallacy that the same word is always used within the same semantic range is easy to fall into. The possibilities for thematic studies are seen in the many fine studies that have been published in the SCM Studies in Biblical Theology and in the IVP series New Studies in Biblical Theology.[4] A number of other thematic studies have shown the variety of subjects and approaches that are possible.[5]

Figure 6 overleaf suggests three parts to a thematic biblical-theological study on the topic of the temple:

1. The theme is established as a significant part of the teaching of the New Testament that requires some understanding of its Old Testament antecedents.
2. The dominant Old Testament expression that, in the case of the temple theme, provides the basis for the New Testament adaptation, is examined for its antecedents and succeeding expressions in salvation history.
3. Each aspect of the progression of the theme can be examined laterally for related themes that enrich our understanding of the theological significance of the original theme. This search for the interconnectedness of themes and theological ideas is important for revealing the unity of revelation within its diversity.

Following the sequence that goes from Christ back into the Old Testament, along with lateral explorations, opens up more possibilities than is likely to be the case if we started with the tabernacle and moved forward. Of course we may start with a prominent theme in the Old Testament and move forward. Either way, we look for the theological significances of the theme in the three

---

4. The SBT series began in 1950 with Oscar Cullmann's study *Baptism in the New Testament*. NSBT is a series edited by Don Carson and published by Apollos and InterVarsity.
5. Thematic approaches to the Old Testament can be found in H. H. Rowley, *The Faith of Israel: Aspects of Old Testament Thought* (London: SCM, 1956), and in Bernhard W. Anderson, *Contours of Old Testament Theology* (Minneapolis: Fortress, 1999). A more comprehensive set of themes taking in the whole biblical witness is Scott J. Hafemann and Paul R. House (eds.), *Central Themes in Biblical Theology: Mapping Unity in Diversity* (Nottingham: Apollos, 2007). Part 3 of *NDBT* (pp. 363–863) is given over to articles on biblical themes.

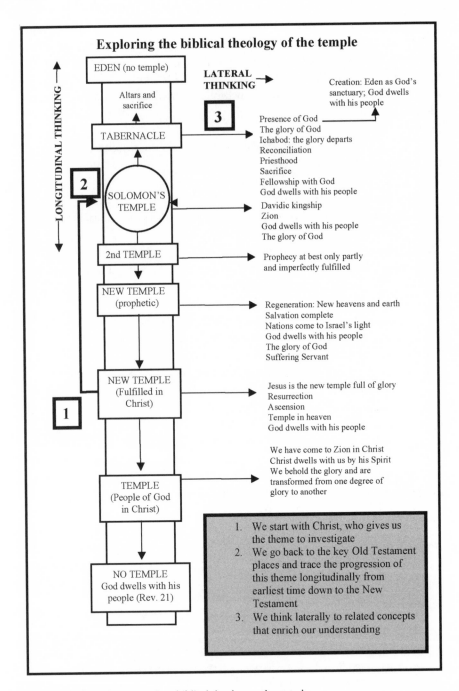

Figure 6: A thematic approach to biblical theology – the temple

stages of revelation: biblical history, prophetic eschatology and the fulfilment achieved by Christ. The figure needs to be understood as falling within
this threefold Robinson schema. For the Christian, the starting point is our
relationship to Christ in the gospel. This is our theological point of reference
since we come to the task as those united to Christ. The new temple in Christ
points us back to the Old Testament antecedents in the history of God's
sanctuary, and in the prophetic view of a coming renewed temple. The lateral
thinking is an exercise in uncovering the interconnectedness of the theme to
many other themes.

A second theme I use as an example of this approach is that of prayer
(see Figure 7 below).[6] In the same way that I have looked at the theme of
the temple we can deal with prayer as a biblical theme that links with many
other aspects of biblical theology. I propose that any theme has potential for
a biblical-theological study. And, I would emphasize, this is not simply to be
able to say that we have done a biblical theology of some particular theme,
but rather to lay bare the real essence of the biblical teaching on this subject.
It also serves to open up the interconnectedness of that theme with other key
themes. Nothing shows up the inner unity of Scripture better than the dem-
onstrating of such relationships within it.

Contextual studies of individual texts, books or corpora

Probably the majority of exegetical commentaries on individual books of the
Bible are biblical-theological studies involving close encounters with the text.
This is an essential aspect of biblical theology, as is the study of meaningful
parts of a book. Canonical corpora such as the Pentateuch, the Book of the
Twelve or Luke-Acts may be studied to try to understand the theology that
links the individual books in each corpus. While close exegetical studies of
limited portions of text are often included within the scope of biblical theology, an evangelical Christ-centred approach will want to show the relevance
of such a study to the wider understanding of the Bible's message about
Christ. The canonical context of any text will be a matter for concern.

As a biblical theologian, and simply as a Christian, I find a commentary or
study of the theology of a book or corpus more meaningful if it is contextual-

---

6. I have outlined my understanding of prayer in biblical-theological perspective
   in my book *Prayer and the Knowledge of God: What the Whole Bible Teaches* (Leicester:
   IVP, 2003). In this book I am also concerned to show the doctrinal relationships
   stemming from our knowledge of God as Trinity to the subject of our response
   to him in prayer.

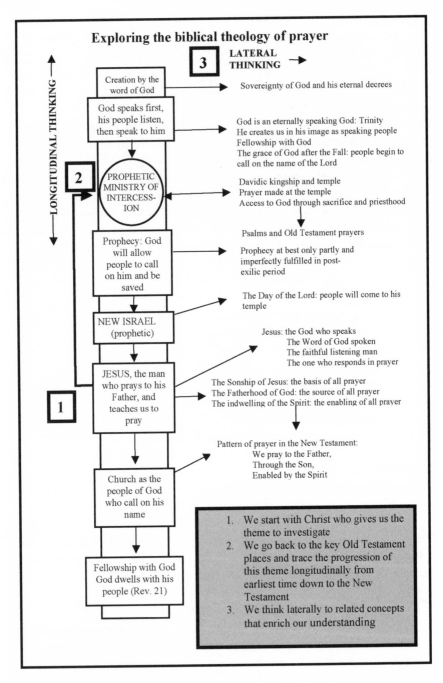

Figure 7: A thematic approach to biblical theology – prayer

ized within the whole canon. It is usual for commentaries to begin with some kind of introduction to the place the book holds within the biblical history and other matters such as authorship, date of writing, literary criticism and cultural concerns. Often such introductions are more concerned with historical and literary matters than with relating the book to the theology of the Bible as a whole. This may reflect the commentator's own views on the unity of biblical theology. Unfortunately many commentaries are restricted to the exegetical treatment of the text and leave the Christian reader without any guidance as to its application to Christians based on its relationship to Christ. The following points can be made about such a biblical-theological quest:[7]

1. While canonical books are usually seen as established literary units, the bounds of some corpora also need to be established if there is to be a meaningful approach to the theology of the corpus in question.
2. Parts of books can be the subject of investigation. Thus we might take any of the individual prophetic oracles in the Latter Prophets and treat them as objects of biblical-theological study. This requires the preliminary stage of deciding the limits of any oracle or text. The canonical question will arise when we come to consider the role of this text in the whole book of which it is a part, and in the complete canon of Scripture.[8]
3. Once the unit is decided upon, the first stage of exegetical study is to make contact with the whole unit. Let the passage or book speak as a whole. Get a feel for what is happening in the text, its structure, its plot, its purpose.
4. Begin the close exegetical reading of the text. If you cannot deal with the Hebrew or Greek, use a good standard translation such as ESV. Then read it in a different standard version. If you find significant differences

---

7. In this I partly depend on guidelines for exegesis prepared by Professor James L. Mays when I was a student at Union Theological Seminary in Virginia (1969–72).
8. It is one of the advantages of the New Literary Criticism that it focuses attention on the whole book or corpus even if there is often scepticism about the unity of original authorship. Its quest is for the theology of the corpus in the literary form that exists in the canon. Thus Isaiah is no longer to be divided into two or three books but is regarded as a single canonical work irrespective of the origin of its parts. One can retain a conservative approach to authorship and structure while benefiting from insights into the theology of the corpus that New Literary Criticism may provide.

in passages that affect your understanding of the theology of the passage, compare versions, check the original language text and, *last of all*, see what good exegetical commentaries have to say about it.[9]

5. Let the hermeneutical spiral operate: close reading may make your overall impressions change, and these changes may in turn affect the way you engage the text closely.

6. You will engage the text for its three main dimensions: the literary, the historical and the theological. Since the text is literature you will need to be concerned with genre differentiation, literary structure, discourse analysis and whatever else the particular genre demands for its understanding.[10] Historical concerns will be with background to the text as well as the role it has in the overall redemptive history presented in the Bible. Literary analysis will also be concerned with how the author, or final editor, has put the book together and with what purpose.

7. Thus far you have been concerned with the questions of exegesis linked with hermeneutics. Specific questions of the theology of the text and the relationship of this to the person and work of Christ should now be uppermost. This relationship emerges more directly in New Testament texts for obvious reasons. Preparing a theological commentary that shows the Christian significance of Old Testament texts is more demanding. It is here that I believe the foregoing discussion in this book is most relevant. The Christian meaning and application of an Old Testament text emerges as we show the links the canon allows us to make between any text and Christ. I suggest the following considerations:

- All reality is God's reality. There is nothing that has no theological significance, even if that significance is the most general thing such as being a creation of God. Ascertain what that significance is to establish its typological link by going through the stages of revelation to the anti-typology found in Christ.
- Thus simply being human is to be typological of Christ. If the human

---

9. There may be the temptation to resort to commentaries before a close study of the text. I am reminded of an anecdote told by Herbert Carson when Vicar of St Paul's church in Cambridge. An elderly Christian struggling with understanding the Bible remarked, 'There's one thing about the Bible; it sure throws a heap of light on them commentaries!'

10. Those able to engage the Hebrew and Greek texts may find the textual apparatus relevant to an informed approach to textual criticism.

in question is peripheral to the theology of the text being examined, its typological value is likely to be very little or virtually nil. But do not be put off too easily. The Bible builds a progressive picture of what sinful humanity is like, and what humanity under grace is like. Both find their fulfilment in Christ, who is the true and faithful Adam/Israel and also the one who was made to be sin for us (2 Cor. 5:21).

- Whatever part of reality the person, event or institution reveals, as portrayed in your chosen text, remember that reality is restored to its perfection in Christ. The Bible portrays reality as God and his created order with humanity as its pinnacle. All relationships between God and creation, and all relationships in creation are fractured because of human sin. Christ restores all things and all relationships. In terms of our macro-typology, Christ is the antitype of every aspect of reality: nothing exists outside this relationship. Everything the Bible deals with comes within this relationship. To put it another way, the incarnate God-man is the representative embodiment of every aspect of reality in perfect relationships. What God has done in Jesus is made to involve us as we are related to Jesus by faith and, by involving us, has ultimate implications for the whole of creation (Rom. 8:19–23).

8. The practical application of any text in Old or New Testament should never be divorced from the relationship of that text to Christ. Avoid the lemming dash over the cliff of direct applications. Of course we want people to be edified by 'all Scripture' (2 Tim. 3:16–17), but we want to get it right. The sufficiency of Christ stretches to his sufficiency as the fulfilling centre of the whole canon of Scripture.

Theologies of either Old or New Testament

It is a fact that the bulk of biblical theologies written from the late nineteenth century onwards have been theologies of one or other Testament. Sometimes this has reflected a critical theological and historical assessment of the relationship of the Testaments. In other cases it may be nothing more than the results of division of labour and specialization in one or other Testament. For some the attempt to deal with the whole Bible is unrealistic simply because of the size of the task. I have already expressed my view on the possibilities of dealing with the whole canon in a way that does not require exhaustive research and exegetical study. From an evangelical point of view, the Old Testament can be dealt with alone but always with the Christian presupposition that it foreshadows Christ and the theology of the New Testament. A theology of the New Testament can scarcely avoid dealing with the constant use of Old Testament texts and allusions by the New Testament writers.

You are not likely to set out to write a theology of one or other Testament from scratch. Such works are the culmination of years of exegetical studies of individual texts and consideration of the theological concerns of books or corpora. Even introductory biblical theologies are likely to arise out of years of preaching or teaching experience. However, some useful introductory biblical theologies have emerged more from a concern to understand the basic structure of biblical revelation.

Should any reader aspire to such a task there are some essentials to remember. First, what kind of work and what readership in mind is planned? Secondly, how would such a work be structured, and of what length? Thirdly, bear in mind that the question of the structure of revelation is not the same as the question of a central theme or unifying concept, though they will probably be related. If planning a work on the Old Testament, your understanding of the matters we have dealt with at length is vital: how do you see the Old Testament relating to the New?[11] Various authors of Old Testament Theologies have engaged the matter of the relationship of the Testaments in different ways. Sometimes it is difficult to see how the author's Christian presuppositions have affected the approach to the theology of the Old Testament.[12]

Theologies of the whole Bible as canon

This is an undertaking that has not been attempted very often. Earlier in this study I mentioned the works by Vos, VanGemeren and Scobie. Brevard Childs has also ventured into this field,[13] and my own attempt at a lay person's

---

11. You may avoid venturing into this area as many Christian OT theologians have done. That implies that it is up to the individual Christian reader of your work to make the connections.

12. Gustave F. Oehler (1883) differentiated his Old Testament theology from a study of Jewish religion in that it is the preparation for the new covenant. Walther Eichrodt (1959) maintained that Old Testament religion must be understood as completed in Christ and as coherent with the New Testament. Gerhard von Rad provides a lengthy section at the end of his Theology dealing with the relation of the Old Testament to the New Testament. Other more recent Theologies of the Old Testament that make some reference to the Christian stance of the writer include those of Th. C. Vriezen (1958), G. A. F. Knight (1959), Walter Kaiser (1978), Elmer Martens (1981, 1994), Walter Brueggemann (1997), Paul House (1998) and John Goldingay (2003, 2006, 2009).

13. Brevard S. Childs, *Biblical Theology of the Old and New Testaments* (London: SCM, 1992).

outline biblical theology, *According to Plan*, comes within this category. An evangelical theologian undertaking this endeavour will presumably want to bring out the essential plan of God revealed in the Bible in such a way that no part of the Bible will be orphaned and left as some kind of embarrassing remainder. My own conviction on the matter is that a canonical biblical theology must be just that: a theology that embraces all parts of the Bible. No book of the Bible can be omitted without compromising the doctrine of the unity of Scripture. No part of any book or corpus can be omitted without compromising the all-sufficiency of Christ as the one in whom God sums up all things.

Epilogue

The bottom line in any discussion on the principles of doing biblical theology is surely its practical value for the edifying of God's people and for their growth in grace and the knowledge of Christ. The essay I contributed to Donald Robinson's Festschrift was entitled 'The Pastoral Application of Biblical Theology'.[14] Robinson expressed his approval of my having taken this line. In this essay I suggested a number of areas that benefit from the application of biblical theology. In the realm of the family it provides a framework for the understanding of the covenant relationships in the home and for the nurturing of children in the spiritual truths of the Bible. In the local church biblical theology is crucial in the ministry to children and teenagers. It is also essential for good adult Christian education. It is important for preaching and worship or liturgy, for pastoral leadership and care. In my essay 'The Pastor as a Biblical Theologian', I emphasized the role of biblical theology in promoting high views of the Bible, of Jesus, of the gospel, of the ministerial task and of the people of God.[15]

Much has happened since my introduction to biblical theology over fifty years ago. I can never lose my sense of gratitude to God for giving me the teachers I had at Moore College. In this book I have sought to show why Don

---

14. David Peterson and John Pryor (eds.), *In the Fullness of Time: Biblical Studies in Honour of Archbishop Donald Robinson* (Homebush West, NSW: Lancer, 1992), pp. 301–317.

15. Richard J. Gibson (ed.), *Interpreting God's Plan: Biblical Theology and the Pastor*, Explorations 11 (Adelaide: Open Book; Carlisle: Paternoster, 1997), pp. 110–129. Similar thoughts are set out in my chapter 'Biblical Theology as the Heartbeat of Effective Ministry', in Scott J. Hafemann (ed.), *Biblical Theology: Retrospect and Prospect* (Downers Grove: IVP; Leicester: Apollos, 2002), pp. 280–286.

Robinson ('Robby' as he is affectionately known) was so important to me. After my first stint overseas I returned to Moore to teach Old Testament and Hebrew in 1963. I was rather intimidated by the task ahead, particularly as I was to take the place of a brilliant scholar, Alan Cole, who had left for missionary service in South-East Asia. I remember sharing my doubts and fears with Robby at the outset: how could I possibly fill Alan Cole's shoes? Robby replied, 'Goldy, when you get up there and look at the students in front of you, say to yourself, "Behold, they know nothing!"' It might have worked for a while; I don't know.

When I returned again to Moore in 1995 it was my custom to begin the first-year course of Biblical Theology by asking the hundred or so new students in front of me, 'Hands up if you have read *Gospel and Kingdom*, or *According to Plan*, or some other basic text in biblical theology.' Usually about 90% of the hands went up. I could no longer think, 'Behold, they know nothing.' I am encouraged to think that we have made progress in propagating Christ-centred biblical theology since the 1960s. Although Moore remains the ministerial training college of the Anglican Diocese of Sydney, it has become both international and interdenominational. We have had many students leave for ministry in all six continents. A steady stream of students from overseas have come to us for training, some specifically to learn about biblical theology, who then have gone back to their countries of origin. Our former students minister in many different denominations and ministry situations. Not all will have been as fired up about biblical theology as I was, but because biblical theology is now so integral to all the programmes at Moore, they will at least have absorbed some of that ethos. Publications by members of the Moore faculty, and by former students, have contributed to the increased awareness that biblical theology can no longer be regarded as an optional subject. Rather it is central to biblical ministry and to the sound proclamation of the gospel.

The establishment of MOCLAM (Moore College en Latinoamérica), as the licensed representative of Moore Theological College in Latin America, has increased the potential for teaching biblical theology using Spanish translations of the MTC Department of External Studies study materials and of key evangelical books published by an associated editorial. While exact numbers are difficult to ascertain, on last count External Studies had in excess of five thousand students in over fifty countries around the world. The founder of MOCLAM, Grahame Scarratt, emailed me recently thus:[16]

---

16. Email dated 28 April 2011.

One comment on Central America and the courses: we now have around 1,000 students (including IFES staff workers and students) studying in this region across about 10 denominations and have been told SO many times that 'the lights turned on' when they did Biblical Theology!!! It TOTALLY transforms one's understanding of the Scriptures. Thank you for your part in that!

Starting from 'special doctrine' as a course for first-year students in the 1950s, and the establishing of a course in biblical theology, the ripples have moved inexorably outwards as the legacy of Donald Robinson has taken on global proportions. I believe this is cause for profound thanks to the God of grace who has revealed himself and his ways in his word. Behind Robinson's achievements lies the history of evangelical Christianity in Australia, and particularly that of Anglicanism, as I mentioned briefly in the preface. We pray that, under God, these beginnings will continue to bear fruit in the wider church. In this way one important aspect of Donald Robinson's biblical theology will find its fulfilment: the gospel that was 'to the Jew first' will continue to be a light to lighten the nations so that the saved of Israel and of the Gentiles will become one new Adam in Christ.

*   *   *

Donald Robinson would from time to time begin or end a lecture or sermon with part of a prayer adapted from the marriage service in the *Book of Common Prayer*. It is a prayer that succinctly sums up his concern that the Scriptures be applied to daily living and that our lives should be transformed by the Word of God: *O God of Abraham, God of Isaac, God of Jacob, bless us your servants, and sow the seed of eternal life in our hearts; that whatsoever in thy holy Word we shall profitably learn, we may in deed fulfil the same, through Jesus Christ our Lord. Amen.*

BIBLIOGRAPHY

ALEXANDER, T. DESMOND (2008), *From Eden to the New Jerusalem: Exploring God's Plan for Life on Earth*, Nottingham: IVP; Grand Rapids: Kregel.

ALEXANDER, T. DESMOND, and BRIAN ROSNER (eds.) (2000), *New Dictionary of Biblical Theology*, Leicester: IVP; Downers Grove: IVP.

ALEXANDER, T. DESMOND, and SIMON GATHERCOLE (eds.) (2004), *Heaven on Earth: The Temple in Biblical Theology*, Carlisle: Paternoster.

ANDERSON, BERNHARD W. (1999), *Contours of Old Testament Theology*, Minneapolis: Fortress.

BAKER, DAVID L. (2010), *Two Testaments, One Bible: The Theological Relationship Between the Old and New Testaments*, 3rd ed., Nottingham: Apollos; Downers Grove: IVP.

BARR, JAMES (1961), *The Semantics of Biblical Language*, Oxford: Oxford University Press.

—(1999), *The Concept of Biblical Theology: An Old Testament Perspective*, London: SCM.

BARTHOLOMEW, CRAIG G., C. STEPHEN EVANS, MARY HEALY and MURRAY RAE (eds.) (2003), *'Behind' the Text: History and Biblical Interpretation*, SHS 4, Carlisle: Paternoster; Grand Rapids: Zondervan.

BARTHOLOMEW, CRAIG G., and MICHAEL W. GOHEEN (2004), *The Drama of Scripture: Finding Our Place in the Biblical Story*, Grand Rapids: Baker.

BARTHOLOMEW, CRAIG G., M. HEALY, K. MÖLLER and R. PARRY (eds.) (2004), *Out of Egypt: Biblical Theology and Biblical Interpretation*, SHS 5, Milton Keynes: Paternoster; Grand Rapids: Zondervan.

BEALE, G. K. (ed.) (1994), *The Right Doctrine from the Wrong Text? Essays on the Use of the Old Testament in the New*, Grand Rapids: Eerdmans.

—(2004), *The Temple and the Church's Mission: A Biblical Theology of the Dwelling Place of God*, NSBT 17, Leicester: Apollos; Downers Grove: IVP.

BEALE, G. K., and D. A. CARSON (eds.) (2007), *Commentary on the New Testament Use of the Old Testament*, Grand Rapids: Baker; Nottingham: Apollos.

BECKER, JOACHIM (1965), *Gottesfurcht im Alten Testament*, Rome: Päpstliches Bibelinstitut.

BOLT, PETER G. (2007), *Thomas Moore of Liverpool: One of Our Oldest Colonists*, Studies in Australian Colonial History 1, Camperdown, NSW: Bolt Publishing Services.

BOLT, PETER G., and MARK D. THOMPSON (eds.) (2000), *The Gospel to the Nations: Perspectives on Paul's Mission*, Downers Grove: IVP; Leicester: Apollos.

—(2008), *Donald Robinson: Selected Works*, vol. 1: *Assembling God's People*; vol. 2: *Preaching God's Word*; *Appreciation*, Camperdown, NSW: Australian Church Record; Newtown, NSW: Moore College.

BRECK, JOHN (2001), *Scripture in Tradition: The Bible and its Interpretation in the Orthodox Church*, Crestwood, N.Y.: St Vladimir's Seminary Press.

BRIGHT, JOHN (1955), *The Kingdom of God*, New York: Abingdon.

—(1959), *A History of Israel*, Philadelphia: Westminster.

—(1967), *The Authority of the Old Testament*, London: SCM.

BRUEGGEMANN, WALTER (1997), *Theology of the Old Testament: Testimony, Dispute, Advocacy*, Minneapolis: Fortress.

CALVIN, JOHN, *Institutes of the Christian Religion*, tr. Ford Lewis Battles, LCC 20–21, Philadelphia: Westminster; London: SCM, 1960.

CARSON, D. A. (1996), *Exegetical Fallacies*, 2nd ed., Grand Rapids: Baker.

CHILDS, BREVARD S. (1970), *Biblical Theology in Crisis*, Philadelphia: Westminster.

—(1985), *Old Testament Theology in a Canonical Context*, London: SCM.

—(1992), *Biblical Theology of the Old and New Testaments*, London: SCM.

CLEMENTS, RONALD (1967), *Abraham and David: Genesis 15 and its Meaning for Israelite Tradition*, SBT, Second Series 5, London: SCM.

CLOWNEY, EDMUND P. (1961), *Preaching and Biblical Theology*, Grand Rapids: Eerdmans; London: Tyndale, 1962.

—(1988), *The Unfolding Mystery: Discovering Christ in the Old Testament*, Leicester: IVP.

—(2003), *Preaching Christ in All of Scripture*, Wheaton: Crossway.

COTTERELL, PETER, and MAX TURNER (1989), *Linguistics and Biblical Interpretation*, London: SPCK.

CRAIGIE, P. C. (1976), *The Book of Deuteronomy*, NICOT, Grand Rapids: Eerdmans.

CULLMANN, OSCAR (1950), *Baptism in the New Testament*, SBT 1, London: SCM.

—(1951), *Christ and Time: The Primitive Christian Conception of Time and History*, London: SCM.

—(1967), *Salvation in History*, London: SCM.

DEMPSTER, STEPHEN G. (2003), *Dominion and Dynasty: A Theology of the Hebrew Bible*, NSBT 15, Leicester: Apollos; Downers Grove: IVP.

DODD, C. H. (1936), *The Apostolic Preaching and its Developments*, London: Hodder & Stoughton.

—(1952), *According to the Scriptures: The Sub-Structure of New Testament Theology*, London: Nisbet.

DUMBRELL, WILLIAM J. (1984), *Covenant and Creation: An Old Testament Covenantal Theology*, Exeter: Paternoster.

—(1985), *The End of the Beginning: Revelation 21–22 and the Old Testament*, Homebush West, NSW: Lancer; Grand Rapids: Baker.

—(1994), *The Search for Order: Biblical Eschatology in Focus*, Grand Rapids: Baker.

—(2002), *The Faith of Israel: Its Expression in the Books of the Old Testament*, 2nd ed., Grand Rapids: Baker; Leicester: Apollos.

EHLEN, ARLIS JOHN (1964), 'Old Testament Theology as *Heilsgeschichte*', *CTM* 35.9, pp. 517–544.

EICHRODT, WALTHER (1959), *Theology of the Old Testament*, London: SCM.

—(1964), 'Is Typological Exegesis an Appropriated Method?', in Claus Westermann (ed.), *Essays on Old Testament Hermeneutics*, English version ed. James Luther Mays, Richmond, Va.: John Knox, pp. 224–245.

ELLUL, JACQUES (1970), *The Meaning of the City*, Grand Rapids: Eerdmans.

FEINBERG, JOHN S. (1988), *Continuity and Discontinuity: Perspectives on the Relationship Between the Old and New Testaments*, Westchester, Ill.: Crossway.

GAFFIN, RICHARD B. (ed.) (1980), *Redemptive History and Biblical Interpretation: The Shorter Writings of Geerhardus Vos*, Phillipsburg: Presbyterian & Reformed.

GIBSON, RICHARD J. (ed.) (1997), *Interpreting God's Plan: Biblical Theology and the Pastor*, Explorations 11, Adelaide: Open Book; Carlisle: Paternoster.

GOLDINGAY, JOHN (2003), *Old Testament Theology*, vol. 1: *Israel's Gospel*, Downers Grove: IVP.

—(2006), *Old Testament Theology*, vol. 2: *Israel's Faith*, Downers Grove: IVP.

—(2009), *Old Testament Theology*, vol. 3: *Israel's Life*, Downers Grove: IVP.

GOLDSWORTHY, GRAEME (1981), *Gospel and Kingdom: A Christian Interpretation of the Old Testament*, Exeter: Paternoster.

—(1984), *The Gospel in Revelation: Gospel and Apocalypse*, Exeter: Paternoster.

—(1987), *Gospel and Wisdom*, Exeter: Paternoster.

—(1991), *According to Plan: The Unfolding Revelation of God in the Bible*, Leicester: IVP; Downers Grove: IVP, 2002.

—(1993), *The Tree of Life: Reading Proverbs Today*, Sydney: Anglican Information Office, rev. ed., Sydney: Aquila, 2011.

—(2000), *The Goldsworthy Trilogy*, Milton Keynes: Paternoster.

—(2000), *Preaching the Whole Bible as Christian Scripture: The Application of Biblical Theology to Expository Preaching*, Grand Rapids: Eerdmans; Leicester: IVP.

—(2000), 'Regeneration', *NDBT*, pp. 720–723.

—(2003), *Prayer and the Knowledge of God: What the Whole Bible Teaches*, Leicester: IVP.

—(2006), *Gospel-Centred Hermeneutics: Biblical-Theological Foundations and Principles*, Nottingham: Apollos; Downers Grove: IVP.

—(2008), 'The Necessity and Viability of Biblical Theology', *SBJT* 12.4, pp. 4–18.

GOPPELT, LEONHARD (1981), *Theology of the New Testament*, vol. 1: *The Ministry of Jesus in its Theological Significance*, Grand Rapids: Eerdmans.

—(1982), *Theology of the New Testament*, vol. 2: *The Variety and Unity of the Apostolic Witness to Christ*, Grand Rapids: Eerdmans.

—(1982), *Typos: The Typological Interpretation of the Old Testament in the New*, Grand Rapids: Eerdmans.

GREIDANUS, SIDNEY (1970), *Sola Scriptura: Problems and Principles in Preaching Historical Texts*, Toronto: Wedge.

—(1988), *The Modern Preacher and the Ancient Text*, Grand Rapids: Eerdmans; Leicester: IVP.

—(1999), *Preaching Christ from the Old Testament: A Contemporary Hermeneutical Method*, Grand Rapids: Eerdmans.

—(2007), *Preaching Christ from Genesis: Foundations for Expository Sermons*, Grand Rapids: Eerdmans.

—(2010), *Preaching Christ from Ecclesiastes: Foundations for Expository Sermons*, Grand Rapids: Eerdmans.

HAFEMANN, SCOTT J. (ed.) (2002), *Biblical Theology: Retrospect and Prospect*, Downers Grove: IVP; Leicester: Apollos.

HAFEMANN, SCOTT J., and PAUL R. HOUSE (eds.) (2007), *Central Themes in Biblical Theology: Mapping Unity in Diversity*, Nottingham: Apollos; Grand Rapids: Baker.

HARRINGTON, WILFRID (1973), *The Path of Biblical Theology*, Dublin: Gill & Macmillan.

HASEL, GERHARD F. (1978), *New Testament Theology: Basic Issues in the Current Debate*, Grand Rapids: Eerdmans.

—(1982), 'Biblical Theology: Then, Now and Tomorrow', *HBT* 4.1, pp. 61–93.

—(1991), *Old Testament Theology: Basic Issues in the Current Debate*, rev. 4th ed., Grand Rapids: Eerdmans.

—(1996), 'Proposals for a Canonical Biblical Theology', *AUSS* 34.1, pp. 23–33.

HEBERT, A. G. (1941), *The Throne of David: A Study of the Fulfilment of the Old Testament in Jesus Christ and His Church*, London: Faber and Faber.

—(1947), *The Authority of the Old Testament*, London: Faber and Faber.

—(1957), *Christ the Fulfiller: Three Studies on the Biblical Types as They Are Presented in the Old and New Testaments*, Sydney: Anglican Truth Society.

—(1957), *Fundamentalism and the Church of God*, London: SCM.

HOUSE, PAUL R. (1998), *Old Testament Theology*, Downers Grove: IVP.

JOHNSON, DENNIS E. (2007), *Him We Proclaim: Preaching Christ from All the Scriptures*, Phillipsburg: Presbyterian & Reformed.

—(2009) (ed.), *Heralds of the King: Christ-Centered Sermons in the Tradition of Edmund P. Clowney*, Wheaton: Crossway.

KAISER, WALTER, C. (1978), *Toward an Old Testament Theology*, Grand Rapids: Zondervan.

KIDNER, DEREK (1985), *Wisdom to Live by: An Introduction to the Old Testament's Wisdom Books of Proverbs, Job and Ecclesiastes*, Leicester: IVP.

KLINE, MEREDITH G. (1963), *Treaty of the Great King: The Covenant Structure of Deuteronomy*, Grand Rapids: Eerdmans.

KNIGHT, GEORGE A. F. (1959), *A Christian Theology of the Old Testament*, London: SCM.

KNOX, DAVID BROUGHTON, *Selected Works*, vol. 2: *Church and Ministry*, Kingsford, NSW: Matthias Media, 2003.

KÖSTENBERGER, ANDREAS J., and PETER T. O'BRIEN (2001), *Salvation to the Ends of the Earth: A Biblical Theology of Mission*, NSBT 11, Nottingham: Apollos; Downers Grove: IVP.

KRAUS, HANS-JOACHIM (1970), *Die Biblische Theologie: Ihre Geschichte und Problematik*, Neukirchen-Vluyn: Neukirchener Verlag.

LAWRENCE, MICHAEL (2010), *Biblical Theology in the Life of the Church*, Wheaton: Crossway.

LONG, V. PHILIPS (1994), *The Art of Biblical History*, Foundations of Contemporary Interpretation 5, Grand Rapids: Zondervan; Leicester: Apollos.

LONGMAN, TREMPER, III (2001), *Immanuel in Our Place: Seeing Christ in Israel's Worship*, Phillipsburg: Presbyterian & Reformed.

MANSON, WILLIAM (1951), *The Epistle to the Hebrews: An Historical and Theological Reconsideration*, London: Hodder & Stoughton.

MARTENS, ELMER A. (1981), *Plot and Purpose in the Old Testament*, Leicester: IVP; 2nd ed., *God's Design: A Focus on Old Testament Theology*, Grand Rapids: Baker; Leicester: Apollos, 1994; 3rd ed., N. Richland Hills: Bibal, 1998.

MILLARD, ALAN R., JAMES K. HOFFMEIER and DAVID W. BAKER (eds.) (1994), *Faith, Tradition, and History: Old Testament Historiography in its Near Eastern Context*, Winona Lake, Ind.: Eisenbrauns.

MOTYER, J. ALEC (1993), *The Prophecy of Isaiah: An Introduction and Commentary*, Leicester: IVP; Downers Grove: IVP.

O'BRIEN, PETER T. (1982), *Colossians, Philemon*, WBC, Waco: Word.

O'COLLINS, GERALD, S. J. (1971), *Foundations of Theology*, Chicago: Loyola University Press.

OEHLER, GUSTAVE F. (1883), *Theology of the Old Testament*, tr. G. E. Day, Grand Rapids: Zondervan.

PACKER, JAMES I. (1958), *'Fundamentalism' and the Word of God*, London: Inter-Varsity Fellowship.

PATE, C. M., J. S. DUVALL, J. D. HAYS, E. R. RICHARDS, W. D. TUCKER and P. VANG (2004), *The Story of Israel: A Biblical Theology*, Downers Grove: IVP; Leicester: Apollos.

PETERSON, DAVID, and JOHN PRYOR (eds.) (1992), *In the Fullness of Time: Biblical Studies in Honour of Archbishop Donald Robinson*, Homebush West, NSW: Lancer.

PORTER, STANLEY E., 'Fear', *NDBT*, p. 497.

POYTHRESS, VERN S. (1987), *Understanding Dispensationalists*, Grand Rapids: Zondervan Academie.

—(1991), *The Shadow of Christ in the Law of Moses*, Brentwood, Tenn.: Wolgemuth & Hyatt.

—(1999), *God-Centered Biblical Interpretation*, Phillipsburg: Presbyterian & Reformed.

—(2008), 'Canon and Speech Act: Limitations in Speech-Act Theory, with Implications for a Putative Theory of Canonical Speech Acts', *WTJ* 70, pp. 337–354.

PROVAN, IAIN, V. PHILIPS LONG and TREMPER LONGMAN III (2003), *A Biblical History of Israel*, Louisville: Westminster.

RAD, GERHARD VON (1962), *Old Testament Theology*, vol. 1, tr. D. M. G. Stalker, Edinburgh: Oliver & Boyd.

—(1964), 'Typological Interpretation of the Old Testament', tr. John Bright, in CLAUS WESTERMANN (ed.), *Essays on Old Testament Hermeneutics*, Richmond, Va.: John Knox, pp. 17–39.

—(1965), *Old Testament Theology*, vol. 2: *The Theology of Israel's Prophetic Traditions*, tr. D. M. G. Stalker, Edinburgh: Oliver & Boyd.

RENDTORFF, ROLF (1993), *Canon and Theology: Overtures to an Old Testament Theology*, tr. Margaret Kohl, Minneapolis: Fortress.

REVENTLOW, HENNING GRAF (1985), *Problems of Old Testament Theology in the Twentieth Century*, tr. John Bowden, London: SCM.

—(1986), *Problems of Biblical Theology in the Twentieth Century*, tr. John Bowden, Philadelphia: Fortress.

RICHARDSON, ALAN (1958), *An Introduction to the Theology of the New Testament*, London: SCM.

ROBERTS, VAUGHAN (2003), *God's Big Picture: Tracing the Story-Line of the Bible*, Leicester: IVP.

ROBINSON, DONALD W. B. (1951), *Josiah's Reform and the Book of the Law*, London: Tyndale.

—(1956), *The Meaning of Baptism*, Beecroft, NSW: Evangelical Tracts and Publications.

—(1985), *Faith's Framework: The Structure of New Testament Theology*, Exeter: Paternoster; Sutherland, NSW: Albatross.

ROLSTON, HOLMES, III (1972), *John Calvin Versus the Westminster Confession*, Richmond, Va.: John Knox.

ROSNER, BRIAN (2005), 'Salvation, History of', in KEVIN J. VANHOOZER (ed.), *Dictionary for Theological Interpretation of the Bible*, Grand Rapids: Baker; London: SPCK, pp. 714–717.

ROUTLEDGE, ROBIN (2008), *Old Testament Theology: A Thematic Approach*, Nottingham: Apollos; Downers Grove: IVP Academic.

ROWLEY, H. H. (1956), *The Faith of Israel: Aspects of Old Testament Thought*, London: SCM.

SAILHAMER, JOHN (1995), *Introduction to Old Testament Theology: A Canonical Approach*, Grand Rapids: Zondervan.

—(2009), *The Meaning of the Pentateuch: Revelation, Composition and Interpretation*, Downers Grove: IVP Academic.

SCHMID, HANS H. (1968), *Gerechtigkeit als Weltordnung*, Tübingen: J. C. B. Mohr.

SCOBIE, CHARLES H. H. (1991), 'The Structure of Biblical Theology', *TB* 42.1, pp. 163–194.

—(2003), *The Ways of Our God: An Approach to Biblical Theology*, Grand Rapids: Eerdmans.

SEITZ, CHRISTOPHER (1999), 'Christological Interpretation of Texts and Trinitarian Claims to Truth: An Engagement with Francis Watson's *Text and Truth*', *SJT* 52.2, pp. 209–226.

—(2007), *Prophecy and Hermeneutics: Toward a New Introduction to the Prophets*, Grand Rapids: Baker Academic.

SMITH-CHRISTOPHER, DANIEL L. (2002), *A Biblical Theology of Exile*, Minneapolis: Fortress.

STEVENSON, J. (ed.) (1975), *Creeds, Councils, and Controversies: Documents Illustrative of the History of the Church A.D. 337–461*, London: SPCK.

STUART, DOUGLAS (1987), *Hosea–Jonah*, WBC 31, Waco: Word.

STUHLMACHER, PETER (1995), *How to Do Biblical Theology*, Princeton Theological Monograph Series 38, Allison Park, Pa.: Pickwick.

VANGEMEREN, WILLEM (1988), *The Progress of Redemption: The Story of Salvation from Creation to the New Jerusalem*, Grand Rapids: Zondervan Acadamie.

VANHOOZER, KEVIN J. (2000), 'Exegesis and Hermeneutics', *NDBT*, pp. 52–64.

—(2005) (ed.), *Dictionary for Theological Interpretation of the Bible*, Grand Rapids: Baker; London: SPCK.

VISCHER, WILHELM (1949), *The Witness of the Old Testament to Christ*, tr. A. B. Crabtree, London: Lutterworth.

—(1969), 'Everywhere the Scripture Is About Christ Alone', in BERNHARD W. ANDERSON (ed.), *The Old Testament and Christian Faith: A Theological Discussion*, New York: Herder & Herder, pp. 90–101.

VOS, GEERHARDUS (1930), *The Pauline Eschatology*, Princeton: Princeton University Press; repr. Grand Rapids: Eerdmans, 1972.

—(1948), *Biblical Theology: Old and New Testaments*, Grand Rapids: Eerdmans; repr. 1963.

—(1972), *The Kingdom of God and the Church*, Nutley, N.J.: Presbyterian & Reformed.

VRIEZEN, TH. C. (1958), *An Outline of Old Testament Theology*, Oxford: Blackwell.

WATSON, FRANCIS (1999), 'The Old Testament as Christian Scripture: A Response to Professor Seitz', *SJT* 52.2, pp. 227–232.

WEBB, BARRY G. (1990), 'Zion in Transformation: A Literary Approach to Isaiah', in DAVID J. A. CLINES, STEPHEN E. FOWL and STANLEY E. PORTER (eds.), *The Bible in Three Dimensions*, JSOTSup 87, Sheffield: JSOT Press, pp. 65–84.

—(1996), *The Message of Isaiah*, BST, Leicester: IVP; Downers Grove: IVP.

—(2000), *Five Festal Garments: Christian Reflections on the Song of Songs, Ruth, Lamentations, Ecclesiastes and Esther*, NSBT 10, Nottingham: Apollos; Downers Grove: IVP.

WHYBRAY, R. N. (1968), *The Succession Narrative*, SBT, Second Series 9, London: SCM.

WILLIAMSON, PAUL R. (2007), *Sealed with an Oath: Covenant in God's Unfolding Purpose*, NSBT 23, Nottingham: Apollos; Downers Grove: IVP.

WRIGHT, CHRISTOPHER J. H. (1992), *Knowing Jesus Through the Old Testament: Rediscovering the Roots of Our Faith*, Downers Grove: IVP.

WRIGHT, G. ERNEST (1950), *The Old Testament Against its Environment*, SBT 2, London: SCM.

—(1952), *God Who Acts: Biblical Theology as Recital*, SBT 8, London: SCM.

—(1969), *The Old Testament and Theology*, New York: Harper & Row.

WRIGHT, N. T. (1992), *The New Testament and the People of God*, London: SPCK.

INDEX OF SUBJECTS

INDEX OF NAMES

INDEX OF SCRIPTURE REFERENCES